MANAGING
Costs &
Resources

tutorial

NVQ LEVEL 4
ACCOUNTING

Janet Brammer
Aubrey Penning
Consultant: Roger Petheram

OSBORNE

Published by Osborne Books Limited
Unit 1B Everoak Estate
Bromyard Road
Worcester WR2 5HP
Tel 01905 748071
Email books@osbornebooks.co.uk
Website www.osbornebooks.co.uk

Cover and page design by Hedgehog

Printed by the Bath Press, Bath

British Library Cataloguing in Publication Data
A catalogue record for this book is available from the British Library

ISBN 1 872962 44 0

CONTENTS

ACKNOWLEDGEMENTS

The authors wish to thank the following for their help with the editing and production of the book: Michael Fardon, Michael Gilbert and Jon Moore. Thanks also go to Andrew Harrington for reading and checking text and to Roger Petheram for reading, checking and contributing many valuable ideas in the writing process.

Thanks are also due to the Association of Accounting Technicians for their help and advice and to the Lead Body for Accounting for permission to reproduce extracts from the Standards of Competence for Accounting.

AUTHORS

Janet Brammer has over ten years' experience lecturing on AAT and ACCA accountancy courses at Norwich City College. She is a Certified Accountant and worked in accountancy practice for a number of years. She has also tutored for the Open University and has written a workbook *Management Information Framework* for the ACCA distance learning scheme.

Aubrey Penning co-ordinates the AAT courses at Worcester College of Technology, and teaches a range of units including MCV and PAR. He has fourteen years experience of teaching accountancy on a variety of courses in Worcester and Gwent. He is a Certified Accountant, and before his move into full-time teaching he worked for the health service, a housing association and a chemical supplier.

INTRODUCTION

Osborne tutorials

Managing Costs & Resources Tutorial has been written to provide a study resource for students taking courses based on the NVQ Level 4 Accounting Unit 8 'Contributing to the management of costs and the enhancement of value' (MCV) and Unit 9 'Contributing to the planning and allocation of resources' (PAR). The companion Osborne text *Financial Statements Tutorial* covers Unit 11 'Drafting Financial Statements'.

Managing Costs & Resources Tutorial is written so that students can study each of the two units independently. Only the first chapter applies to both units, and is an introduction to the background of management accountancy and the techniques that are used in both units.

Chapters 2 to 7 deal with the issues specific to the MCV unit. A substantial section is devoted to standard costing and variance analysis, which is covered in more depth than in the Intermediate Level *Costing, Reports and Returns Tutorial*. The issues relating to quality and its measurement are also covered. The enhancement of value is then considered further through a thorough examination of performance measurement.

Chapters 8 to 11 relate to the PAR unit, and include an examination of the principles of budgets and budgetary control, together with the numerical practicalities that are also so important. The chapters also discuss and demonstrate the various ways that budgets can be developed and their implications. The presentation of budgetary control information is also examined, together with the wider management issues arising from the use of budgets.

The chapters of *Managing Costs & Resources Tutorial* contain:

- a clear text with worked examples and Case Studies
- a chapter summary and key terms to help with revision
- student activities – with answers at the end of the book

The tutorial text – with questions and answers – is therefore useful for classroom use and also for distance learning students. More extended student exercises, without answers in the text, are available in the *Managing Costs & Resources Workbook*, compiled by Janet Brammer.

Osborne workbooks

Managing Costs & Resources Workbook contains extended student activities and sample Central Assessments. The answers to these tasks are included in a separate Tutor Pack.

If you would like a copy of any of our texts, please telephone Osborne Books Sales Office on 01905 748071 for details of how to order, or visit the Osborne online 24 hour shop on www.osbornebooks.co.uk

feedback

Osborne Books is always grateful for feedback on its titles. If you have any comments or queries please telephone us on 01905 748071 or e-mail us on books@osbornebooks.co.uk and we (or our authors) will respond.

Janet Brammer

Aubrey Penning

Spring 2001

OSBORNE WEBSITE

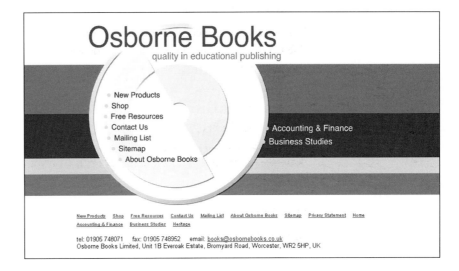

Osborne Books is continually developing its website as a resource for accountancy students.

Visit us on www.osbornebooks.co.uk and see what we have to offer. Let us know if you think the facilities can be improved.

1 MANAGEMENT INFORMATION

NVQ PERFORMANCE CRITERIA COVERED

This chapter introduces the background to management accounting and covers the essential underpinning knowledge that must be used to demonstrate competence in both the units covered by this book.

For this reason the chapter should be read in conjunction with chapters 2 – 7 for the unit 'Contributing to the Management of Costs and Enhancement of Value' (MCV), and in conjunction with chapters 8 – 11 for the unit 'Contributing to the Planning and Allocation of Resources' (PAR).

WHAT IS GOOD INFORMATION?

We all use information every day to manage our lives. We consult train timetables to help us get to work, or review the local fuel prices before filling up our car. As we travel on the train we check our watches to see if the train is running to time, and as we drive we monitor our speed and compare it with the speed limit. We learn to use the information that is useful to us and ignore the information that is not very helpful.

Managers have a wealth of information available to help them to control their organisations. They can obtain information of how much their products or services cost, how much their competitors are charging, and what the current rate of inflation is. They need the right information to help them to do their jobs.

Whether you are an accountancy student or a manager (or both), the best kind of information is that which satisfies the following criteria.

- **Relevant to the user.** If you were hoping to catch a train today, a copy of last year's timetable may not be very relevant, but if you were a statistician undertaking an analysis of train performance over a number of years it would be a vital piece of information.

- **Understandable**. In the same way that the format of a train timetable will help us to understand its content, the way that accounting information is presented to managers is of vital importance. A large part of both the units studied in this book is concerned with presenting management information in an understandable form, and clearly explaining its implications.

- **Timely**. If information is to be acted on it must arrive at the right time. Imagine a car speedometer that only informed the driver of the car's speed via a printout once the journey was completed. Such a system would not help the driver avoid prosecution for speeding, because the information would arrive too late for action to be taken. In the same way receiving accounting information too late to take appropriate action can occur in some organisations and cause major problems.

- **Consistent**. If meaningful comparisons are to be made, the information must be generated using consistent techniques. Government departments are sometimes accused of distorting information by modifying the way that it is compiled from one period to the next. For example comparing the total number of unemployed people is difficult if some groups that were previously included in the figure are no longer counted. An organisation's profits for different periods would also be difficult to compare if the bad debt provision was suddenly changed from 0.1% of debtors to 10% of debtors.

- **Sufficiently accurate for its purpose**. Sometimes a reasonably accurate piece of information is all that is required, whereas in other circumstances it would be insufficient. A manager may only need to know that a supplier is owed about £30,000, but the accounts department will need to know the exact figure if payment is to be made. Accuracy may have a cost attached, in terms of the staff time to produce the information and other costs resulting from the delay created. A balance must be found between the speed and accuracy of information.

SOURCES OF MANAGEMENT INFORMATION

The information needed by managers can be obtained from internal and external sources. The following table gives examples of specific sources, the kind of information that may be available, and what it could be used for. The list is not intended to be exhaustive, so you can probably think of further examples.

INTERNAL SOURCES AND USES OF MANAGEMENT INFORMATION

Source	Information	Use
Purchase Invoices	• Quantity and Cost of Goods Purchased	• Costing Output of Organisation
Wages Analysis	• Time and Cost of Labour	• Costing Output of Organisation
Work Study Reports	• Labour Time to Undertake Activities	• Standard Costs of Output
Unfulfilled Sales Orders	• Type and Quantity of Output Demand	• Planning Future Output
Creditors Accounts	• Amounts Owed and When Due	• Planning future Payments
Stock Records	• Quantity of Goods in Stock & Ordered	• Planning Future Purchases
Production Schedules	• Type and Quantity of Output Planned	• Planning Resource Requirements
Quality Control Records	• Number of Items Rejected	• Monitoring Input and Output

EXTERNAL SOURCES AND USES OF MANAGEMENT INFORMATION

Source	Information	Use
Government Statistics	• Forecast Inflation, Economic Growth, Social trends	• Planning future Activities
Financial Press	• Competitors' Performance	• Comparison and Resulting Action
World Wide Web	• Information and Commentary on Most Issues	• Planning Future Activities
Trade Associations	• Typical Performance in the Trade	• Comparison and Resulting Action
Market Research	• Views of Prospective Customers	• Planning Future Activities

Some of the information generated can be used for more than one purpose. For example the information contained on a purchase invoice can become a part of the information for all of the purposes shown in the diagram below. Note also the references at the bottom of the diagram to financial accounting and management accounting; these concepts are explained in the text which follows.

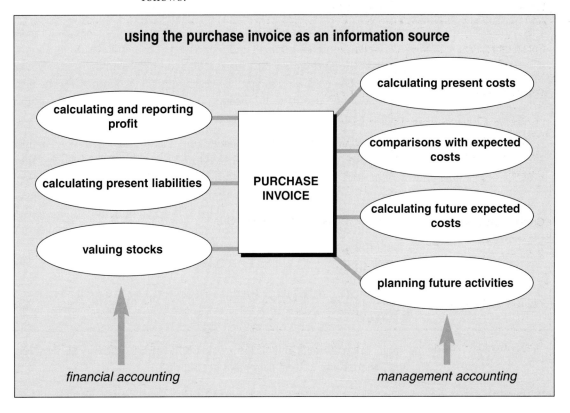

using the purchase invoice as an information source

calculating present costs

calculating and reporting profit

comparisons with expected costs

calculating present liabilities

PURCHASE INVOICE

calculating future expected costs

valuing stocks

planning future activities

financial accounting

management accounting

FINANCIAL ACCOUNTING AND MANAGEMENT ACCOUNTING

If you look at the diagram at the bottom of the previous page you will see that the activities on the left-hand side relate to 'Financial Accounting', while those on the right hand side relate to 'Management Accounting'.

financial accounting

Financial accounting is concerned with recording accounting information so that accounts can be published and used by those outside the organisation. It is governed by legislation and accounting standards, and focuses on the needs of stakeholders from outside the organisation, like shareholders, creditors, and prospective investors. Strict formats and timescales are imposed on organisations that determine exactly how and when the information is produced.

management accounting

Management accounting is the general term used for the production of accounting information for those inside an organisation. Because it is an internal system there are no external rules about how or when the information should be produced. Management accounting exists to help managers plan, monitor, control, and make decisions about the organisation. Its emphasis is on providing information that can help with the future of the organisation. The guiding principal for management accounting information is that it should be **useful** to its readers. If the information fails that simple test, then it has been a pointless waste of time producing it!

This book is concerned with management accounting, and you should therefore keep the idea of the information being useful in your mind throughout your studies for the two units. When responding to tasks in either the MCV unit or the PAR unit you will not need to consider the implications of the Companies' Act or any SSAP or FRS, in fact you will be missing the point if you do. Instead, just make sure that you are communicating information that is useful to an organisation's managers.

financial accounting and management accounting compared

The table opposite sets out a summary of the main differences between financial accounting and management accounting.

FINANCIAL AND MANAGEMENT ACCOUNTING COMPARED

	Financial Accounting	Management Accounting
Users	• External Stakeholders	• Internal
Format	• Summarised	• Specific
Governed by	• Legislation & Standards	• Usefulness
Frequency of Information	• Annual (& possible six monthly)	• As required
Time Focus	• Past	• Future

MANAGEMENT ACCOUNTING SYSTEMS

methods of costing

Management accounting is the branch of accounting that deals with providing internal information within an organisation. Providing costing information is an important area of management accounting, and you will be familiar with the principles of costing from your earlier studies. Just as management accounting has no external rules governing how it should be carried out, cost information can also be developed in various ways. Although costing systems should always be tailored to the needs of the organisation and its managers, there are three general approaches to costing that you will need to become familiar.They all attempt to calculate a cost for the units that the organisation produces. These 'units of output' could be bicycle wheels made by a bicycle component manufacturer, or operations carried out in a hospital.

- **Absorption Costing**

  This is a system that attempts to determine a 'full' cost for each unit of output. It therefore includes both direct and indirect costs, and uses the mechanisms of allocation, apportionment and absorption to incorporate the indirect costs.

- **Marginal Costing**

  This costing system categorises costs according to their cost behaviour, and divides them simply into variable and fixed costs. This system uses a cost for each unit of output based purely on the variable (or 'marginal') costs. All fixed costs are regarded as time based and are therefore linked to accounting periods rather than units of output.

- **Activity Based Costing (ABC)**

  This is a development of absorption costing, and uses a more sophisticated system to deal mainly with the indirect costs. This involves examining the costs to determine what causes them, and using this information to charge the costs to the units of output in an appropriate manner.

You will need to understand the working and implications of these three systems, so we will now examine each one in more detail.

ABSORPTION COSTING

You will probably be familiar with the absorption costing process from your earlier studies, but the following will enable you to recall firstly the terminology and then the steps involved.

terminology:

*   **Direct Costs**

    Costs that are directly attributable to the units of output. They can be divided into Direct Materials, Direct Labour, and Direct Expenses.

*   **Indirect Costs**

    Costs that cannot be directly attributed to the units of production. They are also referred to as overheads. In a manufacturing environment only the indirect costs relating to production are usually absorbed into the product cost.

*   **Cost Centres**

    Parts of the organisation where it is convenient to gather costs. It could be a department or section, or an area where a certain activity is carried out. 'Production' cost centres are where the unit of output has some activity carried out on it, whereas 'Service' cost centres provide a service to other cost centres rather than do anything directly to the units of output.

*   **Absorption Bases**

    The methods available to absorb cost from the production cost centres into the units of output (or products). All absorption bases use expected (or budgeted) costs and activity levels to work out an absorption rate. Examples of absorption bases are Direct Labour Hours, Machine Hours, and Units of Output.

steps in absorption costing

1   Costs are divided into direct costs and indirect costs. The direct costs can immediately form part of the cost of the units of output, while the indirect costs (overheads) will need to be absorbed into the cost of the units via the next stages.

2   Indirect costs are either allocated to one cost centre (if the cost relates to only one cost centre), or apportioned to several cost centres by some fair system (if the cost relates to several cost centres). For example rent costs might be apportioned using the area of the building used by each cost centre.

3   If costs have now accumulated into service cost centres, the total cost of each service cost centre is shared amongst the production cost centres that benefit from the service provided. This is carried out using secondary apportionment. For example the total cost of running the stores service cost centre could be shared out by using the numbers of requisitions from the various production cost centres as a basis for secondary apportionment.

4   The costs that have been gathered in the production cost centres can now be absorbed into the units of output by using a predetermined absorption rate based on the expected activity level. The indirect cost is absorbed from the cost centre into the units of output as they pass through the cost centre. A common basis for this absorption is direct labour hours, so that the longer a product is worked on in the production cost centre, the greater the amount of cost is absorbed.

CASE STUDY

THE ABSORPTION COMPANY: ABSORPTION COSTING

The Absorption Company manufactures several products, one of which is the Sorp. Its factory is divided into two production cost centres (Assembly and Finishing) and one service cost centre (Maintenance). 80% of the activity in the Maintenance cost centre benefits Assembly, while the remainder benefits Finishing.

Before the financial period started the expected indirect costs for the forthcoming year were:

	£
Assembly	208,000
Finishing	72,000
Maintenance	40,000

Each unit of Sorp uses direct material that costs £42. It takes 5 direct labour hours in Assembly and 2 direct labour hours in Finishing to make one unit of Sorp. Indirect costs are absorbed from the production cost centres using a direct labour hour rate. The expected direct labour hours for the year were 120,000 in Assembly and 25,000 in Finishing. All direct labour hours are paid at £8.00.

required:

Calculate the following:

1   The indirect cost absorption rate in each of the two production cost centres.

2   The absorbed cost of one unit of Sorp.

solution

1 the indirect absorption rate

	Assembly	Finishing	Maintenance
Expected Indirect Costs:	£	£	£
Allocated / Apportioned	208,000	72,000	40,000
Secondary Apportionment	32,000	8,000	(40,000)
Total	240,000	80,000	
Expected Direct Labour Hours	120,000	25,000	

Absorption Rates:
Assembly   £240,000 ÷ 120,000   =   £2.00 per direct labour hour
Finishing   £80,000 ÷ 25,000   =   £3.20 per direct labour hour

2 the absorbed cost of one Sorp

		Cost of one unit of Sorp:
Direct Materials		£42.00
Direct Labour:		
Assembly 5 hours @ £8.00	£40.00	
Finishing 2 hours @ £8.00	£16.00	
		£56.00
Indirect Costs:		
Assembly 5 hours @ £2.00	£10.00	
Finishing 2 hours @ £3.20	£6.40	
		£16.40
Total Absorbed Cost		£114.40

MARGINAL COSTING

Marginal costing accepts that there is a fundamental difference between costs that are based, not on the origin of the costs, but purely on the behaviour of the costs when the activity level (or output level) changes. There are three ways that the costs could behave within a range of activity levels:

Variable Costs   Costs where the total amount varies in proportion to the activity level when the activity level changes.Variable costs are also known as marginal costs when using marginal costing.

Fixed Costs   Costs that do not change when the level of activity changes (within certain parameters).

Semi-Variable Costs   Costs where a part of the cost acts as a variable cost, and a part acts as a fixed cost.

All the costs (regardless of whether they might be viewed as direct or indirect) need to be divided into variable costs and fixed costs. Semi-variable costs are divided into their fixed and variable components. There are numerical techniques for dividing them into variable and fixed elements. One of these, the 'high-low' method is studied in chapter 10. Once the total variable and fixed costs have been determined, only the variable (or marginal) costs are linked to the units of output to provide a cost per unit. This enables a 'contribution' towards the fixed costs (and ultimately profit) to be calculated either per unit, or for a specified output level.

Unit Contribution   The difference between the selling price per unit and the variable costs per unit. It is the amount that each unit sold contributes towards the fixed costs of the organisation and profit.

Total Contribution   The difference between the sales income and the variable costs of the units sold in a period. This amount is the total contribution that the sales of all the units in the period make towards the fixed costs of the organisation and profit.

Fixed costs are taken straight to the profit statement, and are deducted from the total contribution for the period to arrive at the profit for the period. For both MCV and PAR you will need to be familiar with Marginal Costing, and recognise and use the formats and terminology that applies to this system.

Marginal costing has considerable advantages over absorption costing when it is used to help with making decisions. Uses of marginal costing are further explored in the unit 'Evaluating Current and Proposed Activities'. That unit is an option for the AAT Technician stage, and is not covered in this book.

CASE STUDY

THE MARGINAL COMPANY: MARGINAL COSTING

The Marginal Company manufactures one product, the Marg. The following costs relate to a financial year, when 100,000 units of Marg are made:

Direct Materials	£350,000
Direct Labour	£230,000
Indirect Costs	£310,000

Investigations into the behaviour of the costs has revealed the following information:
- Direct Materials behave as variable costs.
- Direct Labour behaves as a variable cost.
- Of the Indirect Costs, £270,000 behaves as a fixed cost, and the remainder as a variable cost.

required

1 Calculate the cost of one unit of Marg using Marginal Costing.

2 If each unit of Marg sells for £10, and all the production of 100,000 units is sold, draft a marginal costing statement for the financial year showing the contribution (per unit and in total), and the profit for the year.

solution

1 costing a unit of Marg

Using only the variable (marginal) costs to cost one unit of Marg:

Direct Materials (£350,000 ÷ 100,000)	£3.50
Direct Labour (£230,000 ÷ 100,000)	£2.30
Variable Overheads	
(£310,000 − £270,000 = £40,000 ÷ 100,000)	£0.40
Total marginal cost per unit	£6.20

2 Marginal Costing Statement for the Financial Year.

	Per Unit £	For Year £
Sales	10.00	1,000,000
Less Variable Costs	6.20	620,000
Contribution	3.80	380,000
Less Fixed Overheads		270,000
Profit		£110,000

Note that the fixed costs are not calculated in per unit terms, but are simply deducted in total from the total contribution.

ACTIVITY BASED COSTING (ABC)

background to ABC

Activity based costing was developed in the 1970s and 1980s as an alternative to absorption costing. Since the time when absorption costing was initially developed (at the time of the Industrial Revolution), many aspects of manufacture had changed, and it was felt that absorption costing was not providing information of sufficient quality. The points that were made by advocates of ABC were:

Overheads (indirect costs) typically now account for the major part of product costs, and should therefore be accounted for in a less arbitrary way than they would under absorption costing. For example, simply absorbing based on just one basis (e.g. direct labour hours) does not acknowledge the complexity of costs that can make up overheads.

Both production methods and batch sizes can have a major impact on product costs, yet these are largely ignored by absorption costing. For example the cost involved in setting up equipment will be far greater per unit of output for small production runs than for large ones.

Modern production methods do not lend themselves to the use of absorption rates such as direct labour hours or machine hours. Integrated production systems can often operate with minimal human intervention.

cost pools and cost drivers

ABC works by identifying the indirect activities, and grouping their costs into 'cost pools', one for each major activity. For each cost pool there must be a factor that drives the costs and causes those costs to change. This 'cost driver' is identified and its rate calculated. The rate is then used to charge the output with cost, based on the output's use of the activity.

For example in a stores department (which would typically form one service cost centre under absorption costing), the activities could be determined as

1   Receiving goods inwards, and
2   Issuing goods to production.

The costs of running the stores department would be analysed into the costs for carrying out each of these activities – the 'cost pools'. The cost drivers might be agreed as

1   Number of Deliveries Received (for receiving goods inward), and
2   Number of Requisitions (for issuing goods).

The rate per cost driver would then be calculated by dividing the cost pool by the cost driver for that pool.

Using this technique, a product that required many different components that were delivered separately and then issued frequently to production, would be charged with a high cost from the activities in the stores department. In comparison a product that was made from components delivered together and issued to production in bulk would incur fewer costs.

Using a suitable analysis of costs and their drivers an organisation can adapt the system to its own circumstances. Each different product will then be charged with a more accurate cost based on its use of the activities than if absorption costing had been used.

The diagram below shows how the system works. Study it and then read the two Case Studies that follow. They both illustrate the application of activity based costing, the first in a manufacturing company and the second to a college operating in the service sector.

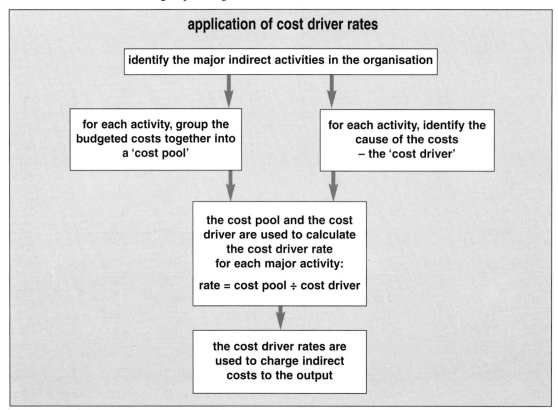

application of cost driver rates

identify the major indirect activities in the organisation

for each activity, group the budgeted costs together into a 'cost pool'

for each activity, identify the cause of the costs
– the 'cost driver'

the cost pool and the cost driver are used to calculate the cost driver rate for each major activity:

rate = cost pool ÷ cost driver

the cost driver rates are used to charge indirect costs to the output

CASE STUDY

ABC COMPANY:
ACTIVITY BASED COSTING

The ABC Company has introduced activity based costing to cost its output. It makes several products on mechanised production lines, including AB, and BC. AB is a product that is usually made in large batches of 1,000 units, since it sells in large quantities. BC is a specialised product selling to a niche market, and is therefore made in small batches of 20 units.

As a part of the introduction of ABC the company has identified one major activity as 'setting up the production equipment'. The cost associated with this activity in a financial year is budgeted at £250,000, and therefore this amount forms the cost pool for setting up production equipment.

The company has identified the cost driver of this activity as 'number of set ups performed', since if the number increases the cost will be proportionally greater. One batch of any product requires one set-up to be performed.

The budgeted figure of £250,000 was based on an estimated 500 set-ups in the financial year.

The unit costs for AB and BC have already been calculated excluding the set up costs, as follows:

AB	£50.00 per unit
BC	£55.00 per unit.

required

Calculate the total cost per unit of AB and BC, including set up costs.

solution

The cost driver rate for set-ups = £250,000 ÷ 500 = £500 per set up

Charging at this rate:

One unit of AB would incur set-up cost of £500 ÷ 1,000 = £0.50

One unit of BC would incur set-up cost of £500 ÷ 20 = £25.00

Incorporating this into the previous costs gives per unit costs of:

	AB	BC
	£	£
Costs excluding set-ups	50.00	55.00
Cost of set-ups	0.50	25.00
Total Cost	50.50	80.00

In this case study set-ups account for approximately 1% of the total cost of a unit of AB, compared to 31% of the total cost of a unit of BC. These differences would not be identified using a traditional absorption costing system that treated set-ups as a part of general overheads.

CASE STUDY

ABC COLLEGE: ACTIVITY BASED COSTING IN THE SERVICE SECTOR

The Activity Based College is a small private college, providing a variety of part-time business related courses. The college has determined that there are four major activities that are undertaken, that have the following cost pools for the financial year and cost drivers.

Activity	Cost Pool	Cost Driver Information
Teaching	£500,000	Teaching Hours (25,000 in year)
Course Preparation	£300,000	New Courses (30 in year)
Lesson Preparation	£100,000	Teaching Hours (25,000 in year)
Student Administration	£100,000	Number of Students (1,000 in year)

The costs for two separate courses are to be calculated using ABC.

The first is the AAT Technician Stage. This course will run for 250 teaching hours, and should attract 20 students. The course has been run previously.

The second is a new course in Taxation for Exporters to Scandinavia. The course will run for 100 teaching hours, and there are 5 prospective students.

required

Calculate the cost per course and cost per student for each of the two courses.

solution

First the cost driver rates need to be established:

Teaching	£500,000 ÷ 25,000	= £20 per teaching hour
Course Preparation	£300,000 ÷ 30	= £10,000 per new course
Lesson Preparation	£100,000 ÷ 25,000	= £4 per teaching hour
Student Administration	£100,000 ÷ 1,000	= £100 per student

Secondly these rates are applied to the courses according to their demand for the activities:

1 AAT Technician Stage

Teaching	£20 x 250 =	£5,000
Course Preparation	(existing course)	-
Lesson Preparation	£4 x 250 =	£1,000
Student Administration	£100 x 20 =	£2,000
Cost for course		£8,000
Cost per student	£8,000 ÷ 20=	£400

2 Taxation for Exporters to Scandinavia

Teaching	£20 x 100 =	£2,000
Course Preparation	£10,000 x 1 =	£10,000
Lesson Preparation	£4 x 100 =	£400
Student Administration	£100 x 5 =	£500
Cost for course		£12,900
Cost per student	£12,900 ÷ 5 =	£2,580

COSTING SYSTEMS AND RECORDED PROFIT

variations in stock valuation

One of the reasons that organisations use a costing system is so that the value of the stock of finished goods (and work in progress) can be calculated and incorporated into profit statements. Since the different approaches to costing that we have examined give different costs per unit, they will result in different valuations of stock, this will in turn affect the profit calculation when stock levels change. A marginal costing system will value stock at just the variable costs, but a system that absorbs fixed costs into the stock valuation can result in fixed costs being charged to a period other than the one in which they were incurred.

the effect of stock valuation on profit

The costs incurred in producing goods in a period, together with the cost of the opening stock must equal the cost of sales for the period, added to the cost of the closing stock.

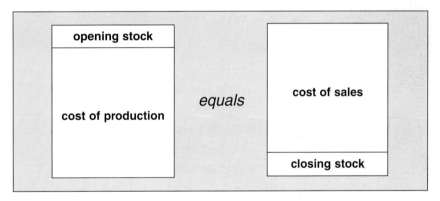

The valuation of the closing stock will therefore affect the cost of sales and therefore recorded profit.

The following case study uses the same data under different costing systems to illustrate the situation.

CASE STUDY

THE ALTERNATIVE COMPANY: COSTING METHODS AND PROFIT

The Alternative Company manufactures a single product, and produces monthly management accounts.

In each of Month 1 and Month 2, 10,000 units were produced, and the following costs were incurred:

Direct Material	£100,000
Direct Labour	£150,000
Fixed Overheads	£250,000
Total Costs	£500,000

Both the costs and the volume of output were in line with the budget.

Units were sold for £70 each, and in Month 1 the whole production of 10,000 units were sold, whereas in month 2 only 8,000 units were sold. There was no stock at the start of Month 1.

Direct Material and Direct Labour are both variable costs.

required

1   Calculate the cost per unit using
    (a) absorption costing using units as an absorption base
    (b) marginal costing

2   Draft management accounts for each month using
    (a) absorption costing
    (b) marginal costing

3   Comment on the reasons for any difference in profits.

solution

1 Calculation of cost per unit

    (a)   Absorption Costing (using all costs)

        £500,000 ÷ 10,000= £50 per unit

    (b)   Marginal Costing (using variable costs only)

        £250,000 ÷ 10,000= £25 per unit

2 Producing management accounts

    (a)   **Absorption Costing**

		Month 1		Month 2
Sales		700,000		560,000
Less cost of sales:				
opening stock	–		–	
cost of production				
(10,000 x £50)	500,000		500,000	
less closing stock	–			
(2,000 x £50)			100,000	
		500,000		400,000
Profit		200,000		160,000

(b)   **Marginal Costing**

		Month 1		Month 2
Sales		700,000		560,000
Less variable cost of sales:				
opening stock	–		–	
Variable cost of production				
(10,000 x £25)	250,000		250,000	
less closing stock	–			
(2,000 x £25)			50,000	
		250,000		200,000
Contribution		450,000		360,000
Less fixed costs		250,000		250,000
Profit		200,000		110,000

3 Comments on the reasons for differences in profit

The profits are identical when there is no change in stock level, as in Month 1, when both opening and closing stocks are zero. However when the stock level changes between the start and end on the period (as in Month 2) the stock valuation has an impact on profit.

The additional reported profit of £50,000 (£160,000 compared with £110,000) by using the absorption system is due to £50,000 of the fixed costs being absorbed into the closing stock and effectively carried into the next period. If the stocks again fell to nil in Month 3 the profit difference would be reversed.

The differences in reported profits are only timing differences – the differences in profit are just reported in different periods.

conclusion

■ Where stock levels increase, absorption costing will record a higher profit than marginal costing, as more of the cost incurred is pushed into the next period.

■ Where stock levels decrease, absorption costing will record a lower profit than marginal costing as more of the costs from the previous period are set against income.

■ Where stock levels are constant, then, providing there has been no change in unit costs, there will be no difference in recorded profit under either system.

You can therefore see that if an organisation uses absorption costing, significantly building up (or reducing) stock levels can distort profits.

MANAGEMENT INFORMATION TECHNIQUES

The techniques described below may be assessable in either of the two units studied in this book. In this chapter we will look at the techniques in outline form. The specific applications will be examined in later chapters. The techniques involve the collection and the analysis of data to provide useful information.

primary and secondary data

Where data is collected specifically for analysis undertaken at that time by an organisation, then the data is known as 'primary data'. Where the data has been collected and provided by another organisation then it is known as 'secondary data'. For example, if a business analyses its sales figures, that is primary data; if it uses inflation figures provided by the Government's statistical services, that is secondary data.

census or sample?

If we want to collect data about a population (not just a population of people, but any large group of items or data) there are two approaches that we could use.

- A **census** could be used to collect data about every item in the population. One example of this technique is the Government's 10 yearly census of all the people in the UK. This provides information which can be used by the Government to plan services. A census provides a complete picture of the 'population', but is expensive, and will often be impractical.
- **Sampling** is a commonly used technique for collecting data from a small number within a 'population', to estimate information regarding the whole 'population'. Market research questionnaires are an example of sampling. Sampling is cheaper to carry out than a full census, but it must be carried out carefully if the results are to be used with confidence.

SAMPLING

The critical issue to consider when examining sampling techniques is that the sample must be as free from bias as practical. If you wanted to estimate the faults in the whole production output of a factory it would not make sense to only sample the output of a machine manned by a trainee on his first day at work!

Some common uses of sampling are to estimate:
- customer satisfaction levels
- quality of production output
- the views of prospective customers of a new product or service

You could be asked to comment on the use of sampling for any of the above uses within these units.

There are various approaches to sampling. The approach taken will depend on the type of population and the resources available. The approach will influence the reliability of the estimates produced.

random sampling

This is the approach that will provide the best estimate. It is based on the rule that every item in the population has an equal chance of being selected. In order for this to happen the exact size of the population must be known, and a 'sampling frame' created by numbering every item. From this frame the sample can be selected using random numbers. This approach could be used (for example) as a way of sampling sales invoices to estimate the likely number of errors in all the sales invoices within a period. This is because the whole population (the number of sales invoices) would be known from the outset. It could not be used to ascertain the views of bald men in Bradford because there is no way of accurately knowing how many there are and who they are.

quasi-random sampling

This approach contains a number of techniques that can provide a good approximation to random sampling. Although they are not quite as accurate as random sampling, they can produce similar outcomes, often using fewer resources. The techniques are:

- **Systematic Sampling**

  Choosing every 'n'th item after a random start. For example selecting sales invoices by starting at number 63, and then checking every 17th invoice from there.

- **Stratified Sampling**

  Dividing the population into groups ('strata' means 'layers'), and then choosing a sample from each of the strata based on its size. For example sales invoices could be grouped according to the location of the customer. If there were more invoices for customers in London than in Devon then the sample for London would be larger. Each group would be sampled independently in this way according to its size.

- **Multistage Sampling**

  Dividing the 'population' into groups, and then randomly selecting several groups as an initial sample. These selected groups are then sub-divided and sub groups randomly chosen (the procedure may be repeated several times). For example sales invoices could be divided into groups based on the location of the customers, and the groups of Yorkshire,

Sussex and Cornwall randomly selected. Within each group towns could then be chosen at random (for example Halifax, Brighton and Truro), and the invoice sample selected from customers within these areas.

non-random sampling

This approach must be used when a sampling frame cannot be established (for example because the size of the population is not known). The results generated by this approach will typically be less reliable than random or quasi-random approaches, but are nevertheless useful. These techniques are often used for market research.

- **Quota Sampling**

  Restricting the sample to a fixed number per strata. For example interviewing people in the street within certain categories (for example age groups, gender etc.) until a predetermined number have been interviewed.

- **Cluster Sampling**

  Selecting one subsection of the population as representative, and just sampling that. For example interviewing dog owners who live in Cardiff as being representative of dog owners throughout the UK.

An actual customer survey that has improved its sampling system is the Top Gear/JD Power survey that examines the customer satisfaction of UK car users. The survey is carried out by a market research organisation in conjunction with the BBC's 'Top Gear' TV motoring series and magazine. The survey has been conducted annually, and initially the data came from inviting viewers and readers to take part. More recently the DVLA became involved and forwarded questionnaires to a random sample of all owners of the cars to be evaluated. This means that any bias caused because previously only Top Gear viewers or readers would respond was eliminated.

TIME SERIES ANALYSIS

Time series analysis involves analysing numerical trends over a time period. It is often used to examine past and present trends so that future trends can be forecast. The term 'trend analysis' is used to describe the technique that we will now examine. At its simplest the concept is based on the assumption that data will continue to move in the same direction in the future as it has in the past.

Using the sales of a shoe shop as an example we will now look a range of techniques of dealing with trends.

an identical annual change

A shoe shop 'Comfy Feet' has sold the following numbers of pairs of shoes annually over the last few years:

1995	10,000
1996	11,000
1997	12,000
1998	13,000
1999	14,000
2000	15,000
2001	16,000

It does not require a great deal of arithmetic to calculate that if the trend continues at the previous rate – an increase of 1,000 pairs a year – then shoe sales could be forecast at 17,000 pairs in 2002 and 18,000 pairs in 2003. Of course this is a very simple example, and life is rarely this straightforward. For example, for how long can this rate of increase be sustained?

average annual change

A slightly more complex technique could have been used to arrive at the same answer for the shoe shop. If we compare the number of sales in 2001 with the number in 1995, we can see that it has risen by 6,000 pairs. By dividing that figure by the number of times the year changed in our data we can arrive at an average change per year. The number of times that the year changes is 6, which is the same as the number of 'spaces' between the years (or alternatively the total number of years minus 1).

Shown as an equation this becomes:

Average Annual Sales Change   =

$$\frac{(Sales\ in\ Last\ Year - Sales\ in\ First\ Year)}{(Number\ of\ Years - 1)} = \frac{(16,000 - 10,000)}{(7 - 1)}$$

=   + 1,000, which is what we would expect.

The + 1,000 would then be added to the sales data in 2001 of 16,000 (the last actual data) to arrive at a forecast of 17,000.

This technique is useful when all the increases are not quite identical, yet we want to use the average increase to forecast the trend. A negative answer would show that the average change is a reduction, not an increase. We will use this technique when estimating the trend movement in more complicated situations.

constructing a graph

The same result can be produced graphically. Using the same shoe shop example we can extend the graph based on the actual data to form a forecast line.

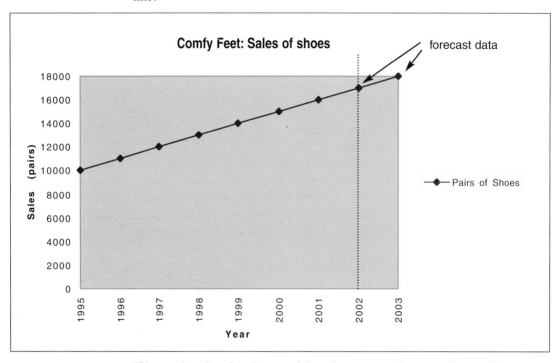

If in another situation the actual data does not produce exactly equal increases, the graph will produce the same answer as the average annual change provided the straight line runs through the first and last year's data points.

using a formula

The data in the example could have been expressed in the following formula:

$$y = mx + c$$

where

y is the forecast amount

m is 1,000 (the amount by which the data increases each year)

x is the number of years since the start year (1995)

c is 10,000 (which is the sales figure in the start year of 1995)

If we wanted a forecast for the year 2003, we could calculate it as:

Forecast   =   (1,000 x number of years since 1995) + 10,000

y (the forecast) =   (1,000 x 8) + 10,000

=   18,000, which is what we would expect.

This formula works because the formula is based on the equation of a straight line.

You would not be asked to develop your own formula or equation in an assessment, but you may be given one to use to work out a forecast. The technique of developing a suitable equation is called 'linear regression'. The technique assumes that a straight line is appropriate.

TIME SERIES ANALYSIS AND SEASONAL VARIATIONS

There are four main factors that can influence data which is generated over a period of time:

- **The underlying trend**

    This is the way that the data is generally moving in the long term. For example the volume of traffic on our roads is generally increasing as time goes on.

- **Long term cycles**

    These are slow moving variations that may be caused by economic cycles or social trends. For example, when economic prosperity generally increases this may increase the volume of traffic as more people own cars and fewer use buses. In times of economic depression there may be a decrease in car use as people cannot afford to travel as much or may not have employment which requires them to travel.

- **Seasonal variations**

    This term refers to regular, predictable cycles in the data. The cycles may or may not be seasonal in the normal use of the term (eg Spring, Summer etc). For example traffic volumes are always higher in the daytime, especially on weekdays, and lower at weekends and at night.

- **Random variations**

    All data will be affected by influences that are unpredictable. For example flooding of some roads may reduce traffic volume along that route, but increase it on alternative routes. Similarly the traffic volume may be influenced by a shortage of fuel caused by protestors.

The type of numerical problems that you are likely to face in assessments will tend to ignore the effects of long-term cycles (which will effectively be considered as a part of the trend) and random variations (which are impossible to forecast). We are therefore left with analysing data into underlying trends and seasonal variations, in order to create forecasts.

The technique that we will use follows the process in this diagram:

incorporating seasonal variations into the trend

```
┌─────────────────────────┐              ┌─────────────────────────┐
│ historical actual data  │              │ forecast of future data │
└─────────────────────────┘              └─────────────────────────┘
              │                                        ↑
              │        ┌──────────────────────┐        │
              │        │ seasonal variations  │        │
              │        └──────────────────────┘        │
              ↓                                        │
┌─────────────────────────┐              ┌─────────────────────────┐
│    historical trend     │  ──────────▶ │  forecast future trend  │
└─────────────────────────┘              └─────────────────────────┘
```

The process is as follows:

1 The historical actual data is analysed into the historical trend and the seasonal variations.

2 The historical trend is used to forecast the future trend, using the techniques examined in the last section.

3 The seasonal variations are incorporated with the forecast future trend to provide a forecast of where the actual data will be in the future.

analysing historical actual data

In an assessment the analysis may have been carried out already, or you may be asked to carry out the analysis by using 'moving averages'. If you are using moving averages it is important that

• your workings are laid out accurately

• the number of pieces of data that are averaged corresponds with the number of 'seasons' in a cycle

• where there is an even number of 'seasons' in a cycle a further averaging of each pair of averages takes place.

The following case study shows the full process.

CASE STUDY

THE SEASONAL COMPANY: MOVING AVERAGES AND FORECAST TRENDS

The Seasonal Company sells various products, including Wellington Boots for use in wet weather. The quarterly management accounts for recent quarters have revealed that the following numbers of these boots were sold.

	Quarter 1	Quarter 2	Quarter 3	Quarter 4
1998	4,000	1,600	2,200	4,800
1999	4,400	2,000	2,500	5,200
2000	4,800	2,400	3,100	5,600
2001	5,200	2,800	3,400	6,000

required

1 Use moving averages to analyse the historical data into the trend and the seasonal variations.

2 Use the data from (1) to forecast the sales for each quarter of 2002.

solution

1 Calculating the trend and seasonal variations

Step 1 The first thing to do is to rearrange the historical data into a single column with spaces in between each of the figures – this is to the right of the date column:

Year	Quarter	Step 1 Historical Sales Data	Step 2 4-point Moving Average	Step 3 Averaged Pairs (Trend)	Step 4 Seasonal Variation
1998	1	4,000			
	2	1,600			
			3,150		
	3	2,200		3,200	−1,000
			3,250		
	4	4,800		3,300	+1,500
			3,350		
1999	1	4,400		3,387.5	+1,012.5
			3,425		
	2	2,000		3,475	−1,475
			3,525		
	3	2,500		3,575	−1,075
			3,625		
	4	5,200		3,675	+1,525
			3,725		
2000	1	4,800		3,800	+1,000
			3,825		
	2	2,400		3,925	−1,525
			3,925		
	3	3,100		4,025	−925
			4,075		
	4	5,600		4,125	+1,475
			4,175		
2001	1	5,200		4,212.5	+987.5
			4,250		
	2	2,800		4,300	−1,500
			4,350		
	3	3,400			
	4	6,000			

Step 2 Calculate the 4-point moving averages. This is the average of each group of four figures, starting with 1998 quarters 1 to 4, followed by 1998 quarter 2 to 1999 quarter 1, and so on. Place each moving average in the appropriate column, alongside the centre point of the figures from which it was calculated. We are using a 4-point average because there are 4 quarters in our data. This also means that the average will fall alongside gaps between our original data. Note that the shaded lines and arrows are drawn here for illustration only – to show where the figures come from.

Step 3 Calculate the average of each adjacent pair of moving averages. These are also known as 'centred moving averages'. This is carried out so that these figures can be placed alongside the centre of each pair, and will therefore fall in line with the original quarterly data (see shaded arrow). If there was an odd number of 'seasons' in a cycle (for example 13 four-weekly periods) then this stage would not be required. We have now calculated the trend figures. Notice that the first trend calculated is in quarter 3 of the first year, and the last one is in quarter 2 of the last year. This is inevitable when calculating a trend from quarterly data using moving averages.

Step 4 Calculate the seasonal variations, and insert them into the last column. These are the amounts by which the actual figures (left hand column) are greater or smaller than the trend figures. Be careful to use the correct + or – sign. The shaded arrows show the figures that are used.

2 forecast the sales for each quarter of 2002

In order to use the data that we have calculated for a forecast we will need to work out some average figures. This is because in this case study you will notice that:

• the trend is not increasing by exactly the same amount every quarter

• the seasonal variations are similar, but not quite identical for each of the same quarters

We can use the technique for calculating the average increase in the trend that we looked at earlier:

Average Trend Change $=$

$$\frac{(Last\ known\ trend - First\ known\ trend)}{(Number\ of\ Quarterly\ trends - 1)} = \frac{(4,300 - 3,200)}{11} = +100$$

We can also average the seasonal variations by grouping them together in quarters:

	Quarter 1	Quarter 2	Quarter 3	Quarter 4
1998			– 1,000	+ 1,500
1999	+ 1,012.5	– 1,475	– 1,075	+ 1,525
2000	+ 1,000	– 1,525	– 925	+ 1,475
2001	+ 987.5	– 1,500		
Totals	+ 3,000	– 4,500	– 3,000	+ 4,500
Averages	+ 1,000	– 1,500	– 1,000	+ 1,500

At this stage we should check that the average seasonal variations total zero. Here they do, but if they do not then minor adjustments will need to be made to the figures.

We can now use the average trend movements and the average seasonal variations to create a forecast. We start with the trend at the last point when it was calculated, and work out where it will be at future points by using the average movements. For example quarter 1 of 2002 is 3 quarters past quarter 2 of 2001, which is when we last knew the trend. We then incorporate the average seasonal variations to complete the forecast.

Forecast Workings:

		Forecast Trend		Seasonal Variations	Forecast
2002	Qtr 1	4,300 + (3 x 100)	= 4,600	+ 1,000	5,600
	Qtr 2	4,300 + (4 x 100)	= 4,700	− 1,500	3,200
	Qtr 3	4,300 + (5 x 100)	= 4,800	− 1,000	3,800
	Qtr 4	4,300 + (6 x 100)	= 4,900	+ 1,500	6,400

All the data and the solution to this Case Study can be shown on a graph, as follows:

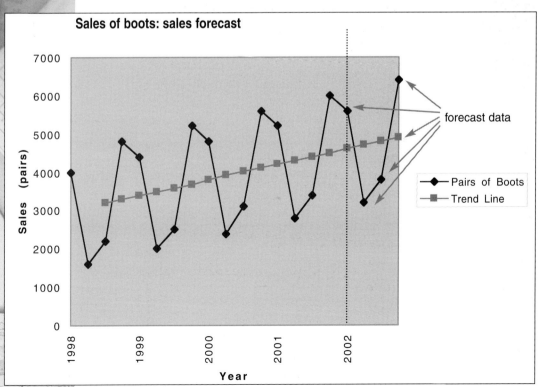

absolute or percentage seasonal variations?

The examples that we have used so far have used the idea of absolute (or 'additive') seasonal variations – ones that are expressed in the same units as the actual data that is being analysed. Sometimes a more accurate forecast can be obtained when the seasonal variations are expressed as a percentage of the trend. This would make sense when the variations naturally become greater as the trend increases. This could occur, for example, if we were analysing the cost of domestic heating over a number of years: as the trend increased (due to cost inflation) the differences between the summer and winter heating costs would also increase at about the same rate.

CASE STUDY

UK ICE CREAM CONSUMPTION

An investigation into the quarterly amount an average UK household spends on ice cream has revealed an underlying trend and percentage variations as follows.

Each quarter the trend increased by £1, and by quarter 4 of 2000 it had reached £50 per quarter.

The seasonal variations, based on percentages of the trend in that quarter were calculated as:

Quarter 1	– 70%
Quarter 2	+ 40%
Quarter 3	+ 60%
Quarter 4	– 30%

required

Forecast the average quarterly spend on ice cream per household in each quarter of 2003.

solution

The calculation here is straightforward. Note that quarter 1 of 2003 is 9 quarters later than the quarter that we already know the trend for, ie quarter 4 of 2000.

		Forecast Trend		Seasonal Variations	Forecast
2003	Qtr 1	£50 + (9 x £1)	= £59	– 70%	£17.70
	Qtr 2	£50 + (10 x £1)	= £60	+ 40%	£84.00
	Qtr 3	£50 + (11 x £1)	= £61	+ 60%	£97.60
	Qtr 4	£50 + (12 x £1)	= £62	– 30%	£43.40

INDEX NUMBERS

Index numbers are used to assist in the comparison of numerical data over time. The most commonly used index is perhaps the Retail Price Index that gives an indication of inflation by comparing the cost of a group of expenses typically incurred by households in the UK from year-to-year. There are many other types of index numbers that have been created for specific purposes, for example:

- the average wage rate for a particular job, or for all employment
- the average house price either by region or throughout the UK
- the market price of shares (eg the FTSE 100 index)
- the quantities of specific items that are sold or used (eg litres of unleaded petrol)
- the quantities of a group of items that are sold or used (eg litres of all motor fuel)

Whatever type of index we need to use, the principle is the same. The index numbers represent a convenient way of comparing figures. For example, the RPI was 82.61 in January 1983, and 159.5 in January 1998. This means that average household costs had very nearly doubled in the 15 years between. We could also calculate that if something that cost £5.00 in January 1983 had risen exactly in line with inflation, it would have cost £9.65 in January 1998. This calculation is carried out by:

$$historical\ price \quad x \quad \frac{index\ of\ time\ converting\ to}{index\ of\ time\ converting\ from}$$

ie £5.00 x (159.5 ÷ 82.61) = £9.65.

You may be told that the 'base year' for a particular index is a certain point in time. This is when the particular index was 100. For example the current RPI index was 100 in January 1987. You do not need to know the base year to do the sort of calculations that are likely to be asked of you.

Index numbers referring to costs or prices are the most commonly used ones referred to in the units studied in this book. If we want to use cost index numbers to monitor past costs of forecast future ones, then it is best to use as specific an index as possible. This will then provide greater accuracy than a more general index.

For example, if we were operating in the food industry, and wanted to compare our coffee cost movements with the average that the industry had experienced, we should use an index that analyses coffee costs in the food industry. This would be much more accurate than the RPI, and also better than a general cost index for the food industry.

CASE STUDY

MARY COX: PENSION CALCULATION

Mary Cox retired in January 1990, and her occupational pension at that point was £6,000 per year. By January 2001 the pension had risen to £8,900 per year. Assume that the index figures for the RPI and the Average Wage Index were as follows:

	RPI	Average Wage Index
January 1990	119.5	230.0
January 2001	175.0	351.2

required

1 Calculate what Mary's pension would have been in January 2001 if it had kept pace with
  (a)   the RPI, and
  (b)   the Average Wage Index since January 1990

2 Discuss the use of
  •   the Retail Price Index and
  •   the Average Wage Index
  as a means of setting Pension levels

solution

1 pension calculation

Converting Mary's 1990 pension in line with each index gives:

(a) Using the RPI   £6,000 x 175 ÷ 119.5   = £8,787 (rounded)

(b) Using Average Wage Index   £6,000 x 351.2 ÷ 230.0 = £9,162 (rounded)

2 discussion of the use of indices:

RPI

The justification for using the RPI to adjust pension levels is that the spending power of the pensioners remains constant as prices rise. The pensioners, it is argued, are equally as well off several years into their retirement as when it commenced. One drawback of using the RPI is that it is based on the average consumption of UK households. Pensioners do not have the same spending profile as typical households, and therefore their costs may move in a different way. For example fuel costs would take proportionally more of a pensioner's income, while other costs may take a lower proportion.

average wage index

If the average wage index was used for setting pensions, the pension would tend to rise slightly faster than general inflation, assuming previous trends continued. This would mean that pensioners slowly became slightly better off than they had been when they first retired, although their improvement would be at the same speed as that experienced by those in work. They would not find the gap between their spending power and that of those in work widening as it does when the RPI is used.

- Managers must select information from the many sources at their disposal. The qualities of good information are that it is Relevant, Understandable, Timely, Consistent, and of sufficient Accuracy for its purpose.

- Information sources for managers are both internal and external. Much of the internal information is from the Management Accounting function of an organisation, and this book is based on many of the techniques used in this area. Management Accounting is guided by its usefulness to managers, and has no external rules or formats that must be followed.

- Management Accounts are based around the organisation's costing system, which can be derived from Absorption Costing, Marginal Costing, or Activity Based Costing. Each system uses different terminology and different ways of calculating the cost of an organisation's output or activities. The different ways that stock can be valued in management accounts effects the amount of profit that is recorded in each period when stock levels change.

- Management Information techniques that you need to be familiar with include methods of sampling, the techniques of time series analysis, and how index numbers can be used.

KEY
TERMS

financial accounting   The branch of accounting that is concerned with reporting performance to those outside the organisation.

management accounting   The branch of accounting that is concerned with providing useful information to managers within the organisation. This book is concerned with some of the main aspects of Management Accounting.

absorption costing   This is a system that attempts to determine a 'full' production cost for each unit of output. It therefore includes both direct and indirect costs, and uses the mechanisms of allocation, apportionment and absorption to incorporate the indirect production costs.

marginal costing

This costing system categorises costs according to their cost behaviour, and divides them into variable and fixed costs. This system uses a cost for each unit of output based purely on the variable (or 'marginal') costs. All fixed costs are regarded as time based and are therefore linked to accounting periods rather than units of output.

activity based costing

This is a development of absorption costing, and uses a more sophisticated system to deal with the indirect costs. This involves examining indirect costs to determine what causes them, and using this information to charge the costs to the units of output in an appropriate manner.

sampling

Sampling is a commonly used technique for using data about a small number of items within a population, to estimate information regarding the whole population.

time series analysis

The examination of historical data that occurs over time, often with the intention of using the data to forecast future data.

trend

The underlying movement in the data, once seasonal, cyclical and random movements have been stripped away.

seasonal variations

Regular variations in data that occur in a repeating pattern. Seasonal variations can be expressed in the same numerical form as the trend (absolute or additive form), or as percentages of the trend.

linear regression

Using a mathematical formula to demonstrate the movement of data over time. This technique is sometimes used to help forecast the movement of the trend.

index numbers

A sequence of numbers used to compare data, usually over a time period.

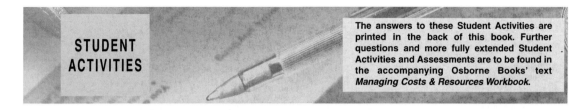

1.1 Suggest where (or from whom) each of the following sources of information might typically be obtained.

   (a)   Monthly Management Accounts

   (b)   Industry Average Performance Indicators

   (c)   Retail Price Index

   (d)   Historical Sales Data

   (e)   Developments affecting Competitors

   (f)   Regional Population Data

1.2 The Radical Company produces a variety of goods, according to customers' demands. Some items have been produced to the same specification for many years, while others are constantly updated to meet the needs of the consumers. Some products have long production runs, while others are produced in small batches for specific customers.

Explain whether you believe that Absorption Costing, Marginal Costing, or Activity Based Costing would appear to be most appropriate for this company.

1.3 The System Company manufactures one product, the Tem. Budgeted production is 4,000 Tems per week. During each of the first two weeks of this year it had costs as follows, exactly as budgeted.

   Direct Materials   £5,000

   Direct Labour   £9,000

   Fixed Overheads   £6,000

The company had no finished goods in stock at the start of week 1. In both weeks it produced 4,000 units. Sales in week 1 were 3,000 units, and in week 2 were 5,000 units, all at £8 per Tem.

Both Direct Materials and Direct Labour behave as Variable Costs.

   (a)   Produce profit statements for each of the two weeks, using

      (i)   Absorption costing, absorbing fixed overheads on a per unit basis.

      (ii)   Marginal Costing

   (b)   Explain briefly the reason for the difference between recorded profits under the alternative costing systems.

1.4 The Supashop that is open 5 days per week has the following cash sales over a period.

	Tues	Wed	Thurs	Fri	Sat
Week 1	£1830	£1920	£2080	£2160	£2160
Week 2	£1880	£1970	£2130	£2210	£2210
Week 3	£1930	£2020	£2180	£2260	£2260

Required

(a) Using moving averages, analyse this data into the trend and seasonal variations.

(b) Use the data from (a) to forecast the cash sales for each day of week 4.

1.5 A computer program has used linear regression to analyse the sales data of Pegasus Limited, a garden ornament manufacturer. Using quarter numbers (quarter 30 is the first quarter of year 2000) the sales trend has been determined as:

Sales Trend (in £) = (Quarter Number x £1,200) + £83,000.

The Seasonal Variations have been determined as the following percentages of the trend.

Quarter 1	– 10%
Quarter 2	+ 80%
Quarter 3	+15%
Quarter 4	– 85%

Required

(a) Use the above data to calculate the forecast of sales for Pegasus Limited in £ for each quarter of 2003.

(b) Comment on any drawbacks of producing sales revenue forecasts directly in money amounts.

1.6   The following historical data relates to sales in units of the Enigma Company.

	Quarter 1	Quarter 2	Quarter 3	Quarter 4
Year 1	500	430	330	280
Year 2	460	390	290	240
Year 3	420	350	250	200
Year 4	380	310	210	160

Required

(a)   Using moving averages, analyse this data into the trend and additive seasonal variations.

(b)   Use the data to forecast the unit sales for each quarter of year 5.

2 STANDARD COSTING – DIRECT COSTS

NVQ PERFORMANCE CRITERIA COVERED

unit 8: CONTRIBUTING TO THE MANAGEMENT OF COSTS AND THE ENHANCEMENT OF VALUE

element 1

collect, analyse and disseminate information about costs

- *valid, relevant information is identified from internal and external sources*

- *trends in prices are monitored for movements and analysed on a regular basis and potential implications are identified*

- *standard costs are compared with actual costs and any variances are analysed*

BACKGROUND TO STANDARD COSTING

Standard costing was developed primarily in manufacturing industry as a formal method for calculating the expected costs of products. It differs from general budget setting (which is normally concerned with the costs of sections of the organisation), because it focuses on the cost of what the organisation produces (the 'cost units').

Standard costing establishes in detail the standard cost of each component of a product, so that a total cost can be calculated for that product.

Standard costing is ideal for situations where components are identical and manufacturing operations are repetitive.

advantages of standard costing

The main advantages of operating with a standard costing system in place are that the standard costs can be used:

- to help with **decision making**, for example as a basis for pricing decisions
- to assist in **planning**, for example to plan the quantity and cost of the resources needed for future production
- as a mechanism for **controlling** costs: standard costs can be compared with actual costs (by calculating variances) so that action can be taken when appropriate.

In addition there may be other benefits to setting up and using a standard costing system:

- The preliminary examination of current production techniques and resources may reveal hidden inefficiencies and unnecessary expenditure.
- The fact that costs are to be monitored may increase the cost consciousness of the workforce (and the management).
- The system lends itself to exception reporting. This is a technique where results are only reported when they are outside a predetermined range so that action can be taken. For example a company may decide that only when costs are more than 2% away from the standard should the variances be reported.

There are therefore a variety of arguments for developing and using a standard costing system. The main uses that a particular organisation intends to make of the system will determine how it goes about setting standards. In chapter 4 we will examine the different ways that standards can be set and how this can effect the interpretation of any variances. At this point we will see what a 'standard cost' consists of, what information we will need to set the standards and where it can be obtained.

COMPOSITION OF STANDARD COSTS

elements of standard costs

The composition of standard costs – whether you are calculating the standard cost of a rubber washer, an aeroplane, or a hip replacement operation – can be analysed into common elements. These are the same elements of cost that you will be familiar with from your earlier studies:

Direct Costs   **Indirect Costs**

Direct Materials   Variable Overheads

Direct Labour   Fixed Overheads

Direct Expenses

In this chapter we will concentrate on the standards and variances for direct materials and direct labour, and in the next chapter we will examine fixed overheads. You do not need to study either the direct expense variances nor the variable overhead variances for this unit.

absorption costing and marginal costing models

The breakdown of costs (shown above) into direct and indirect costs is based on the **absorption costing** model, where a suitable portion of all production costs (indirect as well as direct) is absorbed into the product's cost. A great many standard costing systems use this approach.

You should also be familiar with the **marginal costing** model. Here costs are analysed on the basis of the way they behave in relation to activity levels, and split into variable costs and fixed costs. This then gives the following alternative production cost breakdown:

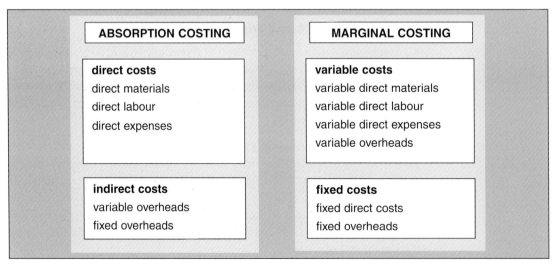

ABSORPTION COSTING	MARGINAL COSTING
direct costs direct materials direct labour direct expenses	**variable costs** variable direct materials variable direct labour variable direct expenses variable overheads
indirect costs variable overheads fixed overheads	**fixed costs** fixed direct costs fixed overheads

Any category of direct or indirect costs could behave as either variable or fixed costs, but once the cost behaviour is established, standard marginal costing is very straightforward to use. The standard costs and variances for direct materials and labour under absorption costing are developed in the same way as variable direct materials and labour under marginal costing. The fixed overhead variances are less complicated under marginal costing, and this is explained further in the next chapter.

standard direct material costs

You can assume when developing a standard direct material cost (and calculating variances) that this cost behaves as a variable cost. For example, it is reasonable to expect that the material cost for 2,000 items will be twice the cost of 1,000 of the same item. This assumption allows us to work out the standard cost for individual units, so that we can then multiply it by the quantity produced. It also explains why the absorption and marginal versions of these standards is effectively the same.

The standard direct material cost for a product comprises two elements:

- the amount of the material, and
- the cost of the material.

For example, a batch of 1,000 rubber washers may require 3 kilos of rubber, which costs £1.00 per kilo. If this data were accepted as the standard figures, then the standard direct material cost for each batch of washers would clearly be 3 kilos x £1.00 = £3.00.

The fact that the data needed to calculate a standard direct material cost is based on two elements determines:

- where the information will come from, and
- how the variances can be calculated.

standard direct labour costs

The composition of the standard direct labour cost for a cost unit is very similar to the material cost. It is also based on the implied assumption that this type of cost is variable, and so twice as many products will cost about twice as much. The standard direct labour cost for a product also consists of two elements:

- the amount of labour time to be used, and
- the labour cost per unit of time (the labour rate).

Using our example of a batch of rubber washers, if the standard direct labour time needed to manufacture them was 2 hours, and the standard labour cost was £5 per hour, then the standard direct labour cost would obviously be £10 per batch. Assuming there were no other direct costs, the total standard direct cost would be:

	£	
Materials	3.00	
Labour	10.00	
	13.00	for one batch of washers

You will be familiar with this idea, and probably find the concept quite elementary, but it is a vital foundation for further understanding.

SOURCES OF INFORMATION FOR STANDARD SETTING

Once we are familiar with the elements that make up a direct cost standard, we can now look at the information sources for each of those elements. The way an organisation chooses to set standards will have an impact on how reliable and accurate they are, and for how long they can remain useful. There will be a range of values that could be used for each figure, and the organisation should have a policy that will guide managers in setting standards, and this will also determine how any variances are ultimately interpreted. This idea is considered further in the next chapter.

The following examples of sources of information should not be learnt as lists. You are advised to think about each one so that you can see how it could be useful. In this way you can then suggest suitable information sources for a situation in a given case study.

the amount of material

The main information sources could be:

- product specifications (the 'recipe' for the product being made)
- technical data from the material supplier (e.g. recommended usage)
- historical data on quantities used in the past
- observation of manufacture

Standard setting may also need to take into account:

- estimates of wastage
- quality of material
- production equipment & machinery available, and its performance

the cost of material

The information sources could include:

- data from suppliers
- records of previous prices paid

- anticipated cost inflation (measured by general or specific price indices)
- anticipated demand for scarce supplies
- production schedules and bulk buying policy (in conjunction with availability of bulk discounts)
- seasonality of prices
- anticipated currency exchange rates

the amount of labour time

Here information sources could include:

- data on previous output and efficiency levels
- results of formal observations (work study, or 'time & motion' study)
- anticipated changes in working practices or productivity levels
- the level of training of employees to be used

the labour cost per unit of labour time

Possible sources of data include:

- current pay rates
- anticipated pay rises
- the expected effects of bonus schemes

To establish an appropriate rate it may also be necessary to take into account:

- equivalent pay rates of other employers in the locality
- changes in legislation (eg minimum wage rates)
- general or industry-specific wage cost indices
- grade of labour (or sub contractors) to be used

THE CALCULATION OF DIRECT COST VARIANCES

Set out on the next page is a summary of the variances that we will be studying for this unit, in the form of diagrams sometimes known as 'variance trees'. The variances differ depending on whether the absorption costing model is being used, or the marginal costing model. Direct expense variances and variable overhead variances are not studied in this unit, and have therefore been ignored in these diagrams.

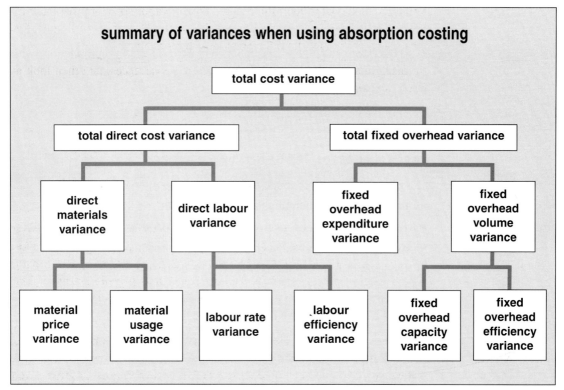

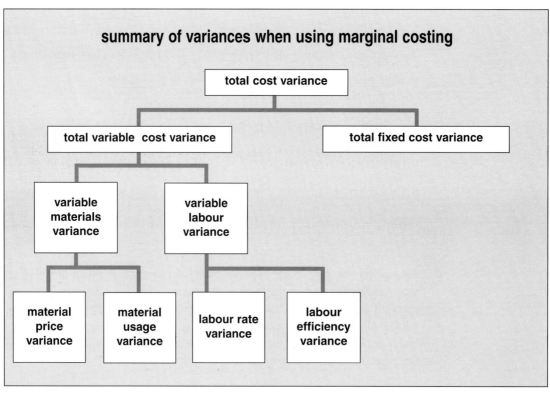

You should be familiar with most of these variances from your earlier studies, but it is important that you are able to calculate them accurately. For this reason, it is worth taking a good look at them again.

In this chapter we will examine the direct cost variances, and then look at fixed overhead variances in Chapter 3.

DIRECT MATERIAL VARIANCE

The total direct material variance is the difference between the standard cost of material and the actual cost of material *for the actual production*.

It would make no sense to compare the actual cost of what was produced with the standard cost of another quantity; we must compare like with like. Often the standard cost figure that we need can be arrived at by multiplying the standard cost for one unit by the quantity of units actually produced. The actual costs will of course already relate to the actual production level.

The total direct material variance can then be analysed into the **direct material price variance**, and the **direct material usage variance**. As their names suggest, the first sub-variance measures the amount of the cost difference due to the price of material, and the second the cost difference due to the amount of material used.

direct material price variance

The direct material price variance =

the standard cost of the actual quantity of material used	*minus*	the actual cost of the actual quantity of material used

It is sometimes useful to express this as:

actual quantity x (standard price – actual price)

This will work if the prices are for a unit of material (for example a kilo or square metre), and the quantity is expressed in the same units. Where the data is not immediately available in this form there is a danger that any rounding carried out will distort the result of the calculation. It is then advisable to use the first version of the formula.

direct material usage variance

The direct material usage variance =

the standard quantity of material for actual production at standard price	*minus*	the actual quantity of material used at standard price

This is often expressed as:

standard price x (standard quantity – actual quantity)

The information for this variance is usually available in this form, so the rounding problems associated with price variances are unlikely to arise.

All the above formulae have been presented so that numerically positive answers will give rise to favourable variances, and a negative answer will mean the variance will be adverse. However it is best to determine favourable or adverse from logic since formulae can be remembered incorrectly. Simply, if it costs more than standard, or the usage is more than standard the direct variance must be adverse.

calculation of variances

The key to calculating the variances accurately is remembering the basis of the formulas. One method that may help is the mnemonic 'PAUS', based on:

Price variances are based on
Actual quantities, but
Usage variances are based on
Standard prices.

One explanation why the variances are calculated in this way is that purchases are sometimes converted to standard price (and a price variance calculated) when the materials are bought. This price variance would relate to the actual materials bought. The materials in stock would then be valued at standard price, and the usage variance would be calculated based on the amounts issued to production at standard price.

A diagram can be used to illustrate how direct material variances are linked. It can be a useful aid to explanation, but should not be used as a means of remembering how to calculate the variances, since when some variances are favourable the diagram can become less easy to follow.

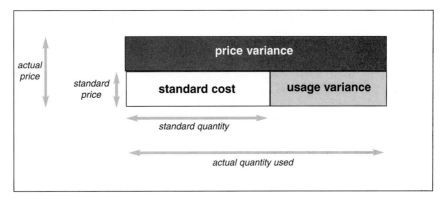

Also remember that the two sub-variances must add up to the total direct material variance. This is a useful check. Assessors have commented that students sometimes calculate some variances, but are confused as to which variances they have calculated.

CASE STUDY

DIRECT MATERIAL VARIANCE: ORME PRODUCTION COMPANY

The Orme Production Company has the following direct material costs results for its product the 'Orme' for the month of September:

	Budget	Actual
Production Level (Ormes)	1,500	1,800
Material Quantity (kilos)	6,000	7,100
Material Cost	£45,000	£54,770

required

Calculate the total direct material variance for the production of 1,800 Ormes, and analyse it into the direct material price variance and the direct material usage variance.

solution

The first stage is to work out the standards for one Orme. We will do this by using the budget data, since the budget would originally have been built up using standard data.

Standard Material Quantity per Orme 6,000 kilos ÷ 1,500 Ormes = 4 kilos
Standard Price of Material per Kilo   £45,000 ÷ 6,000 kilos   =   £7.50

We can then work out the standards for the actual production level. Note that we do not use the budgeted production level for calculating direct variances.

standard material quantity
for actual production level   4 kilos x 1,800 Ormes   = 7,200 kilos.

standard material cost
for actual production level   7,200 kilos x £7.50   = £54,000

The variances can now be calculated:

The total direct material variance =

standard cost of material for actual production level	minus	actual cost of material for actual production level

£54,000 – £54,770 ———————————————————→ = £770 Adverse

The direct material price variance =

the standard cost of the actual quantity of material used	minus	the actual cost of the actual quantity of material used

(7,100 kilos @ £7.50) – £54,770 =

£53,250 – £54,770 ———————————————————→ = £1,520 Adverse

Note that this 'full' version of the formula was used, since the actual price per kilo would work out as £54,770 ÷ 7,100 kilos = £7.7140845 (rounded). It would risk rounding errors to use the formula that requires this figure.

The direct material usage variance =

standard price x (standard quantity – actual quantity)

£7.50 x (7,200 kilos – 7,100 kilos) =

£7.50 x 100 kilos ———————————————————→ = £750 Favourable

Here we were able to use the shorter formula, since all the data was available. Note also that the 'standard quantity' used in the formula refers to the standard quantity for the actual production level.

We can also confirm that the sub variances add up to the total variance:

£1520 Adverse + £750 Favourable = £770 Adverse.

DIRECT LABOUR VARIANCE

The approach for calculating direct labour variances is very similar to direct material variances. The total direct labour variance is the difference between the standard cost of labour and the actual cost of labour for the actual production.

This total labour variance can then be analysed into two sub variances in a similar way to material variances. The direct labour rate variance measures the labour cost difference due to the rate paid, and the direct labour efficiency variance measures the cost difference due to the amount of labour time used. The concept of labour 'rate' is similar to material 'price', and labour 'efficiency' is similar to material 'usage'. This makes remembering the calculation method and interpreting the variances much easier.

direct labour rate variance

The direct labour rate variance =

the standard cost of the actual labour hours used	minus	the actual cost of the actual labour hours used

It is sometimes useful to express this as:

actual labour hours x (standard rate – actual rate)

Note how similar this is to the direct material price variance. This version of the formula will work if both rates are hourly. There is a risk of rounding errors if the actual hourly rate cannot be calculated exactly, in which case it is advisable to use the first version of the formula.

direct labour efficiency variance

The direct labour efficiency variance =

standard labour hours for actual production at standard rate	minus	actual labour hours used at standard rate

This is often expressed as:

standard rate x (standard hours – actual hours)

This also has a strong resemblance to the material usage variance; we are simply considering the quantity of labour hours instead of the quantity of material. We will usually have the information for this variance available in this form, so the rounding problems are unlikely to arise.

Provided we can remember the similarity of the labour sub variances to the material ones, there is probably no need to use any other memory aid. The direct labour sub variances must add up to the total direct labour variance.

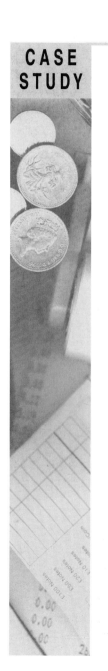

CASE STUDY

DIRECT LABOUR VARIANCE: ORME PRODUCTION COMPANY

The Orme Production Company (see page 47) has the following direct labour data for its product the 'Orme' for the month of September:

	Budget	Actual
Production Level (Ormes)	1,500	1,800
Direct Labour Hours	2,250	2,850
Labour Cost	£15,750	£19,400

required

Calculate the total direct labour variance for the production of 1,800 Ormes, and analyse it into the direct labour rate variance and the direct labour efficiency variance.

solution

The approach here will be almost identical to the calculation of the material variances as carried out earlier. The following calculations are therefore shown with little comment. Make sure that you can see the similarity to the earlier workings, and check that you can see where the figures come from and why they are used.

Standard Labour Hours per Orme	2,250 hours ÷ 1,500	= 1.5 hours.
Standard Labour Rate per hour	£15,750 ÷ 2,250	= £7.00.
Standard Labour Hours for Actual Production Level	1.5 hours x 1,800 Ormes	= 2,700 hours.
Standard Labour Cost For Actual Production Level	2,700 hours x £7.00	= £18,900

The total direct labour variance =

standard cost of labour for actual production level	minus	actual cost of labour for actual production level

£18,900 – £19,400 —————————————————→ = £500 Adverse

The direct labour rate variance =

the standard cost of the actual labour hours used	minus	the actual cost of the actual labour hours used

(2,850 hours @ £7.00) – £19,400 =

£19,950 – £19,400 —————————————————→ = £550 Favourable

This formula version is used here since actual hourly rate could not be calculated without rounding.

The direct labour efficiency variance =

standard rate x (std hours – actual hours)

£7.00 x (2,700 hours – 2,850 hours) =

£7.00 x (– 150 hours) —————————————————→ = £1,050 Adverse

We can also confirm that the sub-variances add up to the total variance:

£550 Favourable + £1,050 Adverse = £500 Adverse.

USING VARIANCES TO RECONCILE ACTUAL WITH STANDARD COSTS

reconciliation statements

It is important that we can show how variances account for all the cost differences between the standard cost of the production and the actual cost. We can do this by using a reconciliation statement. Note that we must compare like with like and use the data for the standard cost of the actual production to compare with the actual cost. The actual cost will of course also relate to the actual production. The reconciliation statement can start with either the standard or the actual cost, and will arrive, via the variances at the other figure. We are accounting for the differences, in the same way that a bank reconciliation statement accounts for the differences between the cash book balance and the bank account balance.

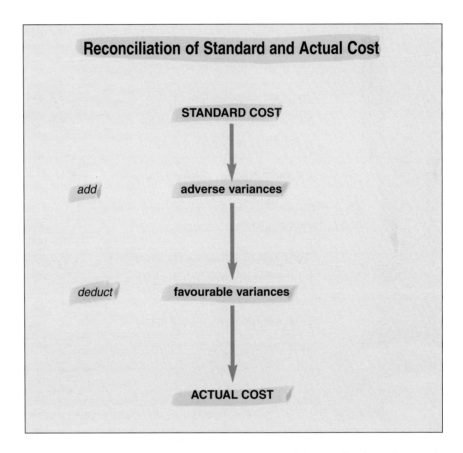

Reconciliation of Standard and Actual Cost

STANDARD COST

add   adverse variances

deduct   favourable variances

ACTUAL COST

If we start the statement with the standard cost of the production, then each adverse variance will be added to this amount, since the actual cost we are working towards will be higher. Any favourable variances will be deducted since this accounts for a lower actual amount. Since a reconciliation only takes a short time to prepare, it is often worth producing since it will show if any variances are inaccurate.

Remember that, like agreement of a trial balance, a satisfactory variance reconciliation is not a guarantee that the variances are correct! Also remember that sub variances are part of main variances, so be careful not to double count them.

In this chapter we are only examining direct cost variances, so our reconciliation will be just based on that part of the cost. We will see later how indirect costs can be incorporated into a full reconciliation.

DIRECT COST RECONCILIATION STATEMENT: ORME PRODUCTION COMPANY

The data given for Orme Production Company in the earlier case studies can be summarised as follows:

	Budget	Actual
Production Level (Ormes)	1,500	1,800
Material Quantity (kilos)	6,000	7,100
Material Cost	£45,000	£54,770
Direct Labour Hours	2,250	2,850
Labour Cost	£15,750	£19,400

required

Using the direct cost variances, reconcile the standard direct cost of the actual production with the actual direct cost.

solution

The two main figures for the reconciliation are as follows:

(1)   Standard direct cost of actual production is made up of:

	Standard material cost for actual production level	= £54,000
plus	Standard labour cost for actual production level	= £18,900
		£72,900

(Both figures as calculated previously, see pages 48-50)

(2)   Actual direct costs of production is made up of:

	Actual direct material cost	= £54,770
plus	Actual direct labour cost	= £19,400
		£74,170

These figures will form the start and finishing point of the reconciliation statement, and the variances will be listed in between. Note that the total direct material and labour variances are formed by totalling the respective sub-variances to avoid duplicating the figures.

Direct Cost Reconciliation Statement for September Production of 1,800 Ormes

	£	£
Standard Direct Cost of Production		72,900
Add adverse direct material price variance	1,520	
Less favourable direct material usage variance	(750)	
Add adverse total direct material variance		770
Less favourable direct labour rate variance	(550)	
Add adverse direct labour efficiency variance	1,050	
Add adverse total direct labour variance		500
Actual Cost of Production		74,170

THE MAIN CAUSES OF VARIANCES

If you are familiar with the sources of data for creating variances, and what each variance means, it should not be necessary to learn lists of possible causes of variances. Instead it should be possible to logically think your way through each situation to see its impact on variances. You may be given a scenario and asked to suggest the possible causes of variances. It is far better to use the facts given to you about the situation to develop a reasoned commentary, than to remember an 'all purpose' list of causes and simply regurgitate it.

Some situations may give rise to more than one variance. For example purchasing cheaper material of lower quality could cause a favourable price variance but an adverse usage variance if there was higher wastage. This is often referred to as the interdependence of variances. It can result in unfair praise or blame if different managers are responsible for each variance.

The following table gives examples of possible causes of variances. Read it carefully, and ensure that you can appreciate the logic of including each item, and its effect. There may be situations where you can envisage the cause creating further variances, since the table is not intended to be exhaustive.

'A' or 'F' refers to whether adverse or favourable variances may result.

Direct Variance: Possible Cause	Material Price	Material Usage	Labour Rate	Labour Efficiency
Poorly set standard	A or F	A or F	A or F	A or F
Different material supplier	A or F			
Different material quality	A or F	A or F		A or F
Different currency exchange rate	A or F			
Poor training		A		A
Higher grade staff		F	A	F
Unexpected pay increase			A	
High general inflation	A		A	
Improved production machinery		F		F
Unexpected bulk discounts	F			
Low bonus payments			F	A

**CHAPTER
SUMMARY**

- Standard costing was developed in manufacturing industry as a method of predicting the cost of products. When comparing actual costs with the expected (standard) costs, it enables variances to be calculated that help explain differences in the costs. There are various other benefits from setting up and using a standard costing system.

- Standard costs can be used based on a traditional absorption costing system, or on a marginal costing system. The main difference arises in the treatment of fixed overhead variances: direct cost variances are calculated in the same way under both types of costing. The direct cost variances for materials and labour can be divided into sub-variances based on the cost per unit of the resource (Price or Rate variances) and the quantity of resource used (Usage and Efficiency variances).

- Information for setting standards can be derived from inside and outside the organisation. This information includes formal and informal historical data and technical specifications, and can be general or specific.

- Direct cost variances (including sub variances) are calculated according to rules that help ensure uniformity. The variances can be used to reconcile the standard cost for the production with the actual costs.

- There can be many causes of variances, some influencing just one variance, while others affect several. The accurate calculation of a variance does not provide information on the cause itself, but the causes can often be deduced by examining the factors surrounding the situation.

**KEY
TERMS**

standard costing	A formal method for predetermining the cost of cost units or products.
variance analysis	The comparison of actual costs with standard costs and the calculation of variances which account for differences in the costs.
marginal costing	A technique that values cost units based on variable costs only. Fixed costs are considered related only to the reporting period of time.

absorption costing

A technique that values cost units based on a suitable part of all the costs of production, whether fixed or variable in behaviour

total direct material variance

The difference between the standard material cost for the actual production and the actual material cost.

direct material price variance

The part of the total direct material variance due to differing material prices. It is based on the difference between standard and actual prices for the actual quantity of material used (or bought).

direct material usage variance

The part of the total direct material variance due to differing quantities of material used. It is based on the difference between the standard quantity of material for the actual production, and the actual quantity of material used, valued at standard price.

total direct labour variance

The difference between the standard labour cost for the actual production and the actual labour cost.

direct labour rate variance

The part of the total direct labour variance due to differing labour rates. It is based on the difference between the actual labour hours at standard rate and the actual labour cost.

direct labour efficiency variance

The part of the total direct labour variance due to differing time being spent. It is based on the difference between the standard labour time for the actual production, and the actual labour time used, valued at standard rate

cost reconciliation statement

A statement reconciling the standard cost of the actual production with the actual cost by using relevant variances.

2.1 Your colleague has accurately produced the following direct cost variances for Week 23.

Direct Material Price Variance	£ 1,585 A
Direct Material Usage Variance	£ 993 F
Direct Labour Rate Variance	£ 2,460 F
Direct Labour Efficiency Variance	£ 1,051 F

The standard cost of one unit is £95.40, and the company produced 1,060 units in week 23.

Required

Calculate the total actual direct costs for the company for week 23.

2.2 Grimley Limited has the following budgeted and actual direct cost and production data for the month of August.

	Budget	Budget	Actual	Actual
Production Units		20,000		19,000
		£		£
Direct Materials	40,000 kg	300,000	37,000 kg	278,000
Direct Labour	10,000 hours	60,000	9,800 hrs	58,600
Total Costs		360,000		336,600

Required

Calculate the relevant direct cost variances and use them to reconcile the standard cost for the actual production level with the actual costs.

2.3 The following comments were made by an inexperienced trainee accounting technician.

Required

State which of the comments are valid, and which are false.

(a) The likelihood of obtaining bulk discounts cannot be relevant when setting direct material price standards.

(b) Work study is often used to assist in setting times for direct labour standards.

(c) The interdependence of variances should be considered when examining the causes for variances.

(d) Material price standards must always be amended when a different supplier is used.

(e) Future production schedules can be used to assist in setting material price standards by helping to gauge the availability of quantity discounts.

(f) Two of the main reasons for using standard costing are to improve planning and control.

(g) Standard costing can be used in conjunction with responsibility accounting. Using this technique each managers would be expected to control the variances occurring in his/her area of responsibility.

(h) Interpretation of variances can help point to the reasons that costs are not in line with the plans.

(i) The inclusion of overtime premium rates when setting direct labour rate standards would depend on the company policy, since many organisations consider that such costs are indirect.

(j) Proposed bonus schemes should be taken into account when setting labour rate standards.

(k) Reconciling standard cost with actual cost is difficult because when variances are a mixture of adverse and favourable the statement may not agree.

(l) If a reconciliation of standard cost for the actual production level with the actual cost agrees this guarantees that all the variances are correct.

2.4   Marge Products Ltd uses marginal costing and has the following budgeted and actual variable cost and production data for the month of August.

	Budget	*Budget*	*Actual*	*Actual*
Production Units		30,000		32,000
		£		£
Variable Materials	3,000 kg	75,000	3,100 kg	81,000
Variable Labour	15,000 hours	75,000	15,900 hrs	77,900
Total Variable Costs		150,000		158,900

Required

Calculate the relevant variable cost variances and use them to reconcile the standard marginal cost for the actual production level with the actual marginal costs.

2.5   Quango Limited has set its direct standard costs for one unit of its product, the quango as follows:
Direct Materials: 96 kg @ £ 9.45 per kilo.
Direct Labour: 5 hours 6 minutes @ £6.30 per hour.

During week 13 the company produced 700 units of quango, and incurred direct costs as follows:

Direct Materials: 71.5 tonnes were used, costing a total of £678,700
Direct Labour: 3,850 hours were worked, costing a total of £24,220

Note: there are 1,000 kilos in a tonne.

Required

Calculate the relevant direct cost variances and use them to reconcile the standard cost for the actual production level with the actual costs.

3 STANDARD COSTING – FIXED OVERHEADS

this chapter covers . . .

In this chapter we examine:

- the problems of dealing with fixed overheads
- the calculation of fixed overhead variances under marginal costing
- the calculation of fixed overhead variances under absorption costing
- the interpretation of fixed overhead variances
- the application of fixed overhead variances to the service sector
- the situations when specific fixed overhead variances are inappropriate

NVQ PERFORMANCE CRITERIA COVERED

unit 8: CONTRIBUTING TO THE MANAGEMENT OF COSTS AND THE ENHANCEMENT OF VALUE

element 1

collect, analyse and disseminate information about costs

- valid, relevant information is identified from internal and external sources.

- standard costs are compared with actual costs and any variances are analysed

FIXED OVERHEADS

the difference between variable and fixed costs

In the last chapter we examined the direct costs of materials and labour. We looked at how standard costing could be used to predict this part of a product's cost and how variances could be calculated to help analyse any differences between the standard cost and the actual cost. Since direct costs will often rise in proportion to the output of products there is logic in calculating a standard for the direct cost for one unit of production, and expecting it to remain the same when multiplied by the number of items produced. For example, it would seem fair to expect that the direct material for 2,000 widgets would cost about 2,000 times more than that for one widget.

You can assume that direct costs will behave in the same way as variable costs, ie they will change in line with the level of activity (the number of products produced). They are therefore different from fixed costs:

Variable Costs   Costs where the total amount varies in proportion to the activity level when the activity level changes.

Fixed Costs   Costs that do not normally change when the level of activity changes.

fixed costs: absorption or marginal costing?

When fixed costs are involved in costing products there are two traditional schools of thought about how they should be dealt with.

Absorption costing attempts to incorporate fixed costs into the cost of the product by absorbing a suitable part of the expected fixed cost into each unit produced.

Marginal costing views fixed costs as time-based rather than product based, and therefore does not attempt to incorporate these costs into each unit produced. Instead it costs each unit based on only the variable costs, and deals with the fixed costs in the profit and loss account for the appropriate reporting period.

using absorption costing for fixed costs

One advantage that standard absorption costing can claim is that the standard cost for a product will be a 'full' cost, and incorporate a portion of all the costs of production. Therefore, provided the actual production level is close to the projected level, and all cost estimates are reasonably accurate, the standard cost of the product will be close to the actual full cost. However, the standard will give an inaccurate forecast of product cost:

- if the costs are not as expected and
- if the production volume is not in line with expectations

For this reason the fixed overhead variances produced under standard absorption costing need to take account of:

- overhead costs
- production volumes

using marginal costing for fixed costs

With marginal costing, by contrast, the volume of production will not affect the standard marginal cost of a product, because the only costs contained in the standard are variable costs – fixed costs are excluded. As fixed costs are dealt with by comparing the expected fixed cost for the period with the actual fixed cost, the only fixed overhead variance that needs to be calculated under marginal standard costing is simply the difference between these two figures.

We will now look in detail at the treatment of fixed overhead variances using marginal costing.

FIXED OVERHEAD VARIANCES – MARGINAL COSTING

fixed overhead expenditure variance

Under standard marginal costing the only fixed overhead variance is usually called the **fixed overhead expenditure variance**. It is very simple to calculate, as follows:

Budgeted Fixed Overhead for period	*minus*	Actual Fixed Overhead for period

The variance would therefore be calculated for the week, month, quarter or other reporting period, and the number of items produced would not form part of the calculation.

If the actual cost was **lower** than the budgeted amount the variance would be **favourable**, and if it was **higher**, it would be considered **adverse**. The variance could be used as part of a reconciliation between actual and standard costs for the production in a period of time.

Note – throughout this and later case studies in this chapter, 'A' and 'F' have been used to denote **A**dverse and **F**avourable variances respectively.

CASE STUDY

FIXED OVERHEAD VARIANCES – MARGINAL COSTING: WENSHAM WHEELBARROWS

Wensham Wheelbarrows manufactures a single product – the 'Wensham' wheelbarrow. The company had the following results for their third quarter. The company used standard marginal costing. Both direct materials and direct labour are considered to behave as variable costs.

	Budgeted	Actual
Number of Units	10,000	12,000
Direct Materials	£ 50,000	£ 65,000
Direct Labour	£ 80,000	£ 94,000
Fixed Overheads	£ 75,000	£ 81,000
Total Costs	£205,000	£240,000

The direct variances have already been calculated (based on information not shown) as follows:

Direct material price variance	£6,000 A
Direct material usage variance	£1,000 F
Direct labour rate variance	£4,000 F
Direct labour efficiency variance	£2,000 A

required

1   Calculate the fixed overhead expenditure variance.
2   Calculate the standard cost of the actual production.
3   Reconcile the standard cost of the actual production with the actual cost of the production.

solution

Step 1

Fixed overhead expenditure variance

= Budgeted Fixed Overhead for period – Actual Fixed Overhead for period

= £75,000 – £81,000

= £6,000 A

This variance can logically be confirmed as adverse since the fixed overheads actually cost more than the amount that was budgeted.

Step 2

At first glance the direct variances that have been given in the Case Study do not seem to fit in with the rest of the data. This is because the budgeted production level is different to the actual level. To see how the direct variances would reconcile we must acknowledge that the standard cost must be based on the actual production level, as follows:

Standard Cost of Actual Production:

Direct Materials (£50,000 ÷10,000) x 12,000	£ 60,000
Direct Labour (£80,000 ÷10,000) x 12,000	£ 96,000
Fixed Overheads	£ 75,000
Total	£231,000

Step 3
We can then reconcile the figures as follows:

Standard cost of Actual Production		£231,000
Direct material price variance	£6,000 A	
Direct material usage variance	(£1,000) F	
Direct labour rate variance	(£4,000) F	
Direct labour efficiency variance	£2,000 A	
Fixed overhead expenditure variance	£6,000 A	
		£ 9,000
Actual cost of Production		£240,000

FIXED OVERHEAD VARIANCES – ABSORPTION COSTING

The fixed overhead variances under standard absorption costing are more complicated than under marginal costing. As mentioned earlier they attempt to take account of:

- differences arising due to cost
- differences resulting from the volume of production.

The variances analyse the differences between the amount of fixed overhead absorbed by a standard absorption costing system, and the actual cost of the fixed overheads.

total fixed overhead variances and expenditure and volume variances

The absorption rate is agreed before the period starts, and is arranged so that the planned level of output will cause enough overhead absorption to exactly match the expected overheads. If the absorption base is units of, then the output will be measured in units, but if the absorption base is labour hours or machine hours, then we must also measure the output in standard labour or machine hours.

If everything goes to plan there will be no under-absorption or over-absorption, and no fixed overhead variances! The plan could be thought of as a pair of weighing scales, as shown in this diagram:

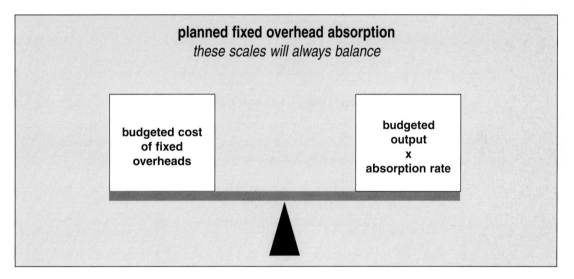

This diagram is based on the planned figures and so will always balance, since the figures are designed to agree. It would not make sense to plan for an imbalance!

will the plan work? – possible imbalances

Once actual figures are used there may be an imbalance due to either

- the fixed overheads not costing what was expected, or
- the output not turning out to be as planned, or (as usually happens)
- a combination of the two.

Since the absorption rate is worked out in advance and used throughout, the rate itself will not be a source of any imbalance.

Once the results for the period are known, then the **planned** figures on the diagram shown above can be replaced by the **actual** figures in the diagram shown below.

under-absorption – adverse variance

The scales in this diagram tip down on the left because actual costs are higher than the amount of cost absorbed and so there is under-absorption.

This will result in the total fixed overhead variance being adverse.

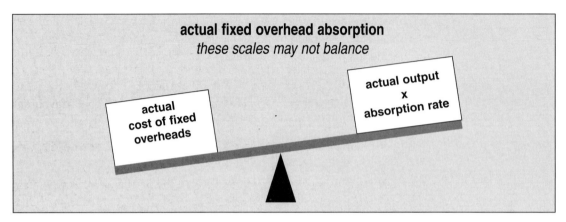

over-absorption – favourable variance

The scales in the next diagram tip down on the right because actual costs are lower than the amount of cost absorbed, and so there is over-absorption. This will result in the total fixed overhead variance being favourable.

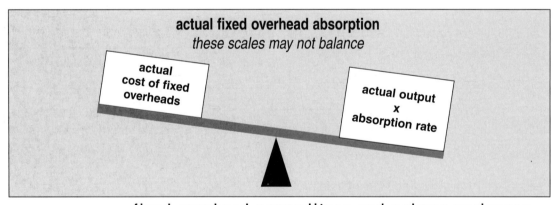

fixed overhead expenditure and volume variances

The imbalances shown in the last two diagrams measure the **total fixed overhead variance** – this is due to the difference between the plan and what actually happens. There are two reasons why the actual results could be different from the plan, and these two reasons combine together to result in the total fixed overhead variance. They are:

1   The actual amount **spent** on fixed overheads may not be the same as the planned (or budgeted) fixed overheads. In the diagrams the left-hand sides of the scales – the actual cost – will be different from the planned figure. This difference is measured by the **fixed overhead expenditure variance**.

2   The actual **volume of output** may not be the same as the planned level of output. This will cause a different amount of fixed overhead to be absorbed than was expected. In the diagrams the figures in the right-hand sides of the scales will differ. This difference is measured by the **fixed overhead volume variance**.

In basic terms, the actual figures on both sides of the scales (last two diagrams) are likely to be different from the plan (first diagram) because of changes in expenditure and output volume levels. It is the **combination** of these two differences/variances which will decide which way the scales will tip and result in an overall **total fixed overhead variance**. A tip to the left will be an overall adverse variance, a tip to the right will be a favourable variance.

The main variances can be summarised when we bring the two diagrams together like this:

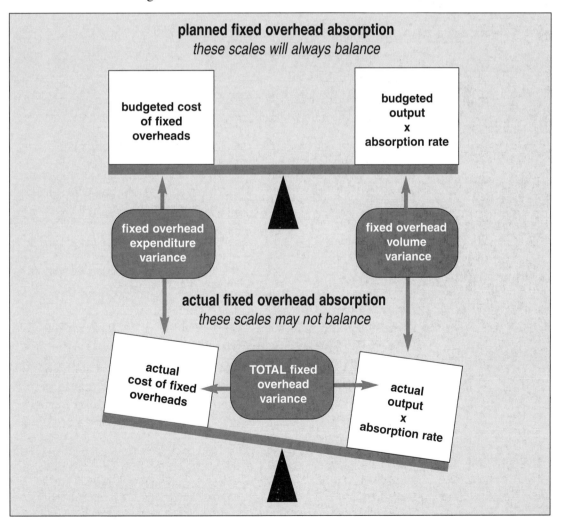

Total **fixed overhead variance** therefore equals

Fixed Overhead Absorbed – Actual Cost of Fixed Overhead

the absorption base

Remember that the amount of fixed overhead absorbed will be based on the actual output multiplied by the absorption rate. The way that the output is measured here will depend on the way that absorption is to take place (the absorption base). If the absorption base is production units, then the output needs to be measured in that form.

If the absorption base is direct labour hours, then the output must be measured in standard labour hours (ie the standard direct labour hours for the actual output). This is often a source of confusion. Remember that what we are measuring is the output; the standard hours for that output is sometimes a convenient way of expressing it.

The same principle will apply if the absorption base is machine hours. The actual output would then need to be expressed in standard machine hours.

Where standard hours are used as an absorption base it is vital to appreciate that absorption will normally take place based on the standard hours for the actual production level, not the actual time taken.

calculation of fixed overhead expenditure and volume variances

The **fixed overhead expenditure variance** is shown on the left-hand side of the last diagram, and is calculated as follows:

Budgeted Cost of Fixed Overheads	*minus*	Actual Cost of Fixed Overheads

If the actual cost is less than the budgeted cost the variance is favourable, and if it is greater the variance is adverse.

The **fixed overhead volume variance** is shown on the right-hand side of the last diagram, and is calculated as follows:

Absorption Rate x (Actual Output – Budgeted Output)

As mentioned above in relation to the total fixed overhead variance, the form in which the output needs to be expressed will depend on the form of the absorption rate. If the absorption rate is expressed in an amount per unit, then the output should also be in units. If the absorption base is some form of standard hours, then the output must be expressed in standard hours, and the volume variance can be written as:

Absorption Rate x (Standard Hours for Actual Output – Standard Hours for Budgeted Output)

The volume variance is therefore a straight comparison of the overheads that would be absorbed by the two output levels (actual and planned).

Some form of standard hours are often used to help measure output because:

- it can be used to convert different kinds of output (eg a carpenter who produces both tables and chairs) into a common form, and
- it enables further analysis of costs (eg by dividing the fixed overhead volume variance, as discussed later)

If an organisation makes a single product then the fixed overhead variances discussed so far will be identical whichever absorption base is used, as illustrated in the next case study.

CASE STUDY

FIXED OVERHEAD VARIANCES: NODGE LIMITED

Nodge Limited manufactures a single product – the 'nodge'. The company had the following budgeted and actual data for the first year of production. Each unit was budgeted to take four direct labour hours to produce, two of which would be using manned machines.

	Budget	Actual
Production Units	20,000	23,000
Standard Direct Labour Hours	80,000	
Standard Machine Hours	40,000	
Fixed Overheads	£ 200,000	£ 195,000

required

Calculate the total fixed overhead variance, and the breakdown into expenditure and volume, assuming the overhead absorption base is:

1   Units
2   Standard direct labour hours
3   Standard machine hours

solution

1 Absorption base of Units

The absorption rate would be £200,00 ÷ 20,000 units = £10 per unit

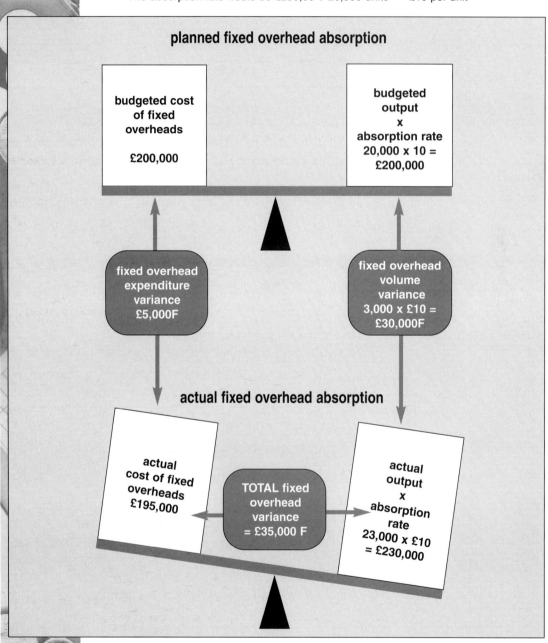

planned fixed overhead absorption

budgeted cost of fixed overheads

£200,000

budgeted output x absorption rate
20,000 x 10 = £200,000

fixed overhead expenditure variance
£5,000F

fixed overhead volume variance
3,000 x £10 = £30,000F

actual fixed overhead absorption

actual cost of fixed overheads
£195,000

TOTAL fixed overhead variance
= £35,000 F

actual output x absorption rate
23,000 x £10 = £230,000

Here the combination of the higher volume achieved and lower actual cost of overheads has resulted in over-absorption and a favourable total fixed overhead variance.

2 Absorption base of Standard Direct Labour Hours

The absorption rate would be £200,000 ÷ 80,000 = £2.50

The standard direct labour hours for the actual production would be

23,000 units x 4 hours = 92,000.

The total fixed overhead variance equals:

Fixed Overhead Absorbed – Actual Cost of Fixed Overhead

(£2.50 x 92,000) – £195,000 = £35,000 F

The volume variance equals:

Absorption Rate x (Actual Output – Budgeted Output)

Since we are measuring outputs in standard direct labour hours, we will insert the following figures:

Actual Output (in standard direct labour hours) is 92,000 (as calculated above)

Budgeted Output (in standard direct labour hours) is 80,000 (the figure given in the Case Study)

The volume variance therefore equals:

£2.50 x (92,000 – 80,000) = £30,000 F

This is the same result that is achieved when we use units as an absorption base.

The expenditure variance is also unchanged at £5,000 F.

3 Absorption base of Standard Machine Hours

The absorption rate would be £200,000 ÷ 40,000 = £5.00

The standard machine hours for the actual production would be:

23,000 units x 2 hours = 46,000

The total fixed overhead variance equals:

Fixed Overhead Absorbed – Actual Cost of Fixed Overhead

£5.00 x 46,000 – £195,000 = £35,000 F

The volume variance equals:

Absorption Rate x (Actual Output – Budgeted Output)

Since we are measuring outputs in standard machine hours, we will insert the following figures:

Actual Output (in standard machine hours) is 46,000 (as calculated above)

Budgeted Output (in standard machine hours) is 40,000 (the figure given in the Case Study)

The volume variance therefore equals

£5.00 x (46,000 − 40,000) = £30,000 F

This is again the same result that is achieved when we use units as an absorption base.

The expenditure variance is again unchanged at £5,000 F.

FIXED OVERHEAD VOLUME SUB-VARIANCES

The full breakdown of the total fixed overhead variance is shown in the following variance tree:

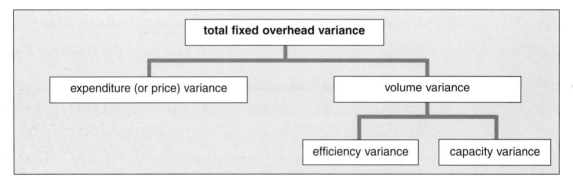

As we saw earlier in the chapter, the Total Fixed Overhead Variance is subdivided between the Expenditure Variance and the Volume Variance.

The Volume Variance can in turn be subdivided into the **Efficiency Variance** and the **Capacity Variance**. These two variances attempt to explain whether any difference in the volume of output can be accounted for through:

- efficient (or inefficient) working or
- by using more or less resources (often labour) than planned

These variances can only be calculated if we are using an absorption base that lends itself to this sort of analysis. If the absorption base is units of production then these variances could not normally be calculated.

We will now look at the two variances in turn.

fixed overhead efficiency variance

The Fixed Overhead Efficiency Variance compares the time the actual production should have taken with the time that it actually took, and multiplies the result by the absorption rate. When standard hours are used it equals:

Absorption Rate x (Standard Hours for Actual Output – Actual Hours Taken)

The notion of efficiency here is identical to that used for direct variances, and if direct labour is the absorption base, then the calculation will use the same hours as the direct labour efficiency variance, but multiplied by the absorption rate.

The logic of whether the variance is adverse or favourable will also be identical; taking less time than standard for the output level achieved is considered efficient and therefore favourable; taking more time is inefficient and the variance is adverse. In conclusion, we are providing a variance that demonstrates how much more (or less) fixed overhead has been absorbed due to the difference in output caused by efficiency.

A Fixed Overhead Efficiency Variance can also be calculated where absorption is carried out through the use of machine hours or some other measure, which is usually time based. The 'efficiency' that is being measured will, of course, depend on the source of the data.

fixed overhead capacity variance

The Fixed Overhead Capacity Variance compares the time that the budgeted production should have taken with the actual hours worked, and multiplies the result by the absorption rate. When standard hours are used it equals:

Absorption Rate x (Actual Hours Taken – Standard Hours for Budgeted Output)

The idea of capacity can be thought of as whether the workplace is filled to capacity with the intended resources. If we are using labour hours then we are examining how we are using the resource of people, by measuring their working hours. If people worked for longer than was originally planned then this produces a favourable variance since we are getting more use out of our factory than we had hoped for. A similar logic applies to the use of machine hours; the longer the machines are used then the better we are utilising that resource.

Since fixed overheads do not vary with output (by definition) the use of the volume variance and its analysis can be a useful reminder to managers that the greater the output the lower the cost per unit because the fixed overhead is spread over more units.

fixed overhead variances – a summary

All the fixed overhead variances can be incorporated into the diagram on the next page, which is based on the format of the diagram on page 67, with the addition of the efficiency and capacity sub-variances.

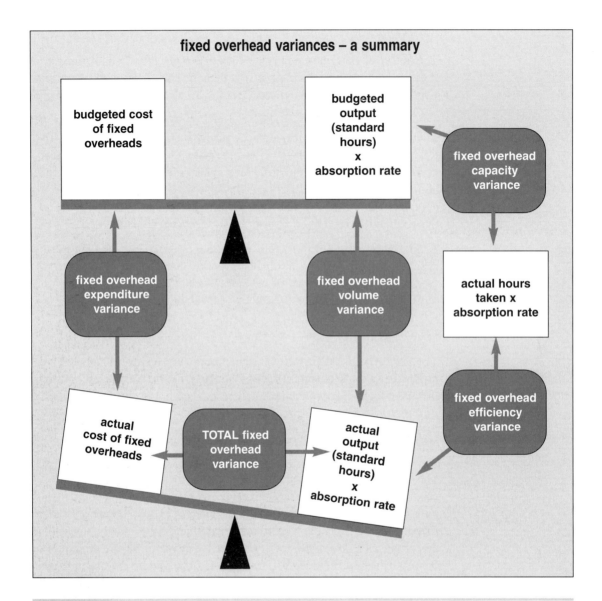

fixed overhead variances – a summary

budgeted cost of fixed overheads

budgeted output (standard hours) x absorption rate

fixed overhead capacity variance

fixed overhead expenditure variance

fixed overhead volume variance

actual hours taken x absorption rate

actual cost of fixed overheads

TOTAL fixed overhead variance

actual output (standard hours) x absorption rate

fixed overhead efficiency variance

CASE STUDY

OVERHEAD VARIANCES AND SUB–VARIANCES: WALMER LIMITED

The Finance Department of Walmer Limited has recorded the following data:

• The budgeted production level is 5000 standard hours. This will enable the absorption rate of £3.00 per hour to absorb the budgeted fixed overheads of £15,000

• Actual fixed overheads amount to £13,000

• Actual output is 5,800 standard hours.

• Actual time taken to achieve output is 5,500 hours.

required

Calculate the Total Fixed Overhead Variance, and analyse it into the sub variances.

solution

We can either use the diagram to help with the calculation, or use the formulae.

using the diagram

Using the diagram on page 74, and inserting first the known figures – and then the variances as differences – gives this result:

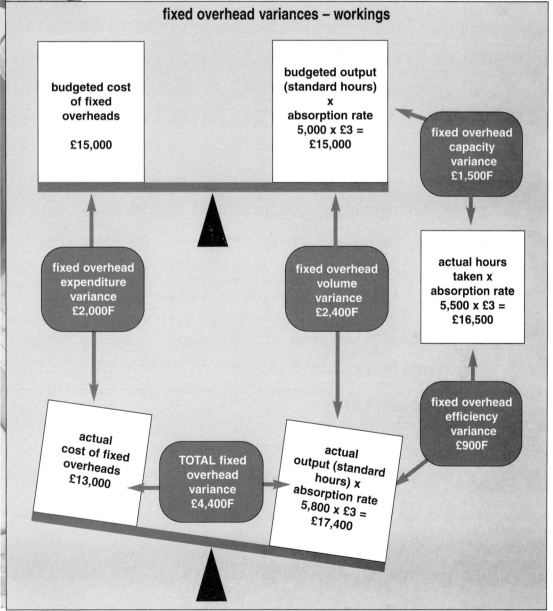

Using the formulae

Using the formulae we can confirm the results shown in the diagram.

The Total Fixed Overhead Variance equals:

Fixed Overhead Absorbed – Actual Cost of Fixed Overhead

(£3 x 5800) – £13,000 $\longrightarrow$ = £4,400 F

The Expenditure Variance equals:

Budgeted Cost of Fixed Overheads – Actual Cost of Fixed Overheads.

£15,000 – £13,000 $\longrightarrow$ = £2,000 F

The Volume Variance equals:

Absorption Rate x (Standard Hours for Actual Output – Standard Hours for Budgeted Output)

£3 x (5,800 – 5,000) $\longrightarrow$ = £2,400 F

Since we have the data on the actual hours taken, we can analyse the volume variance into the fixed overhead efficiency variance, and the fixed overhead capacity variance.

The Fixed Overhead Efficiency Variance equals:

Absorption Rate x (Standard Hours for Actual Output – Actual Hours Taken)

£3 x (5,800 – 5,500) $\longrightarrow$ = £900 F

The Fixed Overhead Capacity Variance equals:

Absorption Rate x (Actual Hours Taken – Standard Hours for Budgeted Output)

£3 x (5,500 – 5,000) $\longrightarrow$ = £1,500 F

Note that the efficiency and capacity variances must add up to the volume variance, and that the volume and price variances must add up to the total fixed overhead variance.

A full summary of the overhead variances reads:

Fixed Overhead Expenditure Variance		£2000 F
Fixed Overhead Efficiency Variance	£ 900 F	
Fixed Overhead Capacity Variance	£1500 F	
Fixed Overhead Volume Variance		£2400 F
Total Fixed Overhead Variance		£4400 F

INTERPRETATION OF FIXED OVERHEAD VARIANCES

Once we understand what the fixed overhead variances are trying to measure, their interpretation becomes quite straightforward. There may be a variety of different underlying causes for these variances in the same way that there are for direct variances, but the individual variances are always trying to measure the same kind of differences.

fixed overhead expenditure variance

The **fixed overhead expenditure variance** shows whether actual spending on fixed overheads was more or less than the budgeted amount.

The fixed overhead expenditure variance is measuring the difference between the budgeted cost of the fixed overheads and the actual cost. An adverse variance indicates that the actual cost is more than was expected, and a favourable variance that the actual cost is less. The reasons for the variances could include poor budgeting, or the fact that actual costs are different due to unforeseen price changes. The cost of these overheads are not expected to change because of differing output levels since they are defined as 'fixed' costs so any difference in output is irrelevant in the interpretation of this variance.

fixed overhead volume variance

The **fixed overhead volume variance** shows the difference between the overheads that would be absorbed by the planned volume of output and the amount absorbed by the actual volume of output.

The fixed overhead volume variance is measuring how much more or less fixed overheads have been absorbed compared to the planned amount of absorption. As the variance name indicates, this is entirely concerned with how the actual volume of output compares with the planned volume. The reason for this is because the system attempts to cost a set amount of overhead onto each unit of output. When the actual output is different to that which was planned, a volume variance will arise.

The effect of lower actual output than was planned would be an amount of overhead that has been left over and not accounted for as part of the output cost. This would mean that ideally (if adjustments could have been made in time) a larger amount of overhead should have been added to each unit. As this is not be possible after the event there is an amount of unabsorbed overhead, which needs to be written off in the accounts. This is why low output causes an adverse variance that results in a further cost to be written off (debited) in the accounts.

output volume greater than budgeted?

If the actual output is greater than expected, the volume variance will be favourable, representing an amount which can be credited to the accounts to compensate for more overhead being absorbed than was planned.

The reasons behind a volume variance will be concerned with either:

- the setting of the budgeted level of output (eg unrealistically high output or output set at too conservative a level), or

- something which caused the actual output to differ from the budget, (eg a shortage or additional levels of some resource, or machine breakdown)

using efficiency and capacity variances to explain the volume variance

The breakdown of the volume variance into efficiency and capacity is an attempt to explain why there had been higher or lower output than the budget forecast.

The **fixed overhead efficiency variance** shows how the efficient use of resources affects the volume of output.

A favourable efficiency variance indicates that output has been created using less resources than had been expected. If the absorption base is standard labour hours then the efficiency relates to labour efficiency. If the absorption base is standard machine hours then any efficiency variance is based on how efficiently the output had passed through the machines.

The **fixed overhead capacity variance** shows how the amount of resources used (compared with the budget) affects the volume of output.

The capacity variance explains how the output has been achieved through the use of more or less resources. When using labour hours as a base a favourable capacity variance indicates that additional output was created through the use of additional labour hours. Since any additional volume of output is beneficial, the fact that this variance is favourable is quite logical; it is just an indication of how the higher output was achieved. It also means that we are using the infrastructure more intensely than was planned, and this must be seen as a beneficial move to spread the fixed overhead costs more widely.

CASE STUDY

INTERPRETATION OF FIXED OVERHEAD VARIANCES: WALMER LIMITED – continued

solution

Using the data in the Case Study on page 74 the following interpretation could be put on the numerical results.

- The fixed overheads actually cost less than the budgeted amount by £2,000. This was demonstrated in the expenditure variance. We do not have any evidence as to whether this was caused by poor estimation of costs, or by changes in the overhead cost structure that occurred after the budget was prepared.

- The actual volume of output achieved was greater than was budgeted, and this caused £2,400 more fixed overhead to be absorbed than was planned. This additional volume was generated through a combination of higher efficiency than the budgeted level (accounting for absorption of an extra £900 of overhead), and the use of more labour hours than was anticipated (accounting for the other £1,500 of additional overhead absorption).

- In all, through the combination of lower cost and greater output a total of £4,400 more fixed overhead was absorbed than the fixed overheads actually cost. This over-absorption is represented by the total favourable variance, which will be credited to the accounts.

THE APPLICATION OF FIXED OVERHEAD VARIANCES TO THE SERVICE SECTOR

Standard costing and variance analysis have their origins in manufacturing industry, but the concepts can often be applied to other sectors of industry, the service sector, for example. The problems which must be dealt with in applying fixed overhead variances to service organisations tend to concern the measurement of output and choice of absorption base. Sometimes the more general term of 'activity level' can be used in these situations instead of 'output', but they both relate to an attempt to measure what the organisations produce, eg holidays arranged and hospital operations carried out.

the use of standard hours

Where some form of standard hours can be used as an absorption base and to measure output, then the techniques already studied can be used without any modification. The interpretation will need to be consistent with the organisation, but the calculation of the variances should follow the usual pattern.

CASE STUDY

FIXED OVERHEAD VARIANCES IN THE SERVICE SECTOR: BELLEVIEW HOSPITAL

situation

A private hospital carries out various surgical procedures in its operating theatre, using a standard team of five staff at all times. Each type of operation has a standard theatre time, and this is used to measure the output (or activity level) of the theatre in a universal manner. All the team record the time that they spend working in the theatre, and this information is also used to help calculate variances.

The fixed overheads of the operating theatre are budgeted at £2,000 per week, during which operations with a standard theatre time of 50 hours are planned to take place. During week 9 the fixed overheads amount to £2,350, and operations with a standard theatre time of 64 hours are completed. The total time logged by the staff on the theatre team that week was 295 hours.

required

Calculate the Total Fixed Overhead Variance, and analyse it into the sub variances.

solution

The only point to be careful about in this Case Study is that the staff hours relate to the total hours worked by five people, whereas the theatre time relates to the time that the team is using the theatre. It would therefore make sense to work out the time that the theatre was in use before progressing. This can be calculated by dividing the total staff hours (295) by the 5 staff in the team (= 59 actual theatre hours).

The absorption rate is £2,000 ÷ 50 = £40 per theatre hour.

using the 'diagram'

Although the overheads amounted to £350 more than planned, the theatre completed more operations than was budgeted, causing additional overhead absorption of £560. This was achieved through a combination of efficient working (carrying out operations with a standard time of 64 hours in only 59 hours) and more intensive use of the theatre than had been expected (using it for 59 hours instead of the planned 50 hours). The net result was over absorption of £210.

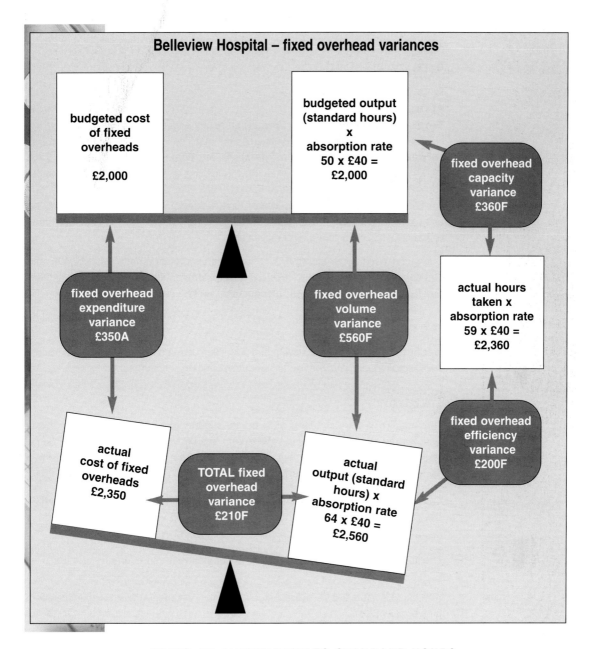

USING AN ALTERNATIVE TO STANDARD HOURS

In some situations it may be appropriate to use some other measure of use of resources rather than standard hours. Where a scenario like this occurs the most important aspect of the solution is to recognise what the output is and how it is being measured. Once this has been clearly established, the problem may be solved by using the same logic as the more traditional approach.

**CASE
STUDY**

ABSORPTION NOT USING STANDARD HOURS: SUNNY BAY FERRY COMPANY

situation

The Sunny Bay Ferry Company operates an hourly passenger service throughout the summer season taking day trippers across the bay. The ferry can accommodate up to 50 passengers, and each return trip takes one hour. The ferry starts running at 10.00 am each day, with the last return trip leaving at 7.00 pm, subject to weather conditions. The company budgets to transport 500 'one-way' passengers per day, and operates all scheduled sailings seven days a week. The fixed overheads of the operation are budgeted at £7,000 per week during the summer, and are absorbed based on a standard return ferry movement.

During the week commencing 3 June the fixed overheads amounted to £7,400, and the ferry carried out 50 return trips (20 having been cancelled due to bad weather). The ferry took 4,000 one-way passengers that week.

required

Identify the output (or activity level), and how it is measured in standard form. Calculate the absorption rate, and the fixed overhead variances, and comment on their meaning.

solution

The output of a ferry company must be the number of passengers it carries; this is what it 'produces'. This company chooses to absorb its fixed overheads based on a standard return ferry movement, which is linked to its budget of 500 one-way passengers per day (3,500 per 7 day week).

The company schedules 7 x 10 return trips per day = 70 return trips per week.

The standard number of passengers on each single trip will therefore be

3,500 ÷ (70 x 2) = 25 passengers.

The absorption rate is £7,000 ÷ 70 = £100 per standard return ferry movement.

In order to apply normal fixed overhead variance calculations, we must first express both the budgeted and the actual outputs in terms of standard return ferry movements (or standard trips).

The budgeted output represents 70 standard return ferry movements (3,500 ÷ [25x2]).

The actual output represents 80 standard return ferry movements (4,000 ÷ [25x2]).

Putting this data into a slightly modified version of the diagram (see page 83) results in the following:

Although the overheads amounted to £400 more than was budgeted, actual output was higher. The company carried more passengers than was planned: 4,000 passengers equating to 80 standard return ferry movements rather than 3,500 passengers equating to 70 standard return trips. This resulted in additional overhead absorption of £1,000.

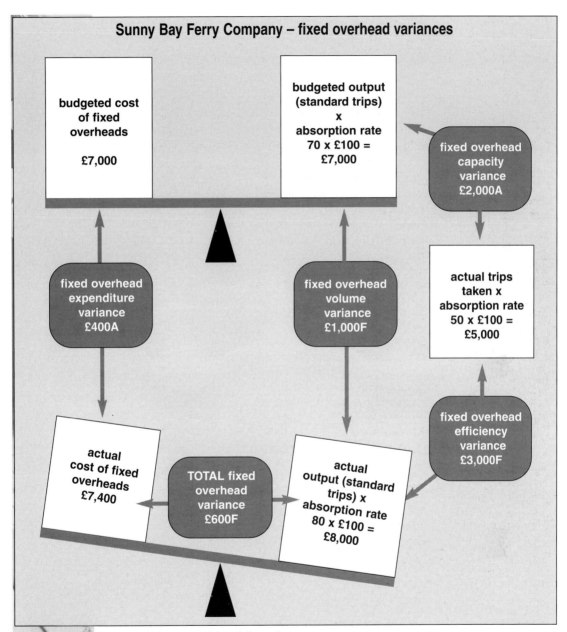

Sunny Bay Ferry Company – fixed overhead variances

budgeted cost of fixed overheads

£7,000

budgeted output (standard trips) x absorption rate 70 x £100 = £7,000

fixed overhead capacity variance £2,000A

fixed overhead expenditure variance £400A

fixed overhead volume variance £1,000F

actual trips taken x absorption rate 50 x £100 = £5,000

actual cost of fixed overheads £7,400

TOTAL fixed overhead variance £600F

actual output (standard trips) x absorption rate 80 x £100 = £8,000

fixed overhead efficiency variance £3,000F

All this was achieved through:

- The carrying of more passengers on each boat trip than standard, measured through the efficiency variance. There were 40 passengers on average on each single trip (4,000 ÷ [50 x 2]) instead of the standard number of 25). This accounted for £3,000 extra being absorbed.
- The cancellation of 20 return trips was reflected in the capacity variance, showing that the boat was not used as much as planned. This accounted for £2,000 less being absorbed.

The net result was over-absorption of £600.

SITUATIONS WHERE CERTAIN OVERHEAD VARIANCES ARE INAPPROPRIATE

It is important to remember that the fixed overhead capacity and efficiency variances are calculated to assist in the understanding of how actual output volume differs from that budgeted, and to what extent overhead has been absorbed. In order that this process is effective, the resource which is used to measure the output (for example standard direct labour hours or standard machine hours) must be **appropriate** in the particular circumstances.

To have an appropriate link between resource and fixed overhead, the chosen resource must be fundamental to the creation of the output. Only then will there be firm links between output and fixed overheads, via the chosen resource.

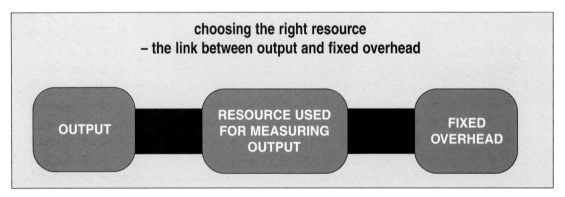

which resource should we use?

It is important to choose the right resource. For example if we were examining the absorption of fixed overheads of a cinema, we would identify the output, then establish (if we could) a fundamental resource used to create the output. It would probably make sense to consider the number of customers as the output. Even if we knew how much time it took to serve a typical customer in the foyer kiosk, it would not be very helpful to use the standard time of kiosk staff per customer as a resource for measuring customers. This is because the customers are attending the cinema to watch a film, and their use of the kiosk is merely supplementary. The costs which make up the fixed overheads of the cinema have very little to do with the efficiency (or otherwise) of the kiosk staff. A better resource for measuring output in this situation might be a standard film showing, using an assumed number of customers. The efficiency variance would then measure the overheads absorbed due to more (or less) customers attending each showing, while the capacity variance would measure the absorption due to there being more or less film showings than planned.

Where a suitable resource for measuring output is not available it is still useful to divide the fixed overhead variance into expenditure and volume variances. The volume variance will then not be split any further.

CASE STUDY

CHOOSING THE RIGHT RESOURCE: SUNNY HILLS PUBLIC GOLF COURSE

situation

The Sunny Hills Public Golf Course is operated on a 'pay as you play' basis. It has extensive fixed overheads primarily concerned with maintenance of the course and running the on-site bar and shop. The output of the course is measured in terms of the numbers of golfers playing a round of golf. No other suitable way of measuring the output has yet been found.

The fixed overheads for the third financial quarter were budgeted at £50,000, and the number of golfers expected to play a round was 2,000. The actual fixed overheads amounted to £53,000 for the quarter, and 1,960 golfers played.

A suggestion has been made to use the standard time to serve a customer at the bar as a way of generating the data for fixed overhead efficiency and capacity variances.

required

1 Calculate the overhead absorption rate, and the total fixed overhead variance for the quarter, divided into the expenditure and volume variances.

2 Comment on the suggestion regarding the data for efficiency and capacity variances.

solution

Since there is no other mechanism for measuring output than the number of golfers, this should be used as the absorption base.

This gives a rate of £50,000 ÷ 2,000 = £25 per round.

The total fixed overhead variance will be the difference between the absorbed overhead (1,960 x £25 = £49,000) and the actual overheads incurred (£53,000) = £4,000 adverse.

This is divided into:

• the expenditure variance (£50,000 – £53,000) = £3,000 adverse

• the volume variance £25 x (1,960 – 2,000) = £1,000 adverse.

The use of standard times by the bar staff would not be appropriate as a mechanism for dividing the volume variance. The bar is supplementary to the main activity (for most golfers, anyway!), and there is no fundamental link between the bar staff's efforts and the number of golf rounds played. A large amount of the fixed overheads will relate to the course itself rather than the bar. To use such a technique would add nothing to the understanding of why the output was not as expected, and what the effect was on overheads absorbed.

- Fixed overhead variances differ from direct variances due to the way that fixed costs behave and the way the chosen costing system deals with them.

- When marginal costing is used, fixed costs are considered time-based, and are not absorbed by the output. The fixed overhead variance under this system is a simple measurement of more or less expenditure than planned and is passed through the accounts.

- When absorption costing is used, fixed overheads are absorbed onto the output based on a predetermined rate. The total fixed overhead variance is the amount by which the amount of overhead absorbed differs from the overhead actually incurred. This can be due to the expenditure on overhead being different to what was planned, or the volume of output being different, or both.

- Where the volume of output can be usefully measured in terms of the use of some fundamental resource (eg standard labour or machine hours), then the volume variance can be broken down into the efficiency variance (measuring the change in volume, and hence absorption, due to the efficiency with which that resource is used), and the capacity variance (measuring the effect of the amount of resource used compared to planned).

- The majority of fixed overhead variance techniques can be applied to the service sector as well as manufacturing, with little modification. Care needs to be taken with interpretation where output is measured in unconventional ways. The meaningful breakdown of the volume variance can be impossible where there is no suitable fundamental resource, which can be used to measure output.

fixed overheads

Indirect Costs which do not vary in proportion to the volume of production or other output.

marginal costing

A technique that values cost units based on variable costs only. Fixed costs are considered related only to the reporting period of time.

**fixed overhead expenditure
variance (marginal costing)**

The only fixed overhead variance generated using marginal costing. It measures the difference between the budgeted expenditure and the actual expenditure on fixed overheads in a reporting period.

absorption costing	A technique that values cost units based on a suitable part of all the costs of production, whether fixed or variable in behaviour.
absorption base	The mechanism by which absorption costing absorbs indirect costs into cost units. It may be simply per cost unit, or (for example) per standard labour or machine hour.
total fixed overhead variance (absorption costing)	The difference between the actual expenditure on fixed overheads, and the amount of fixed overhead absorbed by the actual output. The expenditure and volume variances will combine in this total variance.
fixed overhead expenditure variance (absorption costing)	The difference between the budgeted expenditure and the actual expenditure on fixed overheads in a reporting period.
fixed overhead volume variance (absorption costing)	The difference between the fixed overhead which would have been absorbed by the budgeted output and the fixed overhead which was absorbed by the actual output. The efficiency and capacity variance will combine in this variance.
fixed overhead efficiency variance (absorption costing)	The part of the volume variance attributable to the efficient or inefficient use of the resource used to measure the output. Where this resource is some form of standard hours the variance is based on the amount of overhead that would be absorbed by the difference between the standard hours for the actual output and the actual time taken.
fixed overhead capacity variance (absorption costing)	The part of the volume variance attributable to the amount used of the resource chosen to measure the output. Where this resource is some form of standard hours the variance is based on the amount of overhead that would be absorbed by the difference between the actual time taken and the standard hours for the budgeted output.

3.1   Jo is a self-employed haulage contractor who owns her articulated lorry. Her plans before the financial year started were to drive 50,000 miles in the next year, and absorb the budgeted annual fixed overheads of £10,000 using miles travelled as an absorption base.

In reality she travelled 45,000 miles, and the fixed overheads amounted to £12,000.

(a)   Calculate the budgeted absorption rate per mile.

(b)   Calculate the – fixed overhead expenditure variance,

– fixed overhead volume variance,

– total fixed overhead variance.

(c)   State whether there has been under or over-absorption.

3.2   Joe is a self employed haulage contractor who owns his articulated lorry. His plans before the financial year started were to drive 50,000 miles in the next year in a budgeted time of 2,000 standard hours, and absorb the budgeted annual fixed overheads of £10,000 using standard hours for the miles travelled as an absorption base.

In reality he travelled 45,000 miles, taking 1,850 actual hours and the fixed overheads amounted to £12,000.

(a)   Calculate the budgeted average speed of the lorry in miles per hour.

(b)   Calculate the budgeted absorption rate per standard hour.

(c)   Calculate the standard time it should take to cover 45,000 miles.

(d)   Calculate the – fixed overhead expenditure variance,

– fixed overhead volume variance,

– fixed overhead efficiency variance,

– fixed overhead capacity variance,

– total fixed overhead variance.

(e)   Joe tells you that during the year

(i)   he was sick for 3 weeks and unable to work,

(ii)   there was an abnormal amount of roadworks causing delays,

(iii)   there was a large unanticipated rise in vehicle insurance.

State which variance may be linked to each of the above comments.

3.3   Zorbant Ltd absorbs fixed overheads based on the budgeted fixed overheads of £94,600, and the budgeted number of standard direct labour hours to be worked of 2,200.

The actual output for the period turned out to be 2,500 standard hours, although this took the direct labour workforce 2,600 hours. The actual fixed overheads for the period were £99,000.

Required

(a)   Calculate the fixed overhead absorption rate

(b)   Calculate all relevant overhead variances

(c)   State which of the following comments are valid, based on the above data:

   (i)   The expenditure variance is adverse due to the increased volume of output which has been produced.

   (ii)   The expenditure variance is favourable since the actual fixed overheads are less than were budgeted for.

   (iii)   The expenditure variance is adverse since the actual fixed overheads are more than were budgeted for.

   (iv)   The favourable volume variance reflects the fact that more output was achieved than was budgeted for.

   (v)   The favourable volume variance is due to the overheads being less than anticipated.

   (vi)   The adverse volume variance is due to more output being achieved than was budgeted for.

   (vii)   The capacity variance is adverse since the overheads cost more than expected.

   (viii)   The favourable capacity variance is due to more labour hours being worked than was budgeted for.

   (ix)   The adverse efficiency variance is due to more labour hours being worked than was originally budgeted for.

   (x)   The adverse efficiency variance is due to the actual output taking more labour hours than standard.

   (xi)   The favourable efficiency variance is due to the actual output taking more hours than standard.

   (xii)   The adverse efficiency variance is due to the fact that the overheads cost more than was originally budgeted for.

3.4 G Loop Manufacturing Limited makes a single product, the Gloop, and absorbs fixed overheads on the basis of standard labour hours.

For the year it had budgeted to make 2,000 Gloops, and take 14,000 standard labour hours to do so. It budgeted that its fixed overheads would amount to £448,000.

During the year the company actually made 1,800 Gloops, taking a total of 12,000 actual labour hours.

The fixed overheads for the year actually amounted to £455,000.

Required

(a) Calculate the budgeted absorption rate per standard hour.

(b) Calculate the standard hours to make one Gloop

(c) Calculate the standard hours to make the actual output of 1,800 Gloops.

(d) Calculate:

The fixed overhead expenditure (or price) variance, and

The fixed overhead volume variance, and subdivide it into:

- The fixed overhead efficiency variance and

- The fixed overhead capacity variance.

(e) Reconcile the overhead absorbed by the standard hours for the actual production of 1,800 Gloops, with the actual fixed overheads using the above variances.

3.5 The Maxima Cinema Company operates a cinema with a single auditorium. It has a total budget for its fixed overheads of £12,000 per four-week period. It budgets to show 16 screenings per week, based on 2 per weekday and 3 on Saturday and 3 on Sunday. This makes a budgeted total of 64 screenings per four week period.

The company uses a 'standard screening', based on an expected average of 40 customers attending each screening, to absorb its overheads. The auditorium can accommodate up to 110 people.

During the four-week period ending 31 August there were 72 screenings, including a special late night horror series showing each Friday and Saturday night. In total there were 3,240 attendances in the period, and fixed overheads amounted to £11,800.

Required

(a) Calculate the absorption rate per standard screening.

(b) Calculate how many standard screenings the actual number of customers represents.

(c) Calculate the fixed overhead variances (including efficiency and capacity) and use them to reconcile the actual fixed overhead expenditure with the fixed overhead absorbed.

(d) Comment briefly on the meaning of the variances calculated.

4 STANDARD COSTING – FURTHER ANALYSIS

this chapter covers . . .

In this chapter we examine:

- *the main types of standard that may be set,*
- *the effect of our choice of standard on the interpretation of the variances,*
- *the decisions about when to take action resulting from variances,*
- *the specific problems of*
    seasonality,
    cost inflation, and
    currency conversion,
  and how to analyse and interpret variances accordingly.

NVQ PERFORMANCE CRITERIA COVERED

unit 8: CONTRIBUTING TO THE MANAGEMENT OF COSTS AND THE ENHANCEMENT OF VALUE

element 1

collect, analyse and disseminate information about costs

- *valid relevant information is identified from internal and external sources*
- *trends in prices are monitored for movements and analysed on a regular basis and potential implications are identified*
- *standard costs are compared with actual costs and any variances are analysed*
- *forecasts of trends and changes in factor prices and market conditions are consistent with previous experience of factor prices and market conditions*

element 2

make recommendations to reduce costs and enhance value

- *routine cost reports are analysed, compared with other sources of information and the implications of findings are identified*

SETTING STANDARDS

In the previous chapters we have looked at how standard costing can be used to determine the expected level of costs, and to compare the actual costs incurred with these standard costs by calculating variances. We will now examine in more detail how standards may be set, and how this can have an impact on our interpretation of variances.

types of standard

There are three main types of standard that may be set:

1 **Ideal Standard** makes no allowances for inefficiency or wastage of labour or materials, and therefore assumes perfect conditions.

2 **Attainable Standard** allows for a small amount of normal wastage and inefficiency, but is set at a level that is considered to be a challenging target based on current operating conditions.

3 **Basic Standard** is an historical (and therefore effectively out-of-date) standard that allows comparisons to be carried out over long periods of time.

ideal and attainable standards and actual results

The link between ideal and attainable standards and the actual results is reflected in the difference between strategic and operational management.

Strategic management is concerned with long-term planning and decision-making.

Operational management centres around the day-to-day activities taking place within an organisation. The way in which these types of management may rely on different standards can be illustrated by the following diagram:

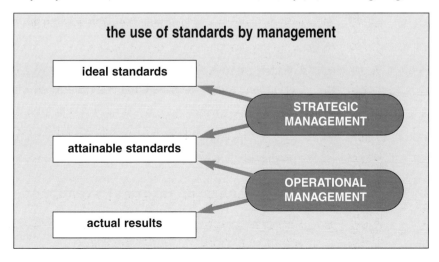

Strategic management can examine ways of moving what is attainable closer to the ideal over the longer term, whilst operational management is more concerned with moving the actual results closer to what is attainable in the short term. Total Quality Management (see pages 122 to 124) is one technique that can be used to bring the actual results closer to the ideal level.

IDEAL STANDARDS AND THEIR IMPLICATIONS

the tendency for dual standards

When an organisation implements a standard costing system, the way that the standard is set will affect the interpretation of the variances. If an ideal standard is used, with no allowances for wastage or inefficiency then the variances for material usage and labour efficiency will tend to be adverse. This in turn will mean that managers will come to expect adverse variances, and that action will only be taken when the variances are outside what they consider a reasonable tolerance level. If the use of an ideal is extended to setting material cost and labour rate standards by using the cheapest prices and the lowest labour rates then the managers will become used to finding that all the variances recorded are adverse. They will tend to ignore the adverse variances that are reasonably small, and concentrate their attention on the larger variances. In this way they will have started to operate a system of informal **dual standards**, whereby the standard that is set is not the one that it is expected will be achieved.

This has important implications when standard costing is used to help a business with its planning. Where standards set at an ideal level are used for planning purposes then the result will always be inaccurate. For example when using ideal standards to specify the amount of materials or labour time that will be required, the resources will tend to be under-estimated. This could result in lower production being achieved than was planned, or that additional resources are needed to complete the required production. This is because the ideal standards do not incorporate any allowance for the wastage or inefficient working that will always occur to some extent. Managers may get around this problem informally by adding an additional amount into their resource requirements. They are then effectively using their own version of a standard. The same situation will occur with material prices and labour costs, so that unless an amount is added to the standard when the anticipated production is costed, the result will almost invariably be under costing.

the dangers of informal standards

It could be argued that making such adjustments as described above is just a logical extension of the setting and use of standards. But problems could arisc if different managers had different ideas of what tolerance levels were acceptable. The use of **exception reporting** whereby results are only reported if they are outside an agreed range is universally recognised as a useful management tool, and can form part of the wider technique of **management by exception**. This is where management time is concentrated on situations in which the actual results vary from the plans. Both these techniques can only work effectively is there is genuine agreement about the level at which results should be reported and acted upon instead of ignored. A situation could develop where not just informal dual standards were in operation, but a range of standards was in use by different managers for different purposes.

---

practical example

Consider the following situation:

The production scheduler may add an allowance of say 10% to the standard usage of materials when planning the amount to be bought for a production run and requisitioning the goods. The production supervisor may consider that a usage variance of up to 8% from standard is reasonable. The production manager views a tolerance level of 5% as being within an acceptable range.

If the variance is reported at 6% then the production supervisor may feel that he/she has performed well, whereas the production manager is expecting answers from him/her as to why the usage is so high. Meanwhile the excess purchases of raw material are sitting in the stores!

This situation would not be a good demonstration of how to use standard costing and variance analysis as a form of responsibility accounting. In order to make different managers responsible for different variances they must be clear as to exactly what standards they are expected to achieve. This can be difficult enough with the impact of the interdependence of variances, without the additional confusion created by having different informal versions of the standards in existence.

ideal standards and motivation

A further area that is influenced by the way that standards are set is that of **motivation**. As discussed earlier, variances resulting from a system where standards are set at an ideal level will generally be adverse. Whether linked to a reward system or not, targets will only tend to work well if they are considered fair and achievable. It cannot be easy to motivate staff at any level to perform well if all you can measure is by how far they have fallen short of the standard on each occasion. The natural human reaction may be to feel that since the standards cannot be achieved there is no point in even attempting to work efficiently. The standards may be felt to be irrelevant by the staff – hardly the atmosphere of cost-consciousness that most businesses would like to develop!

The use of ideal standards will also effectively prevent businesses from setting up a traditional labour bonus system based on paying a percentage of time saved compared with the standard time. It will be clear that if the standards are set at an ideal level, then there will never be any time saved, and therefore no bonus is likely to be payable.

attainable standards and their implications

Setting standards at an attainable level should avoid most of the problems identified with setting ideal standards, and most businesses using standard costing opt for some version of attainable standards. Where the standards are carefully set, the resultant variances should typically be a mixture of adverse and favourable, as the organisation will tend to sometimes exceed the standard and sometimes not quite achieve it.

Not everybody considers what is 'attainable' as being the same thing, and there will be no standard that will be considered fair by everyone. It could be thought of as a range rather than a single point. If standards are set following consultation within the organisation there will always need to be some compromise as different managers and employee groups argue from their own perspectives. There are common problems arising from encouraging participation in the setting of both standards and budgets. While standards which are set by making use of the expertise of a range of participants will tend to be more easily accepted and 'owned', the conflicting needs and desires of the personnel involved can make the standard setting process long and difficult.

basic standards and their implications

Maintaining standards at a 'basic' level will tend to have several disadvantages. Since the standard was set some time ago its relevance may be questionable, and large variances will tend to become normal. This will mean that comparison is most useful if it is based on the **trend** in variances and this procedure will enable managers to identify with ease the way in which costs have changed over a long period.

A clear disadvantage of using basic standards is that the standards themselves may not be comparable with current conditions, and the individual variances may be virtually meaningless. The impact of inflation and changes in working practices will mean that the standard cannot be used as either a target or an estimate of expected cost levels. For these reasons basic standards are rarely used as the only standard by an organisation, but may be used alongside variance analysis which is based on more current data to obtain a longer term view of changes which have occurred.

INTERPRETING VARIANCES

The interpretation of variances, and the taking of appropriate action will be influenced by the way in which the standard was set. We will now examine some of the other issues that need to be considered in interpreting variances and taking appropriate action. The steps involved can be seen illustrated in the diagram on page 98, which is then discussed further.

is the variance significant? – control limits

The first issue to consider is whether the variance is significant enough for any action at all to be worthwhile. The idea of tolerance levels was mentioned earlier, and it is important to establish how large a variance should be in order to justify an investigation into its cause followed by appropriate action. Since any investigation or action will have a cost implication (at least in terms of management time), it would not make sense to do this unless there was an expected benefit that would justify it. **Control limits** within which a variance is acceptable may therefore be set by the organisation (see the diagram below). These limits will quickly identify the variances which need investigating.

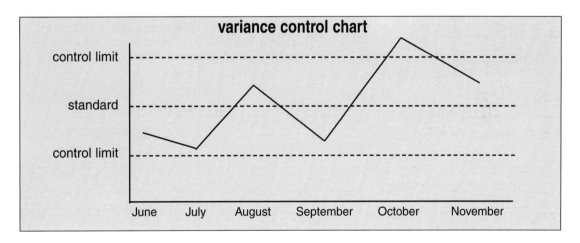

Variances are recorded chronologically from left to right on the chart, either individually or cumulatively. The control levels are agreed in advance. If a variance moves beyond these limits then investigation will be needed and appropriate action can be taken. In the chart shown here the control limit is exceeded in October.

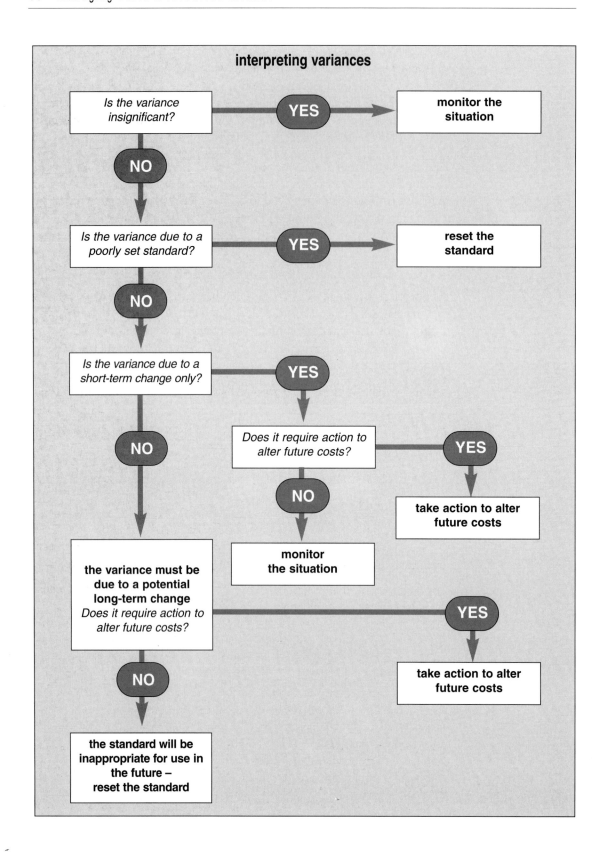

interpreting variances

Is the variance insignificant? — YES → monitor the situation

NO

Is the variance due to a poorly set standard? — YES → reset the standard

NO

Is the variance due to a short-term change only? — YES

NO

Does it require action to alter future costs? — YES → take action to alter future costs

NO

monitor the situation

the variance must be due to a potential long-term change
Does it require action to alter future costs? — YES → take action to alter future costs

NO

the standard will be inappropriate for use in the future – reset the standard

The cumulative effects of variances must also be taken into account. The **trends** in variances that individually are small and may be considered immaterial may point to a situation that requires action. If, for example, efficiency levels amongst the direct labour force are very slowly decreasing then some action (perhaps retraining) will be needed to avoid excess costs occurring over a long period.

modifying standards

An important question to ask is

> *'Is the variance due entirely to the way the standard was set, or is there a current situation that needs investigating?'*

If a poorly set standard is creating a variance out of an otherwise acceptable situation, the most logical approach will be to amend the standard at the next opportunity. Resetting the standard will also be the most appropriate action if there is a long-term change to costs, otherwise 'false' variances will arise in future.

short-term changes

The cause of the variance will dictate whether or not action is required. If the variance is caused by a temporary change that will automatically right itself then clearly no action is needed other than to check later to see that it has. Examples of this could be:

• a price variance caused by a change to another supplier because the normal supplier was temporarily out of stock

• a machine breakdown causing excess wastage of material

If, however, the variance is caused by some temporary change that may recur often enough to cause concern, then action should be taken either to prevent such changes or to alter the standard if the changes are uncontrollable.

An example of this could be individual batches of material that cause excessive wastage. A change of supplier may be a solution, but if all suppliers are having a similar quality problem due to some common situation then the issue may simply need to be acknowledged by monitoring the variances to ensure that they return to their expected level in future. If the material in this example were coffee beans that were affected by poor weather in the world's main coffee growing regions then it would clearly make some sense to monitor the situation over the coming seasons.

long-term changes

Sometimes variances are the result of situations that are potentially long-term. Perhaps there has been a change in working practices or wage rates resulting in different costs, and if the managers consider the situation is acceptable then it would be logical to reset the standards. The same would apply to a general price change that is seen as reasonably permanent and uncontrollable. If, however, a price rise could be avoided by changing suppliers, then there would be no need to alter the standards, provided that managers considered that this was the best solution.

ANALYSIS OF VARIANCES TO ACCOUNT FOR SPECIFIC PROBLEMS

It is often useful to subdivide variances into two parts:

- the part caused by a situation that is known to exist – the 'predictable' variance, caused by a factor such as a seasonal trend
- the part which is due to other causes – the unpredictable 'real' variance

In these cases subdividing the variance will highlight the 'real' variance, which is the information that the management want to be able to see.

There are three main situations where this approach may be appropriate. These are:

- seasonal trends
- inflation
- currency fluctuations

We will explain each of these in turn and illustrate them by means of Case Studies.

SEASONALITY

In Chapter 1 we considered how data could be analysed into trends and seasonal variations to assist with forecasting. Trend analysis can be used to determine more accurate standards for price (or sometimes usage) where these follow seasonal or other regular patterns. The example of foods that follow similar price patterns every year linked to availability is one where price standards could be re-calculated for different periods. A manufacturer of crisps, for example, will look carefully at the fluctuating price of potatoes in different months of the year. The technique is based on applying either absolute or percentage seasonal variations to the standard based on the average price. The price variances can then be recalculated to show the variance

- expected due to the time of year – the seasonal variance, and
- the remainder of the variance that is effectively the 'true' variance.

calculation of material price variance

The analysis of a material price variance would therefore be calculated as follows:

Original Material Price Variance =

Actual Quantity x (Standard Price – Actual Price)

this is then subdivided into:

- *Price Variance due to Seasonality =*
  Actual Quantity x (Standard Price – Seasonally Adjusted Standard Price)

  and

- *Price Variance due to Other Influences =*
  Actual Quantity x (Seasonally Adjusted Standard Price – Actual Price)

The diagram below illustrates these variances and the ways in which they can combine. Sample figures are added to show you how the 'real' variances, due to other causes, can vary enormously when the 'predictable' variance of seasonality is taken out of the equation.

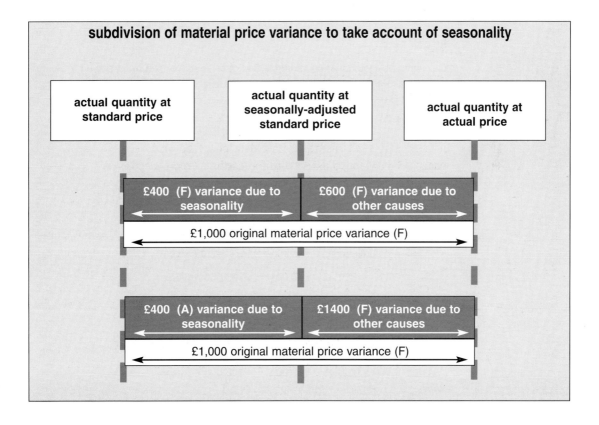

If required, the usage variance could similarly be analysed, based on the seasonally adjusted standard quantities used. The quantity calculations must be multiplied by the standard price in common with all usage variances. This could apply, for example, in a situation where changing seasonal temperatures cause a greater or lesser degree of evaporation of a liquid held in stock.

SUBDIVISION OF THE ORIGINAL MATERIAL PRICE VARIANCE:
MELTO PLASTIC MOULDINGS LIMITED

Melto Plastic Mouldings Limited purchases a liquid raw material which has a standard cost per 100 litres of £60, based on its expected average price over the coming year. Trend analysis of the cost of this liquid over the last five years indicates that the price is seasonal, and that the percentage seasonal variations can be expected to average:

Jan – March	+20%
April – June	+5%
July – Sept	- 8%
Oct – Dec	-17%

In February the company used 900,000 litres, costing £675,000.

required

Calculate the material price variance, and analyse it into the part expected to be due to the seasonality of the price, and the part due to other influences.

solution

900,000 litres ÷ 100 = 9,000 (100 litres).

Actual Price per 100 litres = £675,000 ÷ 9,000 = £75.00 per 100 litres.

Seasonally Adjusted Standard Price (Feb) = £60.00 + 20% = £72.00 per 100 litres.

Original Price Variance:

Actual Quantity x (Standard Price – Actual Price)

9,000 x (£60.00 – £75.00)   = £135,000 Adverse.

Divided into:

• **Price Variance due to Seasonality:**

Actual Quantity x (Standard Price – Seasonally Adjusted Standard Price)

9,000 x (£60.00 – £72.00)   = £108,000 Adverse

and

• **Price Variance due to Other Influences:**

Actual Quantity x (Seasonally Adjusted Standard Price – Actual Price)

9,000 x (£72.00 – £75.00)   = £ 27,000 Adverse.

£108,000 (A) variance due to seasonality	£27,000 (A) 'true' variance
£135,000 original material price variance (A)	

conclusion

This shows that the majority of the original adverse price variance appears to be due to the seasonal nature of the price, although there is a further 'true' adverse element that is as yet unexplained.

In the next Case Study it can be seen that a favourable seasonal variance can in fact disguise an adverse 'true' variance.

CASE STUDY

A SEASONAL VARIATION DISGUISING AN ADVERSE 'TRUE' VARIANCE
MELTO PLASTIC MOULDINGS LIMITED

Melto Plastic Mouldings Limited purchases a raw material that has a standard cost per kilo of £10, based on its expected average price over the coming year. Trend analysis of the cost of this item over the last five years indicates that the price is seasonal, and that the absolute seasonal variations can be expected to average:

Jan – March	+ £4 per kilo
April – June	- £2 per kilo
July – Sept	- £3 per kilo
Oct – Dec	+ £1 per kilo

In June the company used 75,000 kilos, costing £637,500.

required

Calculate the material price variance, and analyse it into the part expected to be due to the seasonality of the price, and the part due to other influences.

solution

Actual Price per kilo = £637,500 ÷ 75,000 kilos = £8.50 per kilo.

Seasonally Adjusted Standard Price (June) = £10.00 – £2.00 = £8.00 per kilo.

Original Price Variance:

Actual Quantity x (Standard Price – Actual Price)

75,000 kg x (£10.00 – £8.50)   = £112,500 Favourable.

Divided into:
- **Price Variance due to Seasonality:**

Actual Quantity x (Standard Price – Seasonally Adjusted Standard Price)

75,000 kg x (£10.00 – £8.00) = £150,000 Favourable

and

- **Price Variance due to Other Influences:**

Actual Quantity x (Seasonally Adjusted Standard Price – Actual Price)

75,000 kg x (£8.00 – £8.50) = £ 37,500 Adverse.

£150,000 (F) variance due to seasonality	£37,500 (A) 'true' variance
£112,500 original material price variance (F)	

conclusion

This shows that the original favourable price variance was misleading, since it was more than accounted for in the seasonal variation of the price. The 'true' variance was in fact adverse.

seasonality – other considerations

From a practical standpoint the seasonal variations need to be predictable enough and significant enough to make the exercise meaningful and worthwhile. There is always a danger that too many versions of standards will create confusion amongst those who should be assisted by their use.

Seasonality can also be applied to the costs involved in fixed overheads. Where, for example, heating costs are significant, and increase substantially in the winter months, the budgeted fixed overhead cost could be varied for each quarter. One major drawback of this approach is that the fixed overhead absorption rate would need to be different for each quarter, and that in turn would lead to different volume variances arising in each quarter even if the production levels were the same. This would add to the difficulties that managers could experience in interpreting fixed overhead variances.

INFLATION

In Chapter 1 we examined the use of index numbers to record and forecast various data including inflation (see page 31). Cost inflation is usually taken into account when setting price standards. Whereas the retail price index (RPI) is a measure of general inflation, an estimate of specific inflation for the industry, or, better still, the specific material or labour index should be used where possible.

Where the allowance for inflation within the standard turns out to be incorrect, then the variances can be analysed into

- the part caused by known price inflation

- the part due to other causes

Calculations may need to be carried out to determine what the price or rate would have been if the 'correct' allowance had been made for inflation. This can be done once the actual change in the appropriate index is applied to the 'pre-inflation' standard. The analysis of the price variance is then similar to that carried out based on seasonality, as follows:

Original Price Variance

Actual Quantity x (Standard Price – Actual Price)

Divided into:

- Price Variance due to Actual Change in Price Index:

  Actual Quantity x (Standard Price – Index Adjusted Standard Price)

  and

- Price Variance due to Other Influences:

  Actual Quantity x (Index Adjusted Standard Price – Actual Price)

This can be summarised as follows:

subdivision of original price variance to take account of changes in inflation
original price variance *actual quantity x (standard price – actual price)*

price variance due to actual change in price index *actual quantity x (standard price – index adjusted standard price)*	**price variance due to other influences** *actual quantity x (index adjusted standard price – actual price)*

CASE STUDY

INFLATION AND THE ORIGINAL PRICE VARIANCE MELTO PLASTIC MOULDINGS LIMITED

Melto Plastic Mouldings Limited set its price standard for a high quality resin when the specific price index for the material was 180. The assumption was made that it would rise to 190 by the time the standard was in use, and therefore the standard decided upon was £38.00 per kilo to take this into account.

In reality the index rose to 186 by the time the standard was in use. During the month 2,000 kilos of the material were used, costing £80,000.

required

Calculate the material price variance, and analyse it into the part due to the actual change in the price index, and the part due to other influences.

solution

'Pre-inflation' standard price = £38.00 x (180 ÷190)   = £36.00 per kilo

Actual Index Adjusted Price Standard = £36.00 x 186 ÷180   = £37.20 per kilo

(or alternatively calculated as £38.00 x 186 ÷ 190 = £37.20)

Actual Price per kilo = £80,000 ÷ 2,000 kilo   = £40.00 per kilo

Original Price Variance:

　　　Actual Quantity x (Standard Price – Actual Price)

　　　2,000 kilos x (£38.00 – £40.00) ⟶ = £4,000 Adverse

This is a combination of:

- **Price Variance due to Actual Change in Price Index**
  Actual Quantity x (Standard Price – Index Adjusted Standard Price)
  2,000 kilos x (£38.00 – £37.20) ⟶ = £1,600 Favourable

and

- **Price Variance due to Other Influences:**
  Actual Quantity x (Index Adjusted Standard Price – Actual Price)
  2,000 kilos x (£37.20 – £40.00) ⟶ = £ 5,600 Adverse

conclusion

original price variance £4,000 adverse	
price variance due to actual change in price index	**price variance due to other influences**
£1,600 favourable	£5,600 adverse

This calculation shows that the original £4,000 adverse price variance masks a larger unexplained adverse variance of £5,600 once you take into account the fact that the rate of inflation has been lower than estimated.

labour rate indexation

A similar calculation can be made for the analysis of labour rate variances. Here the expected index change may be used as a guide to setting standards. Sometimes the actual wage rise agreed by the employer may be more significant than the actual change in the index when analysing the rate variance.

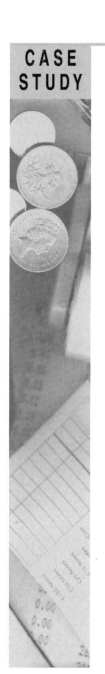

CASE STUDY

LABOUR RATE INDEXATION
MELTO PLASTIC MOULDINGS LIMITED

For the period January to April the appropriate regional wage rate index was expected to rise from 290 to 300, and the standard wage rate was set by Melto Plastic Mouldings at £6.00 per hour to take account of this change. In reality the relevant grade of employees received a pay award averaging 4%.

During April the section of the labour force worked 24,000 hours, and were paid a total of £144,960.

required
Calculate the labour rate variance, and analyse it into the part due to the actual pay award, and the part due to other influences.

solution

'Pre-inflation' standard rate = £6.00 x (290 ÷ 300)	= £5.80 per hour
Actual Pay Award Adjusted Standard Rate = £5.80 + 4%	= £6.032 per hour
Actual Rate per hour = £144,960 ÷ 24,000 hours	= £6.04 per hour

Original Rate Variance:

> Actual Hours x (Standard Rate – Actual Rate)
> 24,000 hours x (£6.00 – £6.04) ——————————————➤ = £960 Adverse

Divided into:

- **Price Variance due to Actual Pay Award:**

  Actual Hours x (Standard Rate – Pay Award Adjusted Standard Rate)
  24,000 hours x (£6.00 – £6.032) ——————————➤ = £768 Adverse

and

- **Price Variance due to Other Influences:**

  Actual Hours x (Pay Award Adjusted Standard Rate – Actual Rate)
  24,000 hours x (£6.032 – £6.04) ——————————➤ = £192 Adverse

conclusion

original labour rate variance £960 adverse	
price variance due to actual pay award £768 adverse	price variance due to other influences £192 adverse

This indicates that the pay award accounts for the majority of the original rate variance. Only the smaller part of the variance appears controllable at this stage.

CURRENCY CONVERSION

Sometimes costs are incurred in a foreign currency, for example when materials are imported by a UK manufacturer from overseas. These costs will normally have to be paid for in the foreign currency at a later date by conversion from £ sterling. The problem here is that currency exchange rates fluctuate over time and price variances will arise when the exchange rate alters.

Currency conversion rates can be considered as a specific index, and the calculations are similar to those used for dealing with price variances caused by inflation (see page 108). When the standard prices are set, an exchange rate is assumed. This may be the one operating at the time, or may be an estimate of the rate that will apply when the price standard is in use. The original standard price may later need to be recalculated after adjusting for the actual currency exchange rate movement. The analysis of the price variance will be as follows:

Original Price Variance:

Actual Quantity x (Standard Price – Actual Price)

This is a combination of:

(a)   **Price Variance due to Exchange Rate Movements:**

Actual Quantity x (Standard Price – Currency Adjusted Standard Price)

and

(b)   **Price Variance due to Other Influences:**

Actual Quantity x (Currency Adjusted Standard Price – Actual Price)

This can be summarised as follows:

subdivision of original price variance to take account of changes in currency exchange rates

| original price variance |
| *actual quantity x (standard price – actual price)* |

price variance due to exchange rate movements	price variance due to other influences
actual quantity x (standard price – currency adjusted standard price)	*actual quantity x (currency adjusted standard price – actual price)*

CURRENCY EXCHANGE RATE FLUCTUATION: CHOPPERDALE FURNITURE COMPANY

Chopperdale Furniture Company imports its direct material (timber) from Nania, and pays in Nania Dollars (Na$). The standard price per tonne of timber was set at £400 when the exchange rate was stable at Na$6 to the £. In December 1,500 tonnes of timber were used at a cost of £570,000. The exchange rate during December averaged Na$7.5 to the £.

required

Calculate the material price variance, and analyse it into the part due to the exchange rate changes, and the part due to other influences.

solution

Standard Price in Nania Dollars	= £400 x 6	= Na$ 2,400 per tonne
Standard price adjusted for December exchange rate		
	= Na$ 2,400 ÷ 7.5	= £320 per tonne
Actual price per tonne	= £570,000 ÷ 1,500	= £380 per tonne

Original Price Variance:
    1,500 tonnes x (£400 – £380) $\longrightarrow$ = £30,000 Favourable

This is a combination of:

- **Price Variance due to Exchange Rate Movements:**
    1,500 tonnes x (£400 – £320) $\longrightarrow$ = £120,000 Favourable

and

- **Price Variance due to Other Influences:**
    1,500 tonnes x (£320 – £380) $\longrightarrow$ = £90,000 Adverse

conclusion

original price variance
£30,000 favourable

price variance due to exchange rate movements	price variance due to other influences
£120,000 favourable	£90,000 adverse

In the case of this company the favourable exchange rate movement as the pound strengthened against the Nania Dollar more than compensated for an adverse price variance due to other reasons, which clearly need investigating.

A COMPREHENSIVE VARIANCE ANALYSIS CASE STUDY

In Chapter 2 we examined direct cost variances, and we have just seen how these variances can be sub-divided. In Chapter 3 we studied fixed overhead variances and their implications. In the following case study we combine the techniques from these three chapters.

CASE STUDY

DELTA PRODUCTS LIMITED: VARIANCE ANALYSIS

Delta Products Limited manufactures a single product, and uses standard absorption costing for planning and monitoring costs. The standard cost of each unit produced is as follows, based on the budgeted production level of 5,000 units per month.

Direct Materials	150 litre @ £1.25 per litre
Direct Labour	5 hours @ £8.00 per hour
Fixed Overheads	5 hours @ £8.50 per hour

The fixed overheads are absorbed based on the standard direct labour hours for the production level achieved.

In September the following data is available on actual production level and costs incurred:

Production Level	5,500 units produced.
Direct Materials	820,000 litres were used, costing £1,020,000 in total
Direct Labour	26,000 hours were taken, costing £208,000 in total
Fixed Overheads	Total expenditure on fixed overheads was £222,800

required

1 Calculate the standard cost of the actual production of 5,500 units.

2 Calculate the following variances, and use them to reconcile the actual costs incurred with the standard cost of the actual production.

- Direct Material Price Variance
- Direct Material Usage Variance
- Direct Labour Rate Variance
- Direct Labour Efficiency Variance
- Fixed Overhead Expenditure Variance
- Fixed Overhead Volume Variance, divided into
- Fixed Overhead Capacity Variance
- Fixed Overhead Efficiency Variance

3 It has been discovered that since the standards were set

(a) new production methods have improved standard material usage by 1%, and

(b) the material price index that relates to the direct materials has fallen from 189 to 187.5.

Neither of these changes was anticipated by the standards.

You are to analyse the Direct Material Price Variance, and the Direct Material Usage Variance into the parts of the variances caused by these factors and the parts caused by other influences.

suggested solution

1 Standard cost of one unit

Direct Materials	150 litre @ £1.25 per litre	=	£ 187.50
Direct Labour	5 hours @ £8.00 per hour	=	£ 40.00
Fixed Overheads	5 hours @ £8.50 per hour.	=	£ 42.50
			£ 270.00

Standard cost of 5,500 units £270.00 x 5,500 units = £1,485,000.

2 The direct cost variances can be calculated as follows

- Direct Material Price Variance

(820,000 litres x £1.25) - £1,020,000   =   £ 5,000 FAV

- Direct Material Usage Variance

£1.25 x ([150 litres x 5,500 units] – 820,000 litres)   =   £ 6,250 FAV

■ Direct Labour Rate Variance

(26,000 hours x £8.00) - £208,000   =   £ 0

■ Direct Labour Efficiency Variance

£8.00 x ([5 hours x 5,500 units] − 26,000 hours)   =   £12,000 FAV

Using the format explained in Chapter 3 to calculate the fixed overhead variances:

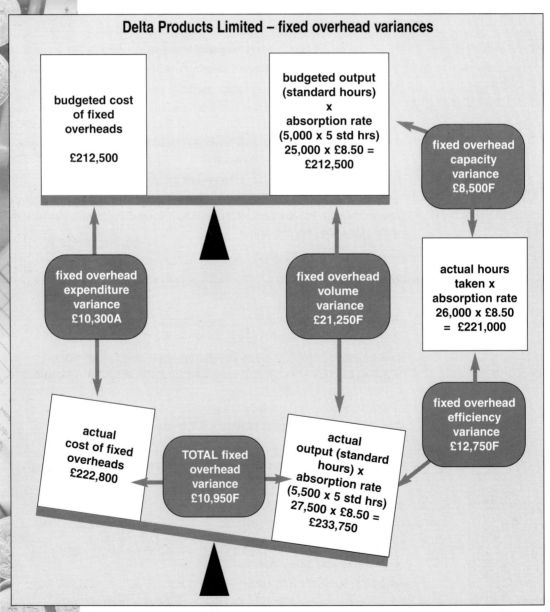

Reconciliation

	£	£	£
Standard cost of production of 5,500 units			1,485,000
Direct Variances:			
Direct Material Price Variance		(5,000) F	
Direct Material Usage Variance		(6,250) F	
Direct Labour Rate Variance		0	
Direct Labour Efficiency Variance		(12,000) F	
			(23,250)
Fixed Overhead Variances:			
Expenditure Variance		10,300 A	
Capacity Variance	(8,500) F		
Efficiency Variance	(12,750) F		
Volume Variance		(21,250) F	
			(10,950)
Actual Cost of Production (£1,020,000 + £208,000 + £222,800)			£1,450,800

3   The 'revised' standard price for the actual quantity used, taking account of the movement of the price index would be:

820,000 litres x £1.25 x (187.5 ÷ 189)   =   £1,016,865

Note: to work out a revised price per litre here would risk rounding errors with the figures given.

The Direct Material Price Variance of £5,000 F can therefore be divided into:

■ Price Variance due to index movement:

Actual Quantity at Standard Price – Actual Quantity at Revised Standard Price

(820,000 litres x £1.25) - £1,016,865   =   £ 8,135 FAV

■ Price Variance due to other influences

Actual Quantity at Revised Standard Price – Actual Quantity at Actual Price

£1,016,865 – £ 1,020,000   =   £ 3,135 ADV

The 'revised' standard usage for the actual production level, based on the new production methods would be:

5,500 units x 150 litres x 99%   =   816,750 litres

The Direct Material Usage Variance of £6,250 FAV can therefore be divided into:

■ Usage Variance due to new production methods:

Standard Price x (Standard Usage – Revised Standard Usage)

£1.25 x ([5,500 units x 150 litres] – 816,750 litres)   =   £10,312.50 FAV

■ Usage Variance Due to other influences

Standard Price x (Revised Standard Usage – Actual Usage)

£1.25 x (816,750 litres – 820,000 litres)   =   £ 4,062.50 ADV

a note on 'rounding'

In the Case Studies in this chapter the figures have been kept simple, and the numbers chosen so that the various standard prices and rates can be calculated without rounding. This has been done so that the general principles may be seen more clearly. Where numbers do not divide easily great care must be taken to avoid inappropriate rounding, and if necessary alternative versions of formulae as shown in Chapter 2 (see pages 45 and 46) should be used. For example, a rounding of a quarter of a penny (0.25p) in the hourly rate would lead to an error of £250 in the rate variance if based on 100,000 hours.

**CHAPTER
SUMMARY**

- •   Standards can be set at an Ideal, Attainable, or Basic level.

- •   The level at which a standard is set has implications for interpretation of variances, and the behaviour of employees.

- •   Actions to be taken resulting from variances will depend on materiality, whether the causes are short or long term, and how controllable they are.

- •   Actions to be taken can be divided into those that will change future costs or those that will require adjustment of the future standard.

- •   Variances can be analysed to determine the variance caused by specific factors such as seasonal factors, inflation, and currency movements. These can then be excluded from the original variance to highlight the variance due to other factors.

ideal standard

A standard set at a level that makes no allowance for losses, and which can only be attainable under the most favourable conditions.

attainable standard

A standard set at a level that assumes efficient levels of operation, but includes allowances for normal loss, waste, and machine downtime.

basic standard

A standard set some time ago which can be used to identify trends or develop other standards.

tolerance level

The range around the standard within which performance is considered acceptable and action does not need to be taken.

exception reporting

The practice of reporting only the information which is significant. In terms of variances it could involve only reporting variances outside the agreed tolerance level (control limits).

management by exception

The use of exception reporting to help concentrate management efforts on significant issues.

interdependence of variances

The fact that a single cause may create two or more separate variances.

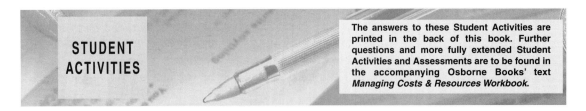

4.1 The following statements were compiled by a trainee accountant:

(a) All variances should always be thoroughly investigated.

(b) Using standards set at a basic level may help to identify long-term trends in costs.

(c) In order to motivate staff, standards should generally be challenging yet achievable.

(d) One advantage of setting up a standard costing system is that an atmosphere of cost-consciousness is generated.

(e) Responsibility accounting means that the accountant is responsible for calculating all the necessary variances.

(f) If a variance has been caused by a short-term change that will naturally right itself then there is probably no need to adjust the standards.

(g) Interpretation problems arising through the interdependence of variances would not exist if variances were calculated accurately.

State whether each of these statements is true or false.

4.2 Aztec plc purchases a natural chemical that has a standard cost per kilo of £16, based on its expected average price over the coming year. Trend analysis of the cost of this item over the last six years indicates that the price is seasonal, and that the seasonal variations can be expected to average the following percentages of the average annual price:

Jan – March	+ 20%
April – June	– 10%
July – Sept	– 40%
Oct – Dec	+ 30%

In March the company used 1,000 kilos, costing £18,000, and in April the company used 1,200 kilos, costing £18,500.

The material price variances for each month have already been calculated, using the standard price of £16. These are £2,000 adverse for March and £700 favourable for April.

You are to analyse the material price variance for each month into the part expected to be due to the seasonality of the price, and the part due to other influences.

4.3   Benson & Co was setting its standards for the next year at a time when the current average pay rate in the organisation was £7.00 per hour. At the time the appropriate regional wage rate index was standing at 140, and expected to rise to 145 in the next year. To take account of this expected increase in costs the new standard wage rate was set at £7.25 per hour.

In reality at the start of the year all employees received a pay award of 4.5%. The regional wage index moved to 150.

During week 12 the labour force worked 3,200 hours, and were paid a total of £23,744.

Required

(a)   Calculate the labour rate variance, and analyse it:

   (i)   by using the actual pay award data into the part of the variance due to the pay award, and the part due to other influences.

   and

   (ii)   by using the actual movement in the regional wage rate index into the part of the variance due to regional wage rate change and the part due to other influences.

(b)   State which analysis is most useful to managers and explain why.

4.4   Retro Limited imports its direct material from Tradland, and pays in Trad Dollars (T$). There has been very little change in the exchange rate of Trad Dollars in the last few years, and therefore the rate assumed in the standards was the one current at the time of T$2.50 to the £. The standard cost of material was based on a cost of T$12.50 per kg.

The following is an extract from a costing statement for the month of September, when the exchange rate had unexpectedly changed to T$2.00 to the £.

	Budgeted	*Actual*
Direct Materials Cost	£15,000	£21,600
Direct Material Usage	3,000 kgs.	3,600 kgs.
Production Level	1,500 units	1,700 units

Required

(a)   Calculate the standard weight of direct materials for the actual production.

(b)   Calculate the standard cost of direct materials for the actual production.

(c)   Calculate the direct material price variance and the direct material usage variance for the month of September.

(d)   Reconcile the standard cost of the direct materials for the actual production with the actual cost of direct materials.

(e)   Analyse the direct material price variance into the part caused by the exchange rate difference, and the part caused through other factors.

5 MEASURING QUALITY

this chapter covers . . .

In this chapter we examine:

- what is meant by quality and value

- the enhancement of value

- the principles of Total Quality Management

- the costs of quality

- ways to reduce costs

- value engineering and value analysis

NVQ PERFORMANCE CRITERIA COVERED

unit 8: CONTRIBUTING TO THE MANAGEMENT OF COSTS AND THE ENHANCEMENT OF VALUE

element 2

make recommendations to reduce costs and enhance value

- routine cost reports are analysed, compared with other sources of information and the implications of findings are identified

- relevant specialists are consulted to assist in the identification of ways to reduce costs and enhance value

- exception reports to follow up matters which require further investigation are prepared

- specific recommendations are made to management and are explained in a clear and appropriate form

QUALITY AND VALUE

The terms 'quality' and 'value' are used in everyday language and generally taken to mean 'how good something is' and 'how much it is worth'. In this chapter, we will consider different ways of measuring how good things are and how much they are worth. We will also examine ways of making improvements in the quality and value of both goods and services.

quality

The quality of a product or service can be considered as its fitness for the customer's purpose.

Another definition is:

Quality is the degree of excellence of a product or service.

The two definitions go together. If we look for 'excellence' in a product or service, we are expecting it to be completely satisfactory for its purpose, as far as the customer is concerned.

quality and customer satisfaction

For a product or service to be of high quality, it does not necessarily mean that it uses very expensive materials or highly skilled staff to provide it. What is important is that it **satisfies the customer**. This means that the product or service must

- be fit for the purpose for which it is purchased
- represent value for money to the customer.

In modern consumer-led societies, customers have access to a wide choice of products and services and make greater demands on suppliers. It is therefore increasingly important for businesses to pay more attention to the requirements of consumers. For example, there is fierce competition for market share between the main supermarket chains in the UK. If they all sell similar products at similar prices, the quality of the service they provide becomes a factor. Attention turns to reducing queues at the tills, providing in-store restaurants and other ways of increasing customer satisfaction.

The way in which customer satisfaction is to be achieved by ensuring that goods are fit for their purpose will depend on the type of product. For example, customers may look for:

- **low prices**

  Some products such as disposable razors and plastic ballpoint pens will be expected to have a short life. Customers expect them to be cheap and they may be made from cheap materials, provided they still work.

- **durability**

  Products such as computers and cars are expected to last much longer and remain reliable throughout their useful life.

- **uniqueness and craftsmanship**

  In certain businesses, expensive raw materials and highly skilled work are an integral part of the value of the product to the customer, for example in hand-made jewellery or furniture.

- **prestige or status**

  Products which represent value to the customer in terms of prestige or status are expected to have expensive packaging, designer labels and high prices, eg perfumes and fashion products.

quality in services

There will also be different ways of considering and measuring quality in the provision of services, depending upon the type of service. Here, customer satisfaction is dependent on customer experience. For example, the features they may look for include:

- **an efficient service**

  Where the service involves answering queries or giving advice, customers expect accurate information, given within a reasonable time. Efficient travel services (rail, bus or air) should run on time. These aspects of a service can be measured against targets.

- **friendly and helpful staff**

  These aspects are also likely to be very important to customers, but are more difficult to measure.

- **a clean and comfortable environment**

  Wherever customers have to visit a service provider or wait for service, for example at a clinic or at a railway station.

quality and value

It can be seen that quality and value to the customer go hand in hand. An organisation can make improvements to the quality of its products or services by reducing the numbers of sub-standard products, responding to customers' demands and by getting things 'right first time'. This is referred to as **quality management**.

In the above discussion, we have concentrated on value to the customer, taking into account both **value in use** and **prestige value**. However, from the point of view of the producer or provider there are other important values to consider. In any organisation, whether profit-making or non-profit-making, control of costs is essential. One 'value' to be put on a product or service is therefore the **cost** of making it or providing it. For profit-making businesses, the selling price or market value is equally important.

In conclusion, the **value** of a product or service can be considered as having four main aspects:

1   value in use (fitness for purpose)   . . . for the customer

2   esteem or prestige value   . . . for the customer

3   cost of production or provision   . . . for the provider

4   exchange value (market value)   . . . for the provider

enhancement of value

Looking at the four aspects of value listed above, it is clear that, from the point of view of the producer or provider, it is desirable to add to the exchange market value of a product or service without increasing the cost. This means that the value in the view of the customers must be enhanced, so that they are prepared to pay a higher price.

In order to **add value**, it is necessary to analyse what customers expect and what they are prepared to pay for. Customers buying a product such as a car may be prepared to pay more for additional features. In service provision, the customers' experience could be improved, perhaps by having more luxurious surroundings, as in first class travel. Enhancement of value without increasing selling prices may be necessary where competitors offer similar products or services to customers, as in the example of supermarket chains described at the beginning of this chapter.

examples

1   List the features of an AAT Tutorial text which give it value to the customer.

2   List the features of an expensive, famous brand watch which give it value to the customer.

3   List the features of a clothes dry cleaning service which contribute to the quality of the service.

suggested answers

1   the AAT text

As the customers for this book are almost certainly AAT students, it is expected that they require:

- the content of the text to cover the required material for the units

- the content to be complete and clearly explained

- that the layout of the book makes it easy to use

- that there are no errors in the book

- that the paper and binding of the book will be of a suitable standard to last the course, without making the book too expensive

2 the watch

Like any other watch, reliable and accurate time-keeping are important for its value in use. In addition, with this type of watch, the brand name adds value in the form of esteem value, as does the fact that it is known that the watch is expensive. Reducing the selling price may therefore detract from its value to the customer. The design and construction should be of a higher standard than cheaper watches, and more expensive materials on the outside of the watch also add value.

3 dry cleaning

In a dry cleaning service, customers would be looking for:

- efficient cleaning and pressing

- no errors resulting in lost items or damage to clothes

- value for money

- convenient time and place to leave and collect clothes

- quick service

- helpful staff

We will now consider in more detail some methods which can contribute to the reduction of costs and enhancement of value.

TOTAL QUALITY MANAGEMENT

Total Quality Management (TQM) means that quality management becomes the aim of every part of an organisation.

The basic principle is one of continuous improvement, in order to eliminate faulty work and prevent mistakes. Mistakes carry a cost:

- wastage of materials
- idle time
- the cost of reworking
- the loss of customer goodwill, resulting in lost sales
- the cost of replacements
- the cost of dealing with customers' complaints

The concept of continuous improvement and getting more 'right first time' will reduce these costs. Other costs will be incurred in quality management, but the intention is that in the long term the organisation will benefit.

implementing TQM

If TQM is to be introduced, it must become the philosophy of everyone in the organisation, and apply to every activity, including administration, purchasing, sales, marketing and distribution, as well as production. Training and motivation of staff is essential, so that an attitude of seeking improvement is encouraged. Everyone should be allowed to put forward ideas. Groups of employees may form 'quality circles' and have regular meetings to discuss their ideas for quality improvements.

Each person within an organisation has customers. These may be *internal* users of his/her work – ie colleagues – as not everyone deals directly with the external customers. If the quality of the work for the next immediate user is monitored, mistakes will be reduced throughout the organisation.

The involvement of all staff of an organisation means that many different types of knowledge and skills are being used. These may be in engineering, design, information technology, materials handling, office management and many other areas. Specialist consultants may also be needed from outside the organisation.

the costs of quality

The costs relating to quality management can be grouped under four headings:

1   prevention costs

2   appraisal costs

3   internal failure costs

4   external failure costs

Prevention and appraisal costs are increased when improvements are made, whereas failure costs will be reduced. We will look at each of the four categories in turn.

Prevention Costs are the costs associated with preventing mistakes and faulty output. They include the costs of:

- design improvements, to reduce numbers of rejects
- systems improvements for services
- the development and maintenance of quality control equipment
- the administration of quality control
- training employees in quality control and new methods of working

Appraisal Costs are the costs associated with assessing quality. They include the costs of:

- inspection of goods inwards and raw materials received
- inspection of work-in-progress
- performance testing of finished goods
- appraisal of the quality of services

Internal Failure Costs are the costs of mistakes within the organisation. They include the costs of:

- investigation and analysis of failures
- re-inspection
- losses due to scrapping sub-standard goods or selling them at lower prices
- losses due to faults in the raw materials purchased
- production delays
- reviewing product design and specification after failures

External Failure Costs are the costs of mistakes which result in sub-standard products or services reaching the external customer. They include the costs of:

- running a customer complaints department
- liabilities in relation to faulty products
- repairs and replacements
- loss of customer loyalty

the benefits of Total Quality Management

Organisations which develop a culture of TQM and continuous improvement expect that the costs will be outweighed by the benefits. The benefits include:

- reduction of Internal Failure Costs
- reduction of External Failure Costs
- improved reputation and goodwill of customers
- increased sales
- better motivated staff due to improved job satisfaction
- reduction of staffing costs in some areas (typically in middle management, as senior management develops closer links to the operational workforce)

CASE STUDY

TYPES OF COST OF QUALITY: MOTORCO PLC

This Case Study is based on Motorco, a large car manufacturing company.

You are required to consider the effect of a number of events.

Identify, for each one, which of the costs of quality (prevention, appraisal, internal failure, external failure) would be affected by the event and state what the effect would be.

the events

1   There is a breakdown of one of the machines which carries out an automated process on the production line.

2   It is found that a particular model has a fault which involves recalling all cars of that type sold so far.

3   In the design of a new model, it is decided that the number of parts in the seat fixing can be reduced, to simplify construction and reduce errors.

4   The company has reduced the number of different suppliers from which materials are purchased.

5   The company has entered long-term contracts with major suppliers of components, and the contract terms include guarantees of the quality of components by the suppliers.

6   The company has introduced a more detailed inspection of the paint finish on all cars.

7   The detailed inspection of paint finish has revealed that one particular colour results in more defects.

8   The company uses Just-in-time stock control, where materials are delivered only as required and stock holdings are kept as low as possible. Essential materials are brought by road. Protesters against Government fuel duty blocked roads for a whole week and supplies were consequently delayed.

suggested analysis of the events

1   Internal failure costs would increase, due to production delays and investigation of the breakdown.

2   External failure costs would increase, due to the cost of repairs, any claims relating to the fault, and possibly loss of customer loyalty resulting from the bad publicity. Internal failure costs would also increase in the form of investigation, review of the product design, repairs and re-inspection. Prevention costs would also increase, as the fault must be eliminated from future production.

3   Prevention costs would be incurred in the change of design, but both internal and external failure costs should be reduced as a result, if errors are avoided.

4   The appraisal costs due to inspection of raw materials received should be reduced if the procedures can be simplified with fewer suppliers.

5   The appraisal costs due to inspection of raw materials can be reduced if the supplier takes this responsibility.

6   Appraisal costs of the inspection will increase, but both internal and external failure costs resulting from defects should decrease.

7   Internal failure costs will be incurred in investigating the defects in this colour paint, in repainting and re-inspecting the cars. There may also be additional prevention and appraisal costs in eliminating the defects when the cause has been found.

8   There will be additional internal failure costs, due to production delays.

THE ACTUAL COST OF QUALITY: ISIS PLC

situation

ISIS plc manufactures clothes for a number of UK retail stores. The company has unfortunately allowed its quality systems to slip in recent years.

The fabric supplies are not inspected before cutting and making up the garments.

The finished garments are inspected, and on average 120 items per month are found to have fabric faults. Of these, 20 have to be scrapped. The remainder are sold as seconds at a discount of £15 on the normal price.

A further 40 garments per month are returned by retailers because of fabric faults, which have been missed by the inspectors in the factory. The retailers do not pay for these and they are not replaced. Some retailers do not reorder from the company.

The returned garments are all sold as seconds at the reduced price.

The variable cost of manufacture is £48 per garment.

A management consultant suggests that ISIS should:

1   Identify the costs of quality, in money terms where possible and state in which of the four types of cost of quality each cost should be categorised.

2   Think about and suggest ways in which improvements could be made.

suggested solution

1   The costs of quality and types of cost

- The cost of scrapping 20 garments is the cost of making them, which is

  20 x £48 = £960 per month.

  This is an internal failure cost.

  Note: We use the variable cost of making the garments, because the fixed costs (by definition) are not increased by making additional items.

- The cost of selling the faulty goods as seconds is £15 per garment, as this the reduction in contribution from the discounted selling price. The cost of seconds found on inspection is:

  100 x £15 = £1,500 per month.

  This is an internal failure cost.

- The cost of selling the other faulty goods, which are returned by retailers, as seconds is:

  40 x £15 = £600 per month.

  This is an external failure cost, because the faulty goods went out of the factory.

Additional external failure costs will result from the lost orders from retailers and loss of reputation amongst customers, but we do not have sufficient information to measure these.

2 how can improvements be made?

The situation could be improved by inspection of the fabric as it is received. This would give rise to appraisal costs. An alternative would be to negotiate contract terms with the supplier to include guarantees regarding the quality of the fabric. Immediate action could be taken to improve the inspection of finished goods and avoid sending faulty goods to retailers. Although this alone would not reduce the total number of substandard goods, it would avoid the external failure cost of lost goodwill and future sales.

MEASURING THE COSTS OF QUALITY

In order to calculate the costs of quality, it is necessary to have recorded the necessary data, such as:

- the numbers of defects,
- the costs of inspection procedures,
- the time spent on repairs and re-working, and so on

This data would not usually be recorded by traditional accounting systems. In a typical system, 'normal' losses would have been allowed for in the costs of production. Wastage of material and scrapping of defective units are then treated as being an unavoidable part of the cost of producing the good output. Costs of inspections and re-working would be included in overheads and not separately identifiable.

New demands are therefore put upon accounting information systems by the introduction of quality management: unless the data is collected, the costs (and benefits) cannot be calculated.

implicit and explicit costs of quality

In the ISIS plc Case Study, information was available which enabled us to give numerical values for certain costs of quality, in particular the costs of scrapping items and of selling them at reduced prices. These failure costs are examples of **explicit costs** of quality. With suitable data, many of the costs of Prevention, Appraisal, Internal Failure and External Failure can be separated out and given in money terms.

However, some costs could not be recorded or given in money terms, although they are equally important. These were the costs of lost future trade and damage to the company's reputation. These are examples of **implicit costs**.

Implicit costs of quality, which are not recorded in the accounting system, include:

- costs which cannot be separated out from other costs, eg the disruptive effects of re-scheduling production when internal failures have occurred

- costs which represent the loss of future benefits (these are called 'opportunity costs'), such as lost sales because customers are dissatisfied

Explicit and implicit costs are explored in more detail in the Case Study which follows.

CASE STUDY

EXPLICIT COSTS AND IMPLICIT COSTS: CLAIR LIMITED

situation

Clair Ltd manufactures double glazed windows and doors, and has a division which installs them in customers' houses.

Clair Ltd buys in the glass sealed units and the locking mechanisms ready made, as well as purchasing the raw materials to make the frames.

When the glass units and locks are received, they are checked for any obvious faults. However, some less obvious faults may be found only when the locking mechanisms are fitted into the frames in the factory and the glass units are put in by the installers.

Defects may also occur in the frames: these are inspected on completion, but further problems may be found by the installers or customers. For example, the frames may not be the exact size required or the locks may not align properly when windows are fitted. If problems arise on installation, they cause delays which upset customers and disrupt the work schedule. If customers have any problems with the products, Clair Ltd's installers have to go back to carry out repairs or replacements.

Clair Ltd's managers feel that it is important to guarantee the quality of both their products and their installation service, but they realise this has a cost. The company records the numbers of:

- purchase returns, ie glass units or locks returned to suppliers

- defective frames, found on inspection before leaving the factory

- products returned to the factory by installers, whether before they are actually installed or later, when they have to be replaced

They also record the costs of:

- inspection of glass units and locks when received

- inspection of finished frames

- the time taken by installers to carry out repairs and replacements.

Required

1   Give three examples of explicit costs of quality which should be identified by the management of Clair Ltd.

2   Give two examples of implicit costs of quality, of which Clair Ltd's managers should be aware, but which are not recorded.

suggested solution

1   Examples of explicit costs of quality include:

■ the variable cost of making frames which are then scrapped at any stage

■ the variable cost of making replacement products

■ the costs of inspections of purchases or production

■ the labour costs of repairs and replacements after installation

2   Examples of implicit costs of quality include:

■ the loss of potential sales when new doors and windows are seen being repaired or replaced

■ the costs associated with the disruption of installers' job schedules when products are found to be faulty: although total time taken could be recorded, it is difficult to separate out different reasons for inefficiency – also the workers may be de-motivated by problems, or may rush their work, reducing the quality of installation

assessing quality

In assessing quality standards, the emphasis is on fitness for purpose and value to the user. Important ways of measuring quality are therefore related to external customer satisfaction, such as the numbers of goods returned or customer complaints. Inside the organisation, quality control and inspection procedures will use measurements which depend on the type of work being carried out. In the Motorco Case Study (see page 125), for example, the number of defects in the paintwork was a measure of quality.

In order to measure the quality of a product or service, it will be necessary to plan in advance in order to collect the relevant data. As we have seen above, the numerical data needed in order to calculate the costs of quality would not normally be available from a traditional accounting system. The same applies to the measurements needed in order to assess quality.

Considerations of quality and value therefore make new demands on information systems, so that the necessary data is collected. In the next chapter, we will be considering in more detail how quality can be assessed.

COST REDUCTION

cost reduction programmes

The aim of standard costing and budgetary control is to keep costs within pre-determined targets. By contrast, the aim of a cost reduction programme is to reduce costs from their previously accepted levels without reducing the value of the product or service.

For example, the value to the customer of the packaging of plain biscuits is that it prevents deterioration or breaking of the biscuits. It may be possible to achieve this with cheaper materials. On the other hand, the superior packaging of expensive chocolates may be important to consumers as chocolates are often given as a gift and the packaging is a sign of perceived quality. Cutting the costs here could reduce the value of the product.

To succeed, cost reduction programmes need the full support of senior management and the co-operation of all other employees. It is essential to plan for cost reduction throughout all areas of the organisation. It may be possible to reduce certain costs with no effect on the product or service at all, for example by reducing the wastage of power for lighting and heating.

approaches to cost reduction

In planning for cost reduction, it is important to ensure that the measures taken will reduce costs in the long term.

Initially, the costs to be considered are likely to be variable costs, because most fixed costs will already have been paid or contracted for a time period.

The only fixed costs which it may be possible to reduce immediately are the 'discretionary' fixed costs. Discretionary fixed costs are those which can be changed by managers. They are the costs of items where there is a choice about the level of expenditure, so that the level can be reduced within a shorter timescale. Examples of discretionary fixed costs include:

• advertising
• non-essential training and staff development
• research and development.

Cutting discretionary costs may increase profits in the short-term, but could be damaging in the long-term. Reducing spending on advertising and product development may lead to loss of market share. Cutting down on training and staff development will result in a less skilled workforce, inefficiency and possibly a high labour turnover. Care must be taken to plan cost reduction programmes, so that the savings are not outweighed by the loss of profits in future.

In general, long-term cost reduction can be achieved by improving productivity and efficiency and making better use of all resources. Changes may be made to working practices in all sections of the organisation, in order to make procedures, and hence the use of materials and of people's time, more cost-effective.

methods of assessing possible cost reductions

Methods which may be applied include:

- **Work Study**

  This is used in manufacturing to determine:

  - the most efficient methods and procedures
  - the best layout of the factory or production line to reduce costs
  - the most efficient ways to use materials, labour and machinery to reduce waste

- **Organisation and Methods**

  This is used in administration to determine ways to improve office methods and procedures, including:

  - form design, office layout, workflows and communication
  - the benefits of computerisation
  - elimination of unnecessary procedures and paperwork

- **Variety reduction**

  This may involve:

  - reducing the product range
  - standardising the components used in different products.

Variety reduction means reducing the number of different products or components which pass through the system. Standardising the components used in different products can be very cost-effective. It can allow for greater use of automation and also economies through bulk purchasing. Cutting the range of products, however, must be balanced with customer needs. The value of all the products to the user must be maintained, or sales and goodwill will be lost.

For example:

- customers expect a range of cars with different features, but the majority of the components can be standardised
- domestic products such as kitchen appliances are produced in different colour finishes and different sizes, but the working parts can be standardised.

other methods of cost reduction

Other aspects of an organisation where planned cost reduction should be considered are:

- **finance costs**: the interest payable on loans and overdrafts, foreign exchange, the cost of capital tied up in stock and the timing of capital expenditure may offer scope for cost reduction
- **energy costs**: savings may be made by energy conservation
- **staffing**: numbers of staff needed and the skill levels required should be considered
- **consumables**: the control of purchases and of stocks of items such as stationery may need to be tightened to make savings
- **authorisation of expenditure**: all expenditure should be subject to proper authorisation at a sufficiently high level of management

Cost reduction programmes, like TQM, involve all staff and hence draw on each person's specialist knowledge of their own job. Production staff can suggest changes in processing to reduce waste, human resource managers can assist with analysing staffing costs, accountants can look at finance costs and so on. Additional specialists may be brought in from outside to solve specific problems or to carry out work study for example.

examples of employee suggestions . . .

■ In a small factory, where production of sports cars is not automated, workers noticed that they were spending unnecessary amounts of time fetching small items such as nuts and bolts from central bins. Placing stocks of these items nearer to the actual work speeded up production.

■ In a large factory, one employee operated a machine to screw two parts of a component together. He realised that one of the four screws used did not actually contribute any strength or have any purpose. By modifying the process and eliminating this screw, both time and materials were saved. The suggestion earned the employee a bonus.

VALUE ENGINEERING AND VALUE ANALYSIS

As stated above, cost reduction programmes must not result in reducing the value of the product or service to the user. The examples of employees' suggestions show that this can be achieved by improving the design of products or processes.

In order to ensure that value is maintained, what constitutes that value must be analysed:

- before production starts (this is **value engineering**)
- or when the product or service is already on the market (**value analysis**).

definitions of value engineering and value analysis

value engineering	Ensuring that new products or services are designed for quality but at low cost, by analysing how every part of the design enhances value.
value analysis	Analysing the value of every part of the design of an existing product or service, and questioning whether its function can be achieved some other way at lower cost.

The aim of both these processes is to build quality into the design of the product or service, while keeping the costs down. Relevant specialists in engineering, design and technology will be consulted.

Clearly it is easier to make alterations at the design stage than afterwards, the aim being to build in value but at lower cost. At the design stage, each part or feature of the product or system is looked at to check that it is necessary and that it contributes value.

In existing products or services, it is possible to analyse the value provided to the customer, and decide whether that level of quality can be kept or improved, when costs are reduced.

For example, the exact colour of a disposable razor may be of no importance to customers, whereas the exact colour of a sofa may be part of its value. Cheaper raw materials which may show colour variations may be acceptable for some products but not others.

practical aspects of value engineering and value analysis

Value engineering and value analysis must look at each product or service in great detail. Typical questions to be asked include:

- Can the function of this product or component be achieved some other way?
- Are all the functions of the product or service essential?
- Can the product be made lighter or smaller, thus using less material? (This may enhance its value.)
- Can components be standardised across a range of products?
- Can the design of the product or the processes involved in a service be modified to save time?

advantages of value engineering and value analysis

The potential advantages of these techniques to the producer or provider are:

- continuous improvements in design and methods
- more efficient use of resources
- higher profits
- enhanced reputation
- extended product life
- improved customer service through standardisation of components
- improved employee motivation

The potential advantages of these techniques to the customer are:

- prices may be reduced without loss of quality
- better design based on satisfying users' needs
- improved performance and reliability
- quicker delivery
- standard components for servicing

We have seen that cost reduction programmes should be planned for the long term. Value engineering and value analysis can be used as part of these programmes, so that the value of products or services to users is maintained or increased, even when costs are reduced.

examples of cost reduction and value analysis

◼ In a hospital outpatients' clinic, the original system meant that each consultant remained in one room, seeing a succession of patients. Time was wasted while patients were prepared for the consultation. The system was changed to one in which two rooms were used and the consultant moved between them. While the consultant saw one patient, the next could be prepared in the other room. The service to patients was improved at reduced cost.

◼ In a factory manufacturing cheap pottery mugs, the handles for the mugs were made separately and attached to the mugs before firing. A moulding process was then developed which allowed the mug to be produced with the handle. This speeded up production and reduced the number of rejects.

◼ Products such as radios and telephones are often produced in a range of exterior designs but offering the same functions. The basic product can then be exactly the same, but housed in different casings. Costs can be reduced by manufacturing the working parts in large numbers, and the value to customers is maintained. This is an example of 'variety reduction'.

CHAPTER SUMMARY

- Businesses can try to ensure that they keep their customers and remain profitable, by making continuous improvements in the quality and value of their products or services.

- The quality of a product or service can be considered as its fitness for the customer's purpose.

- There are costs attached both to poor quality and to making improvements. These costs are grouped under the headings:
  - Prevention costs
  - Appraisal costs
  - Internal failure costs
  - External failure costs

- Some of the costs of quality can be recorded in accounting systems and calculated in money terms. These are called 'explicit' costs of quality. Other costs are 'implicit' costs, which cannot be quantified.

- The intention of quality management is that the additional costs of getting more 'right first time' will be outweighed by the benefits.

- The value of a product or service for the customer is:
  - its value in use (fitness for purpose)
  - its esteem or prestige value

- The value of a product or service for the producer or service provider is:
  - its cost of production or provision
  - its exchange value (market value)

- The value of a product or service can be maintained or enhanced, while at the same time costs are reduced. A careful analysis of value assists with these aims.

- In value engineering (for new designs) and value analysis (for existing designs), the question:'Can the same (or better) value to the user be achieved some other, cheaper way?' is asked about every part of the design. If this can be done, then:
  - the organisation should be able to increase its sales and profitability
  - customers will benefit from the availability of more efficiently designed products and services

KEY TERMS

quality

The quality of a product or service can be considered as its fitness for the purpose for which it is to be used by the customer.

total quality management (TQM)

TQM is a concept that means that continuous improvement is sought in every part of an organisation, attempting to get everything right first time and eliminate mistakes and defects.

costs of quality

These are the costs incurred in making improvements to quality (prevention and appraisal costs) or as a result of mistakes and defects (internal failure costs and external failure costs).

value

A product or service has value to the customer and also to the producer or provider:

. . . for the customer:

- value in use

- esteem or prestige value

. . . for the producer/provider:

- the cost to produce or provide

- exchange or market value

enhancement of value

The value of a product or service to the customer is increased by adding desirable features, eliminating faults or reducing the selling price without loss of quality.

cost reduction

A positive approach to reducing costs in all departments of an organisation, without affecting the quality of output.

value engineering

Ensuring that new products or services are designed for quality but at low cost, by analysing how every part of the design enhances value.

value analysis

Analysing the value of every part of the design of an existing product or service, and questioning whether its function can be achieved some other way at lower cost.

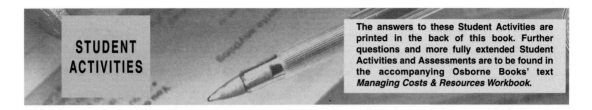

5.1 A Family History Society produces a quarterly journal containing members' contributions, articles and advice about researching family trees. The journal is posted to members. The committee circulated members with a questionnaire about possible changes to the journal. The answers showed members' opinions on various suggestions, including:

■ Whether better quality paper should be used: 78% said No.

■ Whether the number of pages should be increased up to the maximum for the same postage rate: 65% said Yes.

■ Whether the journal should have a crossword: 94% said No.

■ Whether the cover should be printed in colour: 86% said No.

Required

Referring to the case described above to illustrate your answer, explain the terms 'quality' and 'enhancement of value'.

5.2 The costs of quality are divided into four categories:

1 Prevention costs

2 Appraisal costs

3 Internal failure costs

4 External failure costs

Required

State the category to which the each of the following types of cost belongs:

(a) investigation of faults

(b) training production staff to use new equipment

(c) the loss of customer loyalty due to poor quality goods

(d) costs resulting from loss of production due to machine breakdown

(e) inspection of raw materials when received

(f) the cost of scrapping output

(g) claims from customers relating to defective products

5.3 AB Ltd manufactures electronic gadgets, many of which are purchased to give as presents.

AB Ltd has carried out an investigation into the reliability of one of its products, an electronic personal organiser. Investigations show that 1 in every 2,000 organisers quickly develops a fault and ceases to work. It is estimated that 75% of these are returned to the company. A repair which costs the company £10 corrects the fault. The remaining 25% are not returned, but the customers will not purchase AB Ltd's products in future. It is estimated that the costs of advertising in order to replace these customers amount to £50,000 per year. Average sales of organisers are 2,000,000 per year.

Required

List the costs of quality in this case, stating the category of each and the amount where possible. Suggest how AB Ltd could improve this situation and what would be the implications in terms of costs of quality.

5.4 TV-D plc is a digital television company which provides customers who subscribe with a free digital decoder. The decoders are purchased from several suppliers and are delivered to customers' homes. Customers carry out their own installation, but can telephone a helpline for advice. TV-D plc does not inspect or test the decoders. If customers cannot receive the digital service after installation following telephone advice, or if reception fails later, TV-D plc assume the decoder is either faulty or incompatible with the customers' own equipment and replace it. Decoders collected back from customers are scrapped.

Speed of delivery of decoders is an essential feature of the service, as customers kept waiting may choose another company.

In a given period, TV-D plc records the following results:

- New customers placing an order: 8,500

- Existing customers from previous periods: 76,000

- Replacement decoders delivered (to new and existing customers): 3,860

- Cancellations of subscriptions (total for all customers and all reasons): 9,800

- Total cost of customer helpline £1,400,000

- Total cost of delivery of decoders £250,000

- Purchase cost per decoder = £52

Required

(a) Explain briefly what is meant by the term 'explicit cost of quality', giving two examples from the case described.

(b) Explain briefly what is meant by 'implicit cost of quality', giving two examples from the case described.

5.5 PQR and Partners is a large firm of accountants with branch offices spread across several counties. In order to recruit suitable trainees, the firm needs to have a display stand, stocks of literature and several senior staff at every careers convention in the region. Currently, the staff involved take the stand and literature to the convention and set the display up before the starting time. Afterwards, they pack up and return everything to be stored in one of the firm's offices.

One of the staff involved has received an advertising leaflet from Splash Ltd, a company offering to store, transport, and set up the display, then pack it and return it to their own store afterwards. The leaflet points out that the firm's staff need then only attend for the actual opening hours of the convention, and that transporting displays for several firms in one van can save costs.

Required

Referring to the case described above to illustrate your answer, explain what is meant by 'cost reduction' and 'value analysis'.

6 MEASURING PERFORMANCE

this chapter covers . . .

In this chapter we examine:

- how the performance of organisations can be assessed
- the usefulness of comparisons
- benchmarking
- different kinds of measurements
- ratio analysis:
  - analysis of the profit and loss account ratios
  - ratios linking the profit and loss account to the balance sheet
  - working capital ratios
  - interpretation of ratios
  - the limitations of ratio analysis

NVQ PERFORMANCE CRITERIA COVERED

unit 8: CONTRIBUTING TO THE MANAGEMENT OF COSTS AND THE ENHANCEMENT OF VALUE

element 2

make recommendations to reduce costs and enhance value

- routine cost reports are analysed, compared with other sources of information and the implications of findings identified

- relevant performance indicators are monitored and the results are assessed to identify potential improvements

- specific recommendations are made to management and are explained in a clear and appropriate form

MEASURING THE PERFORMANCE OF ORGANISATIONS

performance indicators

It is important to be able to measure the performance of an organisation in a way which allows managers to see where improvements can be made. In chapters 2, 3 and 4 we have studied the analysis of cost variances. These are examples of performance measurements which can be used

- to monitor the use of resources
- to help with control of the business
- to help with planning for the future

A list of variances for one cost centre for one period is not particularly informative. The usefulness of variances depends on being able to compare them with target levels, with the variances for other time periods or with those for other similar cost centres.

In this chapter we will consider different ways of measuring the performance of an organisation (or of a part of an organisation). For example, we can calculate profit as a percentage of sales, sales revenue per employee, the percentage of orders which are delivered late, and many other measures. An individual measurement is called a **performance indicator**. What we have seen above for variance analysis applies to any performance indicator.

A performance indicator may be used for:
- identifying problems
- controlling costs
- measuring the utilisation of resources
- measuring an individual's performance
- planning

Examples of performance indicators include:
- the direct materials usage variance, which may identify a problem relating to wastage of materials
- the administration cost as a percentage of turnover, which may help with control of costs
- the number of hours of machine down time, which is relevant to how well resources are being used
- profit as a percentage of turnover, which may indicate how well a company has been managed
- the number of product units rejected on inspection, which may help with planning production levels

The usefulness of a performance indicator depends on:

• comparing with standards, budgets or targets

• comparing with other periods of time

• comparing with other similar organisations

making comparisons – benchmarking

Comparing performance indicators with standards or targets includes **benchmarking**.

Benchmarks are standards or targets set for one or more areas of activity and should be related to what is important to the organisation.

Benchmarks may be

• set internally and relate to a single aspect of the work, for example: all correspondence to be answered within three working days

• set by external bodies, for example government targets relating to pollution of the environment

• set (either internally or externally) with reference to similar organisations, for example the expected level of profitability calculated as an average for the industry

A single organisation may have a number of benchmarks, including all three types described above:

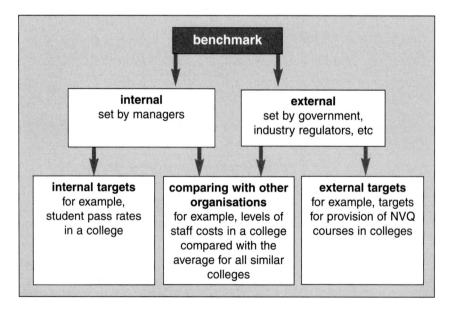

Measurement of how well an organisation (or part of an organisation) has performed in achieving these aims means that it has to record the necessary data to compare with the benchmark.

making comparisons – time series

Comparing the same indicator over a number of periods of time gives a Time Series. In Chapter 1 (pages 22 – 30) it has been shown how a time series may show a trend and possibly a pattern of variations around the trend. A performance indicator may show these features over a number of time periods, adding to the usefulness of the information.

For example, the number of customer complaints can be a useful performance indicator for an organisation. An overall downward trend in the number of complaints shows improvement, even if there are some fluctuations. An overall upward trend would indicate a problem to be investigated.

When items measured in money terms, such as Sales Revenue or Profit, are being compared over a number of years, it may be necessary to take out the effect of inflation. This can be done using index numbers, as shown in Chapter 1 and in Chapter 7.

making comparisons – consistency

Comparisons can give very useful information. However, we must be sure that figures being compared really are 'comparable'. In other words, they must have been prepared in a **consistent** way, so that we are comparing 'like with like'.

For example, the Net Profit figures for a business over a number of years can be compared provided that the same accounting policies have been applied throughout. A change in the policy for depreciation, for example, would affect the profit figures and they would not be comparable.

data for performance measurement

The diagram below shows that there are different kinds of data that may be used for performance measurement.

Quantitative data is data which can be stated in numbers, and this can be split into:

- Financial or Monetary data which is in terms of money and
- Non-financial or non-monetary data, which is in terms of units other than money, such as numbers of hours for example.

Qualitative data is data which cannot be put in numerical terms. It can consist of people's opinions or judgements, for example the views of students about a teacher. Such data is used for performance measurement, particularly in appraisal schemes for types of work where there is no clearcut numerical measure of performance. A combination of quantitative and qualitative data is often used.

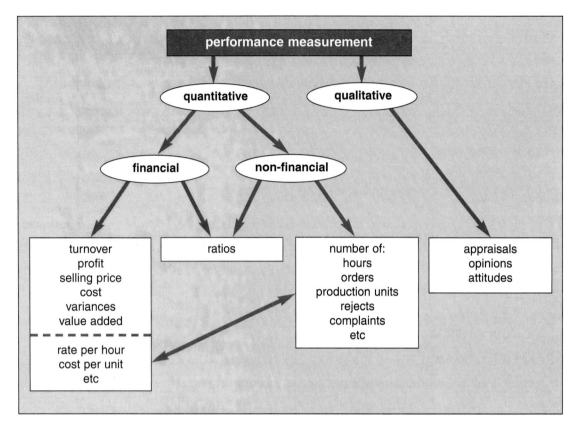

The examples shown in the diagram above include variances as an example of financial data. You have seen in your earlier studies that variances are given in money terms. The other point to note about variances is that each variance comes from two pieces of information and is the difference between them. An alternative way of comparing two pieces of information is to calculate a ratio or percentage, and this is one of the most common ways of arriving at a useful measure of performance. Percentages are particularly useful when comparisons are being made.

tutorial note

In order to express a ratio as a percentage, it is necessary to multiply by 100. This can be done using the '%' function on a calculator.

In all the formulas which follow, we have shown 'x 100' as well as indicating that the answer is a percentage by using the % sign.

When using these formulas:

either multiply by 100

or   use the % button on your calculator.

PERFORMANCE INDICATORS AS PERCENTAGES: LITTLE LIMITED AND LARGE LIMITED

Little Ltd and Large Ltd are companies which operate in the same industry. For a given period, we have the following data:

	Little Ltd £000s	Large Ltd £000s
Turnover	465	2,550
Gross Profit	185	895

At a glance, it is not easy to compare these figures because of the difference in size. If we calculate the gross profit as a percentage of turnover, we obtain more useful information for comparison:

Little Ltd   Gross profit percentage $= \dfrac{185}{465}$ x 100% = 39.8%

Large Ltd   Gross profit percentage $= \dfrac{895}{2,550}$ x 100% = 35.1%

We can then see that Little Ltd is translating a greater proportion of its turnover into gross profit than Large Ltd. This is an example of a performance indicator.

RATIO ANALYSIS

Ratio analysis generally refers to the calculation of a set of ratios or percentages using data from the financial and management accounts of a business. The trading and profit and loss account and the balance sheet are used in the analysis, which can then be used to evaluate the performance of the business, particularly by:

• comparing with budgets or targets

• comparing with other periods of time

• comparing with other similar organisations

In the case of limited companies, people outside the company can look at the final accounts and calculate ratios, for example when deciding whether to buy shares in the company.

In order to make meaningful comparisons between organisations or between time periods, the accounts must have been prepared on the same basis – applying the principle of consistency by comparing like with like.

sources of data for ratios

In this chapter we consider the ratios which can be calculated from the Profit and Loss Account and the Balance Sheet of a business. We will do this in a number of stages:

1 We will consider first the ratios calculated from the Profit and Loss Account separately, before linking sales and profits with the Balance Sheet.

2 The key measure of profit in relation to the assets shown on the Balance Sheet is Return on Capital Employed.

3 Our third section on ratio analysis will include ratios relating to the current assets and current liabilities of the organisation.

The diagram below illustrates these groups of ratios and the sources of data for their calculation, and the stages in which we will look at them.

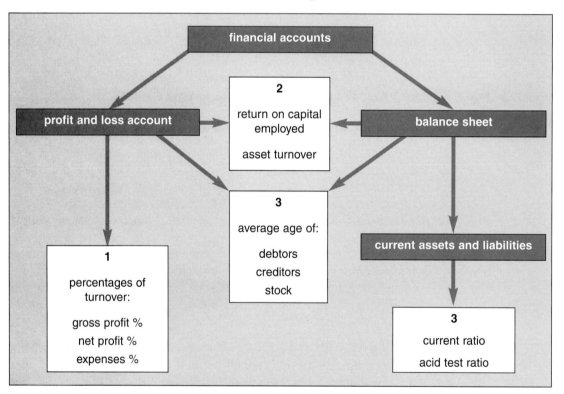

CALCULATION OF RATIOS: THE PROFIT AND LOSS ACCOUNT

Profit percentages are calculated on the basis of Turnover (Sales Revenue). This can be done for Gross Profit and Net Profit. In the accounts of a company, several versions of profit are given, before and after interest and tax. To measure the performance of the company, the 'Operating Profit' or

'Profit before interest and tax' is used for many ratios, because this is the profit from the main trading activities of the company. In the formulas below, the terms 'Sales' and 'Turnover' mean the same thing.

■ *gross profit margin (percentage)* $=$ $\dfrac{gross\ profit}{sales} \times 100\%$

■ *net profit percentage* $=$ $\dfrac{net\ profit}{sales} \times 100\%$

■ *or Operating Profit percentage* $=$ $\dfrac{operating\ profit}{sales} \times 100\%$

Profit percentages are indicators of the profitability of the business.

Any other figure from the Profit and Loss Account can also be calculated as a percentage of Sales, particularly if it appears to need investigation. For example, if Selling Expenses have increased from one period to the next, it may be useful to calculate for each period

■ *selling expenses as a percentage of sales* $=$ $\dfrac{selling\ expenses}{sales} \times 100\%$

■ *or any type of expense as a percentage of sales* $=$ $\dfrac{expense}{sales} \times 100\%$

Similarly, if details of the costs of materials and wages are available, we can calculate, for any type of cost:

■ *Cost as a percentage of sales* $=$ $\dfrac{cost}{sales} \times 100\%$

Whether costs behave as fixed or variable costs in relation to activity levels (see Chapter 1) makes a difference to how we would expect the ratios to behave. A higher turnover figure often results from a higher volume of sales, which would mean that total variable costs would also be higher. Total fixed costs, however, would not be expected to change with the volume. In percentage terms, this means that we would expect:

• a variable cost to remain relatively stable as a percentage of turnover

• a fixed cost as a percentage of turnover to decrease as turnover increases

Calculation of the Profit and Loss Account ratios will show how the revenue from sales has been split between the elements of cost and the profit. The following Case Study illustrates this.

CASE STUDY

RATIO ANALYSIS OF THE PROFIT AND LOSS ACCOUNT: AYEBRIDGE LIMITED

Ayebridge Limited is a manufacturer of electronic circuits used in domestic products. The following Profit and Loss Account for the year ended 30 June 2001 includes some detail of the cost of sales.

Ayebridge Ltd: Profit and Loss Account for the year ended 30 June 2001

	£000s	£000s
Sales		6,000
Less: Cost of Sales:		
Materials	800	
Labour	900	
Production overheads	1,700	
Cost of Sales		3,400
GROSS PROFIT		2,600
Selling and Distribution	813	
Administration	967	1,780
OPERATING PROFIT		820

required

Analyse the Ayebridge Limited Profit and Loss Account given above, using ratio analysis.

solution

Using the formulas listed on page 147, we obtain:

Gross profit margin (percentage) = $\dfrac{\text{Gross profit}}{\text{Sales}} \times 100\% = \dfrac{2,600}{6,000} \times 100\% = 43.3\%$

This shows that 43.3% of the Sales Revenue remains as Gross Profit after the Cost of Sales has been deducted (see diagram on the opposite page).
The Cost of Sales therefore represents 100% – 43.3% = 56.7% of the Sales Revenue. In this example it is possible to calculate percentages for the three elements of the cost of sales, as follows:

■ Materials cost as a percentage of sales = $\dfrac{800}{6,000} \times 100\% = 13.3\%$

■ Labour cost as a percentage of sales = $\dfrac{900}{6,000} \times 100\% = 15.0\%$

■ Production overheads as a percentage of sales = $\dfrac{1,700}{6,000} \times 100\% = 28.3\%$

(Allowing for a rounding difference, these total the cost of sales percentage of 56.7%)

In order to draw any conclusions from these calculations, we would need more information for comparison. We would need the same format of Profit and Loss Account for Ayebridge Limited for other years, or as a budget for the year ended 30 June 2001. Alternatively, we could compare Ayebridge's figures with averages for the industry or with those for other similar businesses, if available. The same applies to the remaining percentages:

■ Operating profit percentage = $\frac{820 \times 100\%}{6,000}$ = 13.7%

Each of the two categories of expense could also be calculated as a percentage of sales:

■ Selling and Distribution as a percentage of sales = 13.6%

■ Administration as a percentage of sales = 16.1%
(Check that you can calculate these).

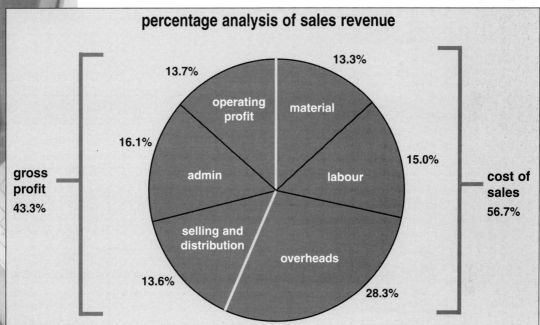

Case Study continued – comparison with the previous year.

Consider the table below, which shows information for Ayebridge Limited for the year ended 30 June 2000, together with answers from our calculations for the year ended 30 June 2001.

	30 June 2000	30 June 2001
Gross profit percentage	41.0%	43.3%
Operating profit percentage	15.4%	13.7%

The Gross Profit percentage has therefore increased from 41% in the previous year, to 43.3% in the year ended 30 June 2001. This improvement means that a lower proportion of the Sales Revenue has been used for Cost of Sales. This could result from increasing selling prices or from reducing costs. With more detailed information for the previous year this could be analysed further.

The Operating Profit percentage, however, has decreased from 15.4% in the previous year to 13.7% in the year ended 30 June 2001. This could be because the expenses have increased, but it could also be due to a reduction in the total sales revenue, or both. Increased selling prices may reduce demand for the products, and this could result in lower total sales revenue.

These comments show that the calculated percentages alone are not enough. To see exactly what has happened, we would need to look back at the original data as well.

CASE STUDY

RATIO ANALYSIS OF THE PROFIT AND LOSS ACCOUNT: BEETON LIMITED

The following information relates to Beeton Ltd, a chain of retail stationery shops.
Note: whenever you are given data for different time periods, make sure you check which is the earlier and which the later time period. Here the earlier year is on the right, but this is not always so. If you do not check, you may discuss a completely opposite case!

Beeton Ltd: Trading and Profit and Loss Account for the year ended:				
	31 March 2001		31 March 2000	
Sales		4,200		3,400
Less: Cost of Sales				
Opening Stock	450		410	
Purchases	2,896		2,250	
Less: Closing stock	(490)	2,856	(450)	2,210
GROSS PROFIT		1,344		1,190
Expenses:				
Selling and Distribution	157		128	
Administration	200	357	280	408
OPERATING PROFIT		987		782

required
Analyse the Profit and Loss Account, for each of the given years, by calculating (correct to one decimal place)
- the gross profit margin on sales
- the operating profit as a percentage of sales
- two other percentages to aid your analysis

Identify where possible the reasons for changes in the profitability of Beeton Ltd.

solution

Year ended:	31 March 2001	31 March 2000
Gross Profit Margin on Sales	32%	35%
Operating Profit percentage	23.5%	23%
Expenses as % of Sales:		
Selling and Distribution	3.7%	3.8%
Administration	4.8%	8.2%

The **Gross Profit margin** on sales has decreased in the year to 31 March 2001. This may be due to having to reduce selling prices in order to increase sales demand. It could also be caused by increases in purchasing costs, or a combination of these reasons.

The **Operating Profit percentage** has increased slightly. It can be seen from the Profit and Loss Accounts and from the expense percentages that this level of operating profit percentage has been maintained by a considerable reduction of Administration costs. This cost has been reduced by £80,000, even though sales have increased. The effect is to cut the Administration as a percentage of sales from 8.2% to 4.8%. The Selling and Distribution costs are at a similar level in relation to sales in both years.

RATIOS LINKING TURNOVER AND PROFITS TO THE BALANCE SHEET

From your studies of financial accounting, you will be familiar with the idea that the Balance Sheet of an organisation represents the equation:

assets – liabilities = capital

and that the Capital represents the owners' interest in the business.

We can therefore look at the Balance Sheet from either side – as the net assets or as the capital provided by the owners.

- 'Assets' include both fixed and current assets.
- 'Liabilities' include current and long-term liabilities.

Long-term liabilities, such as loans, can be viewed as a long-term source of finance for the organisation by rearranging the equation as:

fixed and current assets – current liabilities

= long-term liabilities + capital

This version of the equation will be used in calculating the Return on Capital Employed on the next page and examples will show how it works.

tutorial note

The Balance Sheet of an organisation shows its assets, liabilities and owners' capital on a specific date.

It is important to remember, when using a Balance Sheet for ratio analysis, and when interpreting the ratios, that the position shown on that date may not be typical. A single transaction the next day, such as a payment to a creditor, will alter the position. Bearing this in mind, we calculate a number of ratios using the Balance Sheet.

return on capital employed (ROCE)

Return on Capital Employed is a key ratio which shows how well the management of an organisation has used the assets (or the resources shown on the Balance Sheet) to generate profits.

To calculate ROCE, the profit is expressed as a percentage of the capital employed in the business.

The difficulty comes in deciding which 'profit' figure to use, and what is meant by 'capital employed'. If comparisons are being made, between companies for example, then the ROCE must be calculated in the same way for each company (as far as is possible from the available information).

The principle of comparing 'like with like' also means that the assets included in the capital employed must be those relevant to the profit being measured. Usually, the measurement of management performance would mean that the **Operating Profit** is used, and the Capital Employed would take account of the **assets used in the main activities of the organisation**.

For instance, if there is any income from investments, this would be excluded from the profit figure and the investment assets themselves would be excluded from the capital employed.

Allowing for such adjustments, the capital employed figure to use in straightforward cases is equal to the **Fixed Assets plus the Net Current Assets**. By 'net current assets' we mean 'current assets less current liabilities'.

Referring back to the Balance Sheet equation on the previous page,

fixed assets plus net current assets

= fixed and current assets – current liabilities

= long-term liabilities + capital

We are looking at the 'capital employed' either as the assets being used to generate profits or the funds which are being used to finance those assets.

For our purposes in this unit, we therefore have the formulas:

$$ROCE = \frac{operating\ profit}{fixed\ assets + net\ current\ assets} \times 100\%$$

or

$$ROCE = \frac{operating\ profit}{capital\ on\ balance\ sheet + long\text{-}term\ liabilities} \times 100\%$$

You may find the term 'Profit before interest and tax' instead of Operating Profit in some examples. It is advisable to make your method clear when calculating ROCE, because of the possible variations in the definitions.

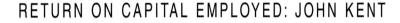

CASE STUDY

RETURN ON CAPITAL EMPLOYED: JOHN KENT

John Kent is a sole trader who runs a plumbing business employing two other people. He financed part of the purchase of his vans with a long-term loan from his father. We have the following simplified balance sheet:

Balance Sheet of John Kent as at 31 March 2001		
	£	£
Fixed Assets:		
Vehicles at cost	50,000	
Less: provision for depreciation	12,500	37,500
Equipment at cost	6,800	
Less: provision for depreciation	1,200	5,600
		43,100
Current Assets	8,400	
Current Liabilities	(3,900)	
Net current assets		4,500
Long term loan		(30,000)
		17,600
Capital as at 31 March 2001		17,600

required

Show the calculation of the Capital Employed as at 31 March 2001 for John Kent from the above balance sheet using:

■ Fixed Assets plus net current assets

■ Capital on Balance Sheet plus long-term liabilities

solution

■ Fixed Assets plus net current assets = £43,100 + £4,500 = £47,600

■ Capital on Balance Sheet plus long-term liabilities
= £17,600 + £30,000 = £47,600

Note: These two views of the balance sheet give the same figure for Capital Employed (at 31 March 2001)

ROCE AND THE BALANCE SHEET OF A LIMITED COMPANY: WING LIMITED

This case study illustrates some of the features of a limited company balance sheet, using a simplified version.

Balance Sheet of Wing Ltd as at 31 March 2001

	£000s	£000s
Fixed Assets (Net Book Value)		750
Current Assets	95	
Current Liabilities	68	
Net current assets		27
		777
Long term loans		150
		627
Capital and Reserves:		
£1 Ordinary Shares issued and fully paid		350
Reserves		200
Profit and Loss Account		77
		627

Note that the Balance Sheet total of £627,000 represents for Capital and Reserves:

• Share Capital which has been introduced into the company (by investors buying shares)

• Reserves, which represent amounts of capital or profits which have been set aside to be used in future

• Profit and Loss Account, which represents accumulated profits retained within the business (other than those set aside in reserves)

required

Determine the Capital Employed for Wing Ltd as at 31 March 2001 and calculate the Return on Capital Employed. (Note: Operating Profit for the year was £233,100).

solution

Wing Ltd has long-term loans of £150,000 which are being used, along with the accumulated total capital, to finance the operating activities of the company. Therefore the Capital Employed is:

Balance Sheet total + Long term loans = £627,000 + £150,000 = £777,000

or Fixed Assets + Net Current Assets = £750,000 + £27,000 = £777,000

Applying the formula:

$$Return\ on\ Capital\ Employed = \frac{Operating\ profit}{Capital\ employed} \times 100\%$$

$$= \frac{£233,100}{£777,000} \times 100\% = 30\%$$

asset turnover

Asset Turnover is another important ratio which links the balance sheet with the profit and loss account.

Asset Turnover is the number of times the value of the assets has been obtained in Turnover (Sales).

Again there may be different definitions of the value of the assets, but we will use the fixed assets plus net current assets as above.

$$asset\ turnover\ =\ \frac{turnover}{fixed\ assets\ +\ net\ current\ assets}$$

CASE STUDY

ASSET TURNOVER: WING LIMITED

In the Wing Limited Case Study (see opposite), if the Turnover for the year ended 31 March 2001 was £1,165,500, then:

$$asset\ turnover\ =\ \frac{£1,165,500}{£750,000\ +\ £27,000}\ =\ 1.5\ times$$

ROCE and operating profit margin

There is an important link between ROCE, Asset Turnover and the Operating Profit margin (ie Operating Profit as a percentage of Sales):

ROCE = operating profit margin x asset turnover

because

$$\frac{Operating\ Profit}{Fixed\ \&\ net\ current\ assets}\ =\ \frac{Operating\ Profit}{\cancel{Sales}}\ x\ \frac{\cancel{Sales}}{Fixed\ \&\ net\ current\ assets}$$

The sales (turnover) figure can be cancelled in the calculation of the right hand side of this equation (see lines).

The following diagram illustrates these connections:

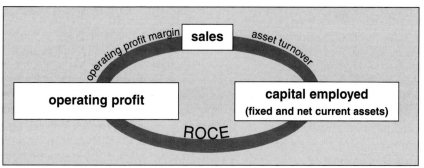

It is easiest to see this using the figures from the Wing Limited Case Study:

$$\frac{£233,100}{£777,000} \times 100\% = \frac{£233,100}{£1,165,500} \times 100\% \times \frac{£1,165,500}{£777,000} = 20\% \times 1.5 = 30\%$$

This relationship means that the ROCE can be increased either by increasing the Operating Profit Margin or by improving the Asset Turnover or both. In other words, using the assets more effectively to generate sales or spending less of the sales revenue on operating costs can both improve ROCE.

There is a further illustration of the calculation and interpretation of the ROCE and Asset Turnover in a Case Study later in this chapter (page 163).

CALCULATION OF RATIOS: CURRENT ASSETS AND LIABILITIES

The ratios and percentages usually calculated from the Balance Sheet include several which relate to the current assets and current liabilities. These can be grouped under the heading 'Working Capital Ratios'.

Working Capital is the part of the capital of the business which circulates between the stock, debtors, cash and trade creditors. These current assets and liabilities are constantly changing, unlike the fixed assets which change only occasionally.

The circulation of working capital is often illustrated by the Cash Cycle:

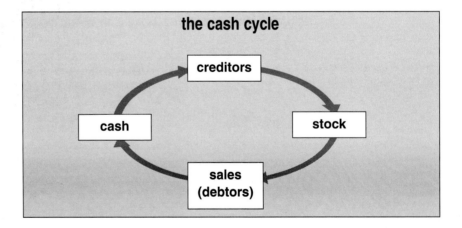

The diagram of the cash cycle above represents how creditors (suppliers) provide stock. When stock is sold it results in an increase in debtors. When debtors pay, the cash increases. When creditors are paid, the cash moves along to the creditors. This decreases the creditors' balance, but it will increase again when more stock is provided . . . and so on.

calculation of working capital ratios: the current ratio

$$\text{The current ratio} \ = \ \frac{\textit{current assets}}{\textit{current liabilities}}$$

This is kept as a ratio and written in the form x : 1, where x is the answer obtained above. It shows the **number of times that the current liabilities are covered by the current assets**.

It is often said that the current ratio should be about 2 : 1, and this may be appropriate for some organisations. However, in certain types of business, the current assets are not expected to be so high in relation to the current liabilities. In a supermarket, for example, the level of debtors will be low in comparison to creditors, and stocks are not held for long periods.

The ratio of 2 : 1 can be used as a guide for organisations where stock does not sell so quickly and where sales as well as purchases are likely to be on credit. In a given case, look for comparisons (with other time periods or other similar organisations) rather than judging a single figure against this guideline.

The current ratio is affected by the level of stock included in the current assets. Stock is considered to be the least 'liquid' of the current assets, because it is further from becoming cash. In the diagram of the cash cycle above, it can be seen that Debtors are one step nearer to cash. Cash itself is the most 'liquid' current asset, because it can be used immediately to pay the creditors. The measurement of 'Liquidity' is important, because it indicates the ability of the organisation to pay its current liabilities when they fall due.

CASE STUDY

CURRENT RATIO: A LTD, B LTD, C LTD

A Ltd, B Ltd and C Ltd are similar companies, which have current assets as shown:

	A Ltd	B Ltd	C Ltd
	£000	£000	£000
Stock	170	100	50
Debtors	90	140	110
Cash at bank and in hand	40	60	140
	300	300	300

Each of the three companies has current liabilities of £150,000.

required

Calculate the current ratio for each of the three companies and compare the liquidity position of the three companies.

solution

For each company,
    current assets = £300,000 and current liabilities = £150,000.
    Each of the three companies therefore has a current ratio of 2 : 1.

However, A Ltd has built up stocks to a high level and we cannot be sure that these can easily be sold, in order to convert them into debtors and then into cash. When the stocks are taken out, A Ltd's current assets do not cover its current liabilities.

B Ltd has a better liquidity position, provided the debtors are well controlled.

C Ltd has the most liquid current assets and could pay most of its creditors immediately.

calculation of working capital ratios: the quick ratio

The ratio which is used to measure liquidity compares the current assets *other than stock* with the current liabilities, as follows:

$$\textit{Quick Ratio or Acid Test Ratio} = \frac{\textit{current assets} - \textit{stock}}{\textit{current liabilities}}$$

As a guide, a level of 1 : 1 for the quick ratio is quoted, but a business with frequent cash inflows may operate satisfactorily on a lower quick ratio.

Comparison with similar businesses gives more useful information, but it must be remembered that a single large transaction can alter the position significantly and the Balance Sheet may not be typical.

CASE STUDY

CALCULATION OF THE QUICK RATIO: A LTD, B LTD, C LTD

Referring to the data given for A Ltd, B Ltd and C Ltd in the last Case Study, we can calculate their quick ratios:

A Ltd: $\dfrac{300 - 170}{150}$ = 0.87, giving a quick ratio of   0.87 : 1

B Ltd: $\dfrac{300 - 100}{150}$ = 1.33, giving a quick ratio of   1.33 : 1

C Ltd: $\dfrac{300 - 50}{150}$ = 1.67, giving a quick ratio of   1.67 : 1

These calculations illustrate the discussion of the liquidity of the companies above.

RATIOS LINKING THE PROFIT & LOSS ACCOUNT & BALANCE SHEET

debtor collection

In the last Case Study, B Ltd has a high proportion of debtors and we noted that these should be well controlled. This means that the cash should be received within the time allowed by the normal credit terms for customers. It is possible to *estimate* the time being taken for debtors to pay, by using the formula:

$$debtors'\ collection\ period\ =\ \frac{trade\ debtors}{credit\ sales}\ x\ \ 365\ days$$

A separate figure for 'Credit Sales' may not be available, and Total Sales would have to be used, although this is not appropriate if cash sales are a significant part of the total.

If customers are normally allowed two months' credit, for example, the debtors collection period should not be much above 60 days (remembering that the closing debtors figure may not be typical). As usual, comparison over time is more useful and may show whether control of debtors is improving or not.

In effect, debtors are *borrowing from* the business, because sending goods without receiving payment is like lending money. Conversely, creditors are *lending to* the business. It makes sense, therefore, to try to collect the money back from debtors more quickly than paying amounts due to creditors. However, creditors who are not paid on time may refuse to supply goods or services in future.

creditors' payment period

The **Creditors' Payment Period** can be estimated in a similar way to the Debtors' Collection Period, but here it is credit purchases which are relevant.

$$creditors'\ payment\ period\ =\ \frac{trade\ creditors}{credit\ purchases}\ x\ \ 365\ days$$

A separate figure for Credit Purchases may not be available, in which case Total Purchases or (less appropriately) Cost of Sales may have to be used.

stock holding ratios

Another step in the Cash Cycle can be estimated in terms of days: this is the length of time taken for stock to be sold, or the average age of stock. The stock figure used in the formula may be the average of the opening and closing stock, which is calculated in the usual way for an average (mean) of two items, by adding them together and dividing the total by 2:

$$average\ stock = 0.5\ x\ (opening\ stock + closing\ stock)$$

If the opening stock is not known, the closing stock figure is used.

$$average\ age\ of\ stock\ =\ \frac{average\ stock}{cost\ of\ sales}\ x\ 365\ days$$

or,

$$average\ age\ of\ stock\ =\ \frac{closing\ stock}{cost\ of\ sales}\ x\ 365\ days$$

Note the correspondence between the pairs of figures used in the last three ratios:

- debtors are related to credit sales
- creditors are related to credit purchases
- stock is related to cost of sales

As an alternative to calculating the average age of stock, we can look at the number of times per year that the stock is 'turned over' or sold. This is called **stock turnover** or **stockturn** and is calculated as:

$$\textit{Stock Turnover} \quad = \quad \frac{\textit{cost of sales}}{\textit{average stock}} \quad \textit{or} \quad \frac{\textit{cost of sales}}{\textit{closing stock}}$$

The result of this calculation gives the **Stock Turnover as a 'number of times per year'**.

A higher stockturn indicates that stock is moving more quickly, and this corresponds to a lower average age of stock. The speed with which stock should be sold depends on the type of business, for example fresh fruit must be sold within a few days, whereas non-perishable goods may be kept for longer periods. Once more, we need comparison with other years or other similar organisations to be able to comment further.

ratios: the whole picture

We now look at a Case Study which incorporates a number of the ratios described so far in this Chapter. It shows how ratios can be used in business decision making.

CASE STUDY

RATIO ANALYSIS: TUBS AND POTS LIMITED

Tubs and Pots Ltd supply plant holders to local garden centres. The company has now been offered a contract to supply a national chain of home and garden superstores. The following information shows extracts from the Balance Sheet and the Profit and Loss Account as forecast for the next year:

- on the basis of continuing with the current local trade ('Current Trade')
- on the basis of acceptance of the contract ('With Contract')

	Current Trade	With Contract
	£	£
Current Assets:		
Stock	6,000	20,000
Trade Debtors	14,000	52,000
Cash at Bank	4,000	
	24,000	72,000

Current Liabilities		
Trade Creditors	12,000	70,000
Bank Overdraft		7,000
	12,000	77,000
Sales (all Credit Sales)	70,000	204,000
Opening stock	4,000	4,000
Purchases (all Credit Purchases)	40,000	140,000
Less: Closing stock	(6,000)	(20,000)
Cost of Sales	38,000	124,000

required:

Task 1

Using the above information, calculate the following ratios for the current trade and for the acceptance of the contract:

1 Current Ratio
2 Quick Ratio
3 Debtors' Collection Period
4 Creditors' Payment Period
5 Average age of stock (using the closing stock)
6 Gross Profit
7 Gross Profit percentage (on Sales)

Task 2

Identify the changes which will take place in the business of Tubs and Pots Ltd if the contract is accepted and comment on the findings.

solution

Task 1: calculation of ratios

Check that you can carry out these calculations, before looking at the workings at the end of the solution.

		current trade	with contract
1	Current Ratio	2.0 : 1.0	0.9 : 1.0
2	Quick Ratio	1.5 : 1.0	0.7 : 1.0
3	Debtors' Collection Period	73 days	93 days
4	Creditors' Payment Period	110 days	183 days
5	Average age of stock	58 days	59 days
6	Gross Profit	£32,000	£80,000
7	Gross Profit percentage (on Sales)	45.7%	39.2%

Task 2: analysis of ratios

The forecasts show that, with the contract, **sales** would increase to nearly three times the current level and the management of the company would need to consider whether such expansion within one year is feasible. There would also be higher **stock levels** and the company would go into an **overdraft** situation. Building up stocks means that **purchases** are increased to more than three times the current level, which could have

contributed to the need for an overdraft. Another reason for the overdraft could be purchases of fixed assets.

The indicators we have calculated show that both the **current and quick ratios** would be adversely affected by the contract, such that the current liabilities are not covered by the current assets. The **Debtors' Collection Period** increases to about 3 months with the contract, and the Creditors' Payment Period to about 6 months. The adjustment to stock levels would keep the **average age of stock** about the same. With the contract, there is a decrease in the **Gross Profit Margin** (Gross Profit as a percentage of Sales).

The managers of Tubs and Pots Ltd need to investigate the risks attached to acceptance of this contract. If fixed assets are purchased, longer-term finance would be more suitable than an overdraft. They also need more working capital to avoid the problems with liquidity. The increased collection period indicates that the national chain would take longer to pay for the goods than the current customers. It appears risky to plan for a 6 month creditors' payment period unless such terms have been agreed with the suppliers.

It would be important to consider the length and security of the contract. The forecasts given are for one year only and show that Gross Profit Margin would decrease. This could be caused by the national chain insisting on paying lower prices for the goods. Over a number of years it may be possible to improve on this, by reducing costs. Expansion on this scale would not be worthwhile unless the contract was secure for the long term. The management of Tubs and Pots Ltd should also consider the effect on their current trade with their local customers.

Workings		*current trade*	*with contract*
1	Current assets	£24,000	£72,000
	Current liabilities	£12,000	£77,000
2	Current assets – Stock	£18,000	£52,000
	Current liabilities	£12,000	£77,000
3	Debtors x 365	£14,000 x 365	£52,000 x 365
	Credit sales	£70,000	£204,000
4	Creditors x 365	£12,000 x 365	£70,000 x 365
	Credit purchases	£40,000	£140,000
5	Closing stock x 365	£6,000 x 365	£20,000 x 365
	Cost of sales	£38,000	£124,000
6	Sales – Cost of sales	£70,000 – £38,000	£204,000 – £124,000
7	Gross Profit x 100%	£32,000 x 100%	£80,000 x 100%
	Sales	£70,000	£204,000

We will now look at a long Case Study which gives practice in calculating and interpreting *all* the ratios. In central assessments, it is usual for the tasks to concentrate on one aspect of performance, such as profitability or liquidity.

CASE STUDY

COMPREHENSIVE RATIO ANALYSIS: BAMBERDALE PLC

Bamberdale plc is a large manufacturing company in the chemicals industry producing a range of different products. The following information is available for the years ended 30 September 2000 and 2001. (Note as before that the earlier year is shown on the right).

The Profit and Loss Account for a limited company is immediately followed by the appropriation account, showing the amount of dividends to be paid out of profits to shareholders. The remaining profit is retained within the business and is added to the Retained Profits, which are part of the capital of the company. The term 'Debentures' under long-term liabilities in this example refers to long term loans, (which are often secured on the assets in a similar way to a domestic mortgage). For ease of working the information is shown in a simplified format.

Bamberdale plc Profit and Loss Account for the year ended 30 September

	2001		2000	
	£m	£m	£m	£m
Turnover		2,660		2,200
Opening Stock	400		277	
Purchases	1,945		1,723	
Less: Closing Stock	350		400	
Cost of Sales		1,995		1,600
Gross Profit		665		600
Selling and Distribution	120		105	
Administration	240	360	210	315
Operating Profit		305		285
Interest charges		25		20
Profit before taxation		280		265
Taxation		84		62
Profit after taxation		196		203
Dividends		90		64
Retained Profit for the year		106		139

Bamberdale plc Balance Sheet as at 30 September:

	2001		2000	
	£m	£m	£m	£m
Fixed Assets at Cost	1,370		763	
Provision for Depreciation	770	600	500	263
Current Assets:				
Stock	350		400	
Debtors	200		210	
Cash at Bank	26		97	
	576		707	
Current Liabilities:				
Trade Creditors	236		224	
Taxation	84		62	
Dividends	90		64	
	410		350	
Net current assets		166		357
Long term liabilities:				
Debentures		200		160
		566		460
Financed by:				
Ordinary shares issued and fully paid		300		300
Retained Profits		266		160
		566		460

required

Carry out an analysis of the ratios studied in this chapter (listed below) for Bamberdale plc and comment on the results.

The ratios to be used are:
1   Gross Profit Margin
2   Operating Profit %
3   Selling and Distribution % (of Sales)
4   Administration % (of Sales)
5   ROCE
6   Asset Turnover
7   Current Ratio
8   Acid Test Ratio
9   Debtors' Collection Period
10   Creditors' Payment Period
11   Average age of stock (use average stock)

solution

The following indicators are calculated from the information given, using the formulas in this chapter. (Check that you can carry out these calculations, before looking at the workings at the end of the solution).

		30 Sept 2001	30 Sept 2000
1	Gross Profit Margin	25.0%	27.3%
2	Operating Profit %	11.5%	13.0%
3	Selling and Distribution % (of Sales)	4.5%	4.8%
4	Administration % (of Sales)	9.0%	9.5%
5	ROCE	39.8%	46.0%
6	Asset Turnover	3.47 times	3.55 times
7	Current Ratio	1.4 : 1	2.0 : 1
8	Acid Test Ratio	0.6 : 1	0.9 : 1
9	Debtors' Collection Period	27 days	35 days
10	Creditors' Payment Period	44 days	47 days
11	Average age of stock	69 days	77 days

comments

We can look first at the **original figures**, before considering the ratios. It is clear that, in the year ended 30 September 2001, **Turnover** has increased, and so have the **Gross Profit** and **Operating Profit** figures. On the Balance Sheet, we can see that fixed assets have been purchased during the year, and there are also additional **long term loans** (debentures). Current assets have decreased, particularly the **Cash at Bank**. It seems that the extra loans have partly financed the new fixed assets, but cash has also been used for this. These assets have helped to generate higher sales and this has resulted in higher profits. However, the ratios will show how well the company has used its assets in comparison to the previous year, and what percentage of the higher sales has been translated into profits.

ratio analysis

1   **Gross profit margin** has decreased, which suggests that selling prices have been reduced (this could result in more demand for the products and therefore higher turnover). Alternatively, purchase costs may have gone up, or both.

2, 3 & 4   The **expenses** have increased approximately in line with turnover, being at similar percentage levels. Together with the lower gross profit margin, this has resulted in a decrease in the **operating profit percentage**. The increase in the amount of **administration** expenses could be investigated, as it might be expected that the majority of these costs would be fixed.

5   **ROCE** has decreased from 46.0% to 39.8%. This is due to the fact that the **capital employed** has increased. (The **operating profit** has also increased, but because we are dividing it by a much larger number, the resulting percentage has gone down). We saw that we can look at the capital employed from the point of view of the fixed and net current assets being used or the financing of those assets. The fixed assets being used in the year ended 30 September 2000 were probably older and therefore the accumulated depreciation had considerably reduced

their value on the balance sheet. In the following year, a significant factor is that there are **new fixed assets** included on the Balance Sheet as at *30 September.* There is no information as to whether these were acquired early or late in the year, which would make a difference to the amount of profit they could generate.

Looking at the increase in capital employed from the finance point of view, it is due to the £40m increase in **debentures** and the £106m **retained profit** for the year ended 30 September 2001.

6   The **asset turnover** has decreased slightly, but considering the effect of the additional fixed assets as discussed above, it seems that the company has continued to use its assets to generate sales at a similar level.

7 & 8   The **current and acid test ratios** have both deteriorated and may cause concern at these levels. The main reasons are the decrease in cash and the increase in **current liabilities**, particularly tax and dividends. Some of the cash may have been used for the purchase of fixed assets. Cash will be required to pay the tax and dividends when they fall due and this could prove to be a problem.

9,10 & 11 There has been an improvement in the **collection of debtors** and **stock** is being turned over slightly more quickly. The **payment period for trade creditors** has changed only slightly and the net effect is that the circulation of working capital has been speeded up.

More general discussion of this case study could include some of the following points:

■   In general, the year ended 30 September 2001 has been one of expansion for Bamberdale plc.

■   Sales have increased at a rate which corresponds with the expansion, and therefore to reverse the decline in profitability, opportunities for cost reduction should be investigated.

■   It will be important to review the ROCE in the next year, ending 30 September 2002, to check that it does not continue a downward trend. The current year's decrease can be explained by the effect of increased capital employed and next year should see an improvement if the new assets generate sufficient profits.

■   The main problem at 30 September 2001 is liquidity. As at the balance sheet date the company appears to need more cash. The improvement in collection of debtors is helpful, but the company may still have difficulty in paying its tax liability and the dividends. The dividend has increased by over 40% on the year before, and this is a policy decision on the part of the directors. They now need to obtain the necessary cash to cover it. Possible ways of doing this include selling fixed assets, issuing more shares or taking out more loans. What they choose to do will of course affect next year's results and ratios.

Workings (£m)

		30 Sept 2001	30 Sept 2000
1	Gross Profit x 100% / Sales	665 x 100% / 2660	600 x 100% / 2200
2	Operating profit x 100% / Sales	305 x 100% / 2660	285 x 100% / 2200
3	Selling & Dist. x 100% / Sales	120 x 100% / 2660	105 x 100% / 2200
4	Administration x 100% / Sales	240 x 100% / 2660	210 x 100% / 2200
5	Operating profit x 100% / Capital employed	305 x 100% / 566 + 200	285 x 100% / 460 + 160
6	Turnover / Fixed & net current assets	2660 / 600 + 166	2200 / 263 + 357
7	Current assets / Current liabilities	576 / 410	707 / 350
8	Current assets – Stock / Current liabilities	226 / 410	307 / 350
9	Debtors x 365 / Credit sales	200 x 365 / 2660	210 x 365 / 2200
10	Trade Creditors x 365 / Credit purchases	236 x 365 / 1945	224 x 365 / 1723
11	Average stock x 365 / Cost of sales	0.5 x (400+350) x 365 / 1995	0.5 x (277+400) x 365 / 1600

NOTES ON CALCULATION AND INTERPRETATION OF RATIOS

behaviour of ratios

The comments on the last Case Study are very detailed, but they are based on a few basic properties of ratios. It is important to be able to analyse the ratios by this method, as shown below.

A ratio or percentage is calculated from two figures and shows how one amount relates to the other. There may be some other link between the two figures, for example:

Gross Profit = Sales – Cost of Sales

The gross profit margin shows what percentage of the sales is left after cost of sales is taken out. If the gross profit margin decreases, it means that the cost of sales is taking out a bigger part of the sales and therefore we conclude that either selling prices have been reduced or costs of sales have increased or both.

Each percentage is calculated by dividing one figure by another. Using the usual terms for fractions we could write this as:

$$\frac{Numerator \ x \ 100\%}{Denominator}$$

The percentage will **increase**:

either if the **numerator increases** relative to the denominator

or if the **denominator decreases** relative to the numerator.

The percentage will **decrease**:

either if the **numerator decreases** relative to the denominator

or if the **denominator increases** relative to the numerator.

In the Bamberdale Case Study, the ROCE decreased from

$$\frac{285 \ x \ 100\%}{620} = 46.0\% \quad to \quad \frac{305 \ x \ 100\%}{766} = 39.8\%$$

Although the numerator has increased, the much greater increase in the denominator has had the dominant effect and this is what has been highlighted in the discussion. If you find making comments on ratios difficult, try to see how this method applies to the other ratios in the Bamberdale Case Study.

Further examples of how percentages change:

■ $\frac{120 \ x \ 100\%}{200} = 60\%$ and $\frac{130 \ x \ 100\%}{200} = 65\%$

Here the numerator (on top) increases, the denominator (on the bottom) is unchanged, and the percentage increases.

■ $\frac{120 \ x \ 100\%}{200} = 60\%$ and $\frac{114 \ x \ 100\%}{180} = 63\%$

All figures decrease, but the decrease in the denominator dominates, causing the percentage to increase.

In an assessment on this unit, it is not likely that you would be expected to calculate and comment in detail on all the ratios as in the Bamberdale Case Study. This is a comprehensive example to practise all aspects, but whichever aspect is assessed, the basic method of interpretation can be used.

HINTS ON USING FORMULAS

In Central Assessment tasks, you often have to use two items of data to calculate *one* figure which you need. In ratio analysis, such calculations may involve using a given ratio and one of its parts to calculate the other part.

A general method to use for such questions is to write down the formula and insert the figures you are given. You should then be able to deduce the required amount.

Note: If you are not used to using equations, remember that you can move figures from one side of the '=' sign to the other, provided that you change

- addition into subtraction and vice versa
- division into multiplication and vice versa.

For example, in the Bamberdale Case Study, we could ask 'What would the Operating Profit have been in the year ended 30 September 2001 if the ROCE had remained at 46.0%?'

First, write down the formula:

$$ROCE = \frac{operating\ profit \times 100\%}{capital\ employed}$$

Then insert the known figures:

$$46.0\% = \frac{operating\ profit \times 100\%}{£766m}$$

Then, moving £766m to the top left-hand side of the equation changes division to multiplication. The required Operating Profit is therefore:

46.0% x £766m = £352.36m

Your answer can always be checked by seeing that it satisfies the required condition. To check this answer: £352.36m ÷ £766m x 100% = 46.0%.

practical examples

See if you can work out the following:

1 If the Turnover is £98,000, what Gross Profit is required to give a Gross Profit Margin of 40%?

2 If the Operating Profit is £45,000 and this is 25% of Turnover, what is the Turnover?

3 If the Current Ratio is 2.2 : 1, and the Current Assets total £88,000, what is the total of the current liabilities?

solutions to examples

1 Gross Profit Margin $= \dfrac{\text{Gross Profit} \times 100\%}{£98,000} = 40\%$

Therefore Gross Profit = 40% x £98,000 = £39,200.

2 Operating Profit = £45,000 = 25% x Turnover

Therefore Turnover = £45,000 x 100 ÷ 25 = £180,000

3 $\dfrac{\text{Current Assets}}{\text{Current liabilities}} = 2.2$

$\dfrac{£88,000}{\text{Current liabilities}} = 2.2$

Therefore   £88,000 ÷ 2.2 = Current Liabilities = £40,000.

(In each case the answer can be checked).

LIMITATIONS OF RATIO ANALYSIS

In the introduction to this section, it was emphasised that one set of ratios alone does not give very useful information. Ratios for other time periods or other organisations are useful for comparison, as are target ratios.

The principle of **comparing like with like** should be applied in ratio analysis, but this is not always straightforward. Some of the ratios can be defined in different ways, so the particular definition used should be made clear. Even so, detailed information may not be given, for example to split sales into cash sales and credit sales.

When using the **published accounts of companies**, it is not possible to guarantee that we are comparing like with like, as different policies (including those regarding depreciation, stock valuation and goodwill, for example) will affect the results. Also there is the possibility that the Balance Sheet does not show a typical position.

Discussion of a particular case may include looking for ways in which the ratios could have been distorted. For example, high levels of spending on research, training or marketing may reduce profits in one period, but bring much greater benefits in a later period. The reverse is also true: cutting these costs may improve the profit ratios in the short-term, but in the long-term sales and profits would suffer.

When making comparisons over different time periods, the ratios are based on historical costs as shown in the accounts. If there has been inflation during the time periods, a better comparison can be made by making adjustments for this before calculating the ratios. (See Chapter 7).

Before drawing firm conclusions from ratio analysis, these limitations should be borne in mind. However, the analysis can give useful information, particularly in showing how items in the financial statements relate to each other and in identifying trends. In the next chapter, we consider other types of performance indicator, but again their usefulness depends on comparability.

CHAPTER SUMMARY

- Numerical (quantitative) data can be used when measuring performance: this data may be in terms of money or other units.

- Opinions and judgements which are not numerical (qualitative) are also important when measuring performance.

- Comparisons are more useful than single sets of data, provided the data being compared has been prepared on a consistent basis, to compare like with like. Comparison may be made with standards, budgets or targets; with other periods of time; with other similar organisations.

- The methods and techniques used for performance measurement include Ratio Analysis - ie the calculation of percentages and ratios from the financial accounts.

- The next chapter continues the study of performance measurement, with examples of alternative forms of performance indicator and consideration of methods applicable to various types of organisation.

KEY TERMS

performance indicator	an individual measurement used to evaluate the performance of an organisation or part of an organisation
benchmarking	the setting of standards or targets for the activities of an organisation
trend	the underlying behaviour of a series of figures over time

comparability
the principle of comparing like with like, that is comparing data prepared on consistent bases

quantitative data
data which can be measured in numerical terms, including financial and non-financial data

qualitative data
data which cannot be measured in numerical terms, such as opinions and attitudes

ratio analysis
the analysis of the financial accounts of an organisation by calculating ratios and percentages

gross profit margin (percentage)
$$\frac{\text{Gross Profit} \times 100\%}{\text{Sales}}$$

net profit percentage
$$\frac{\text{Net Profit} \times 100\%}{\text{Sales}}$$

operating profit percentage
$$\frac{\text{Operating Profit} \times 100\%}{\text{Sales}}$$

ROCE
(return on capital employed)
$$\frac{\text{Operating profit} \times 100\%}{\text{Fixed assets} + \text{net current assets}}$$

asset turnover (number of times)
$$\frac{\text{Turnover}}{\text{Fixed assets} + \text{net current assets}}$$

current ratio
$$\frac{\text{Current assets}}{\text{Current liabilities}}$$

acid test or quick ratio
$$\frac{\text{Current assets} - \text{stock}}{\text{Current liabilities}}$$

debtors' collection period
$$\frac{\text{Trade debtors} \times 365\text{days}}{\text{Credit sales}}$$

creditors' payment period
$$\frac{\text{Trade creditors} \times 365\text{days}}{\text{Credit purchases}}$$

average age of stock
$$\frac{\text{Average stock} \times 365\text{days}}{\text{Cost of sales}}$$

or $\dfrac{\text{Closing stock} \times 365\text{days}}{\text{Cost of sales}}$

stock turnover (number of times)
$$\frac{\text{Cost of sales}}{\text{Average stock}}$$

or $\dfrac{\text{Cost of sales}}{\text{Closing stock}}$

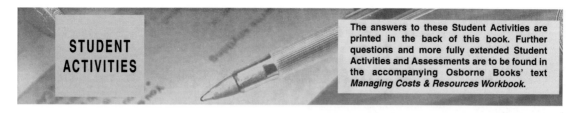

The answers to these Student Activities are printed in the back of this book. Further questions and more fully extended Student Activities and Assessments are to be found in the accompanying Osborne Books' text *Managing Costs & Resources Workbook.*

STUDENT ACTIVITIES

6.1 Explain briefly what is meant by the following terms relating to performance measurement:

(a) Consistency

(b) Benchmarking

(c) Qualitative data

6.2 The following information relates to Raven Ltd for a given period:

Sales revenue = £500,000,

Gross profit margin = 24%,

Operating profit = £50,000

Which of the following four statements is correct for Raven Ltd for the given period?

(a) Cost of sales = £620,000, Expenses = £170,000

(b) Cost of sales = £70,000, Expenses = £380,000

(c) Cost of sales = £380,000, Expenses = £70,000

(d) Cost of sales = £330,000, Expenses = £170,000

6.3 The following profit and loss accounts relate to a small retail shop selling stationery and gifts:

Toni Jones Profit and Loss Account for the year ended:

	31 May 2001		31 May 2000	
	£000s	£000s	£000s	£000s
Sales		525		450
Less: Cost of Sales				
Opening stock	50		30	
Purchases	408		335	
Less: Closing Stock	(80)	378	(50)	315
Gross Profit		147		135
Less: Expenses:				
Administration	25		24	
Selling	38	63	30	54
Net Profit		84		81

Required

For Toni Jones for the given years, calculate:

      (a)   Gross Profit percentage

      (b)   Net Profit percentage

      (c)   each expense as a percentage of Sales

Comment briefly on the original figures and on the percentages calculated.

6.4   Ace plc is an electrical goods manufacturing group and the information below relates to one of its subsidiaries, Jack Limited.

Jack Ltd: Summary Profit and Loss Account for the year ended 30 June 2001

	£000s	£000s
Turnover		2,500
Less: Cost of Sales		
Opening Stock	30	
Cost of Production	650	
Less: Closing Stock	(90)	590
Gross Profit		1,910
Administration	780	
Selling and Distribution	505	1,285
Operating Profit		625

Jack Ltd: extract from Balance Sheet as at 30 June 2001:

	£000s	£000s	£000s
Fixed assets	*Land and Buildings*	*Plant*	*Total*
At cost	900	2,000	2,900
Additions	-	1,000	1,000
	900	3,000	3,900
Accumulated depreciation	-	1,380	1,380
	900	1,620	2,520
Current Assets:			
Raw materials stock	10		
Finished goods stock	90		
Debtors	160		
Cash at bank	110		
	370		
Current liabilities	(50)		320
Net Assets			2,840

Required

(a)   Calculate the following ratios for Subsidiary Jack Ltd for the financial year

   •   Gross Profit margin

   •   Operating profit margin

   •   Return on Capital Employed (ROCE)

   •   Asset turnover

   •   The average age of debtors

   •   The average age of finished goods stock (using average stock)

(b)   The directors of Ace plc consider that ROCE and Asset Turnover are important performance measures, and Subsidiary Jack Ltd has failed to meet the group targets, which are:

Target ROCE   26%

Target Asset turnover   1.5 times

Identify one factor which may have affected the performance of Subsidiary Jack Ltd in relation to these targets in the year ended 30 June 2001.

(c)   Calculate the Turnover which Subsidiary Jack Ltd would have obtained if it had achieved the target level of Asset turnover.

(d)   Assuming Subsidiary Jack Ltd maintained the same operating profit margin, calculate the ROCE which would have resulted from the Turnover calculated in (c) above.

6.5   Using formulas, calculate the answers to the following:

(a)   If the Gross Profit Margin is 35% and the Turnover is £200,000, what is the Cost of Sales?

(b)   If the Stock is £4,200, the Current Liabilities total £7,000, and the Acid Test Ratio is 0.9 : 1, what is the Current Ratio?

7 MEASURING PERFORMANCE – FURTHER ASPECTS

this chapter covers . . .

In the last chapter we gave examples of quantitative performance measures (financial and non-financial) and qualitative measures. In this chapter we will consider the other possible ways of measuring aspects of the performance of individuals or of organisations, including:

- *financial performance indicators such as*
  - *adjustment to real terms using index numbers,*
  - *calculating averages and value added*
- *non-financial performance indicators*
- *qualitative measures*
- *productivity and efficiency*
- *unit cost*
- *control ratios: efficiency, capacity and activity*
- *performance measurement in service organisations*
- *the assessment of quality*
- *the balanced scorecard*
- *performance measurement in non-profit making organisations.*

NVQ PERFORMANCE CRITERIA COVERED

unit 8: CONTRIBUTING TO THE MANAGEMENT OF COSTS AND THE ENHANCEMENT OF VALUE

element 2: make recommendations to reduce costs and enhance value

- *routine cost reports are analysed, compared with other sources of information and the implications of findings identified*

- *relevant performance indicators are monitored and the results are assessed to identify potential improvements*

- *specific recommendations are made to management and are explained in a clear and appropriate form*

FINANCIAL INDICATORS

Data given in terms of actual amounts of money (or other units) is sometimes referred to as absolute data, and ratios or percentages as *relative* figures. We have included discussion of the financial indicators of absolute Turnover and Profit in the previous chapter, with ratios, because the most useful information comes from considering the absolute and relative figures together. Other financial indicators include selling prices, costs and variances. As before, the usefulness of these depends on:

- comparing with standards, budgets or targets
- comparing with other periods of time
- comparing with similar organisations

financial indicators: adjustment to real terms

In comparing financial data over periods of time, it may be necessary to 'deflate' the figures, that is take out the effect of inflation, so that the comparison is of 'like with like'. A suitable index is used to put all the data in terms of the value of money in the same year, often described as 'real terms'. This method is described in Chapter 1.

Financial data adjusted by using an index in this way, to obtain comparable figures, could then be used for the calculation and analysis of ratios, as illustrated in Case Study that follows.

CASE STUDY

ADJUSTING TO REAL TERMS: TURNER LIMITED

Turnover and Net Profit figures are given for Turner Ltd for the five years ended 31 December 2001 to 2005. A suitable index for Turner Ltd's industry is also given.

	2001	*2002*	*2003*	*2004*	*2005*
Turnover (£000s)	435	450	464	468	475
Net Profit (£000s)	65	70	72	75	78
Industry Index	133	135	138	140	143

required

Calculate the Turnover and Profit in terms of year 2005 values and comment on the results. Illustrate the results for the Turnover on a graph for the five years shown.

solution

To put each figure into 2005 terms, it is divided by the index for its own year and multiplied by the index for 2005, ie 143. (The base year is not used). For example:

Turnover Year 2001 $\quad \dfrac{435}{133} \quad \times \quad 143 = 467.7$

Turnover Year 2002 $\frac{450}{135}$ x   143 =   476.7 and so on.

In year 2005 terms:

	2001	2002	2003	2004	2005
Turnover (£000s)	467.7	476.7	480.8	478.0	475.0
Net Profit (£000s)	69.9	74.1	74.6	76.6	78.0

The adjusted figures compare like with like in terms of the value of the pound, and the Net Profit still shows an increasing trend throughout, but the Turnover decreases in the last two years. The following graph shows both the original and adjusted turnover figures. (A similar graph could be drawn for the net profit).

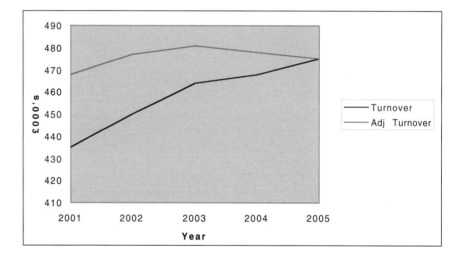

After adjusting the net profit and turnover to year 2005 terms, we can calculate the net profit percentage, using the adjusted figures:

2001   (69.9 ÷ 467.7) x 100% = 14.9%
2002   (74.1 ÷ 476.7) x 100% = 15.5%
2003   (74.6 ÷ 480.8) x 100% = 15.5%
2004   (76.6 ÷ 478.0) x 100% = 16.0%
2005   (78.0 ÷ 475.0) x 100% = 16.4%

This shows an increasing trend in the 'real terms' net profit percentage.

financial Indicators: calculating averages

Although total amounts of money such as sales, profits and costs may be used for performance measurement, it is often more informative to calculate an average 'per employee', 'per hour', 'per unit of output' and so on. This is a simple calculation which relates the financial data to the size of the organisation in some way.

practical examples

1   If sales orders amount to £32million for the year and there are 16 sales representatives, then

   Average sales orders per representative = £32m ÷ 16 = £2m

2   If materials cost £87,000 in total for output of 29,000 units of a product, then

   Average cost of materials per unit = £87,000 ÷ 29,000 = £3

3   If training costs for the year total £171,000 and there are 450 employees, then

   Average expenditure on training per employee = £171,000 ÷ 450 = £380

financial indicators: value added

Value added is a financial measure of the difference between the value of outputs and the value of inputs. It shows the increase in monetary value which has resulted from the work done and the use of assets within the organisation. For the calculation of value added, 'inputs' are defined as 'materials and bought-in services'. These have been brought into the organisation *from outside*. The monetary value of outputs is sales revenue or turnover, which is their value as they go to *outside customers*.

Value added = Turnover – (cost of materials used and bought in services)

The average value added per employee can also be used as an indicator of productivity within the organisation. (For more about productivity see later in this chapter).

CASE STUDY

VALUE ADDED: TURNER LTD

The following information is given for Turner Ltd for the year 2005.

Turnover	£475,000
Number of employees	22
Cost of materials used	£100,000
Total cost of bought-in services	£155,000

required

Calculate the total value added and the value added per employee for the year 2005 for Turner Ltd.

solution

Value Added = £475,000 – (£100,000 + £155,000) = £220,000
Value Added per employee = £220,000 ÷ 22 = £10,000

NON-FINANCIAL INDICATORS

A **non-financial indicator** is a measurement which is expressed in numbers, but not in money terms, the possible units being very varied: for example hours, transactions, units of product, customers and so on.

Non-financial indicators can take many forms, because they can be designed to measure aspects of any kind of work. They are useful in both manufacturing and service industries and can be applied in both profit-making and non-profit making organisations. They are particularly useful for measuring quality, which was discussed in Chapter 5.

Some examples of possible non-financial indicators are given below. Several indicators may be used together for the same activity. You may have other examples from the workplace.

Activity or aspect to be measured	Non-financial indicator
Automated production	Hours of machine down time
Absenteeism	Employee-days absence
Telephone helpline	Average time in seconds taken to answer calls
Quality of service	Number of customer complaints
Input of data to computer	Number of errors per 1000 inputs
Customer satisfaction	Number of repeat orders
Quality of output	Number of units rejected per 1000

Further examples of non-financial indicators will occur when different types of organisation are considered later in this chapter.

QUALITATIVE (NON-NUMERICAL) MEASURES

Some aspects of work are very difficult to measure in terms of numbers, for example: motivation of others, team working, helpfulness to customers.

When numerical indicators are not suitable, **opinions** and **attitudes** have to be recorded, perhaps by customer surveys. Surveys often ask customers to give ratings, say on a scale of 1 to 5, but these are only an aid to obtaining an overall view, not an accurate measurement.

Appraisal schemes within an organisation may involve collecting feedback from colleagues. For example, those present at a meeting may be asked their opinion as to the how well the person chairing the meeting carried out that task. Work relationships can affect the judgements given (and vice versa), so the usefulness of this feedback may be limited.

MEASUREMENT OF PRODUCTIVITY AND EFFICIENCY

The terms 'productivity' and 'efficiency' are used in various ways, but generally relate to how much output is being achieved from the inputs. Here we are referring to the productivity and efficiency of a whole organisation. (The efficiency of an employee or a group of employees can be measured by the labour efficiency variance or the efficiency ratio. The efficiency ratio is defined later in this chapter.)

Productivity is likely to be measured in terms of **units of output**, or related to quantity of output in some way.

For example, productivity could be measured by relating units of output to the number of employees or the assets used to produce them, by calculating: 'units of output per employee' or 'units of output per £ value of fixed assets'.

Efficiency implies that the measure should indicate the **value** of the outputs in relation to the inputs, because it is not 'efficient' to produce more units if they are worth less than their cost, for example if they cannot be sold. This suggests that the efficiency of the organisation as a whole is linked to **profits**, and how well resources have been used to generate the profits.

Measures of efficiency could therefore include Return on Capital Employed (ROCE) and operating profit percentage, which we have studied in detail in Chapter 6. Where ROCE is used, a business with newer fixed assets, giving a higher capital employed, may appear less efficient than a similar firm with older assets. (See page 153).

The choice of performance indicators for productivity and efficiency will depend on the information available. This is illustrated in the next Case Study below.

CASE STUDY

PRODUCTIVITY AND EFFICIENCY: LIDO LTD AND NEW LTD

Lido Ltd and New Ltd are two companies owned by Wells plc. Lido Ltd and New Ltd are similar companies using the same accounting policies and both manufacture the same component, which is sold to the motor industry. The following information relates to the year ended 31 May 2001 for the two companies:

	Lido Ltd	New Ltd
Units produced and sold	20,000	50,000
Number of employees	34	78
	£000s	£000s
Net book value of fixed assets	350	1,600
Net current assets	75	20
Capital employed	425	1,620
Turnover	640	1,600
Operating profit	128	256

required

1 Calculate for each company for the year ended 31 May 2001 the following indicators:

- Units produced per employee
- Asset turnover
- Operating profit margin (percentage of turnover)
- Return on capital employed
- Operating profit per employee
- Units per £1,000 of NBV of Fixed Assets

State how each of these indicators might be relevant to the *productivity* or *efficiency* of the companies (abbreviated to 'P' and 'E' in the table below).

2 Explain briefly one reason why the productivity and efficiency measures calculated may give opposite rankings to the two companies.

solution

calculations	Lido Ltd	New Ltd	P or E?
1 Units produced ÷ number of employees	588	641	P
Asset Turnover	1.51	0.99	E
Operating profit as % of turnover	20.0%	16.0%	E
ROCE	30.1%	15.8%	E
Operating profit ÷ number of employees	£3,765	£3,282	P & E
Units per £1,000 of NBV of fixed assets	57	31	P

comments

- *Units produced per employee* are a measure of output and therefore productivity.
- *Asset turnover* shows how efficiently the assets have been used to generate sales, so could be used to assess efficiency.
- *Operating profit margin* and *ROCE* are both measures of efficiency because they relate the value of outputs to inputs and resources used.
- *Operating profit per employee* could be said to relate to productivity as it compares the results of production with the number of employees; it is probably more suitable to measure efficiency because the profit figure is being used.
- *Units per £1,000 NBV of fixed assets* is an alternative measure of productivity, relating the output to the fixed assets used to produce it.

why are the ratings opposite?

2 Lido Ltd has higher Operating profit margin and ROCE, indicating that it is more efficient. New Ltd has higher productivity according to the units produced per employee, (although the units per £1,000 value of fixed assets was higher in Lido Ltd).

The reason for the different rankings is the *difference in the value of the fixed assets.* New Ltd has much higher value fixed assets, and would therefore have higher depreciation charges in the profit and loss account. The result is that the efficiency measures of asset turnover, ROCE and operating profit margin are lower in New Ltd, whereas the output per employee is higher. The relative age of the assets could affect both productivity and efficiency measures. If the higher value is because New Ltd has newer fixed assets, particularly plant and machinery, this may also account for the fact that each employee can produce more output.

unit cost

Another way of comparing output with inputs is to calculate the *cost per unit of output*. This can be applied to products or services, provided the output achieved can be measured in some way.

The cost of inputs is divided by the number of units of output. This may be done for the total cost, or for some particular element of cost, for example

Production labour cost per unit =

total cost of production labour divided by number of units of output

Comparing unit costs between similar organisations or divisions could be part of the assessment of efficiency, provided that the principle of comparing like with like is applied.

practical example

In a given period, the output of a division is 15,000 product units.

The costs of production are as follows:

Direct materials	£97,500
Direct labour	£63,750
Production overheads	£85,500
Total production cost	£246,750

Therefore, for these costs, the Unit Cost could be calculated as follows:

Direct materials:	£97,500 ÷ 15,000	=	£6.50 per unit
Direct labour:	£63,750 ÷ 15,000	=	£4.25 per unit
Production overheads:	£85,500 ÷ 15,000	=	£5.70 per unit
Total production cost:	£246,750 ÷ 15,000	=	£16.45 per unit

CONTROL RATIOS: EFFICIENCY, CAPACITY AND ACTIVITY

efficiency ratio

In the discussion above, 'efficiency' refers to an organisation's performance and this relates to its profitability. In this section, we consider the efficiency of the workforce (or a part of it) in terms of the hours used to produce the output. One performance indicator to measure this is the Labour Efficiency Variance studied in Chapter 2. The variance shows the difference between the *standard hours for actual production* and the *actual hours*, valued at the standard labour rate. The same two figures in hours can be compared in percentage terms instead of calculating the difference. This gives the efficiency ratio:

$$efficiency\ ratio\ =\ \frac{standard\ hours\ for\ actual\ production}{actual\ hours\ worked}\ x\ 100\%$$

If the ratio is exactly 100%, the employees have worked at the standard level of efficiency. If it is less than 100%, they have worked more slowly – this would result in an adverse variance. If it is more than 100%, they have worked more quickly than the standard – corresponding to a favourable variance.

activity ratio and production volume ratio

The standard hours for actual production can also be compared with the original plan for the period, the budgeted hours. This an indicator of how actual output compares with the budgeted output and is known as the **activity ratio**. The formula is:

$$\frac{standard\ hours\ for\ actual\ production}{budgeted\ hours}\ x\ 100\%$$

This can alternatively be expressed in terms of volume of output and is known as the **production volume ratio**:

$$\frac{actual\ output}{budgeted\ output}\ x\ 100\%,$$

capacity ratio

The third control ratio compares the actual 'capacity' which has been used with the planned amount.

Capacity (here being measured in terms of direct labour hours) is the amount of available resources being used. Full capacity would mean that all possible resources were being used. Budgeted capacity (probably less than full capacity) would be set in line with planned levels of production and sales.

The capacity ratio shows what proportion of the planned resources have actually been used. This is particularly important when there are significant fixed costs which have to be paid to make these resources available.

capacity ratio = $\dfrac{actual\ hours\ worked}{budgeted\ hours}$ *x 100%*

CONTROL RATIOS: EAC LTD

EAC Ltd produces a single product, for which the standard direct labour time is 2 hours per unit. For a given period, EAC Ltd budgeted for a total of 68,000 hours. The actual results for the period showed that 34,600 units were produced and the actual total direct labour hours worked were 71,000 hours.

required
Calculate the standard hours for the actual production in this case and hence calculate the three control ratios.

solution
The standard hours for the actual production of 34,600 units would be
34,600 x 2 = 69,200 hours

Therefore, using the above formulae, the control ratios would be:

Efficiency Ratio = $\dfrac{69,200}{71,000}$ x 100% = 97.5%

Activity Ratio = $\dfrac{69,200}{68,000}$ x 100% = 101.8%

Capacity Ratio = $\dfrac{71,000}{68,000}$ x 100% = 104.4%

The control ratios for EAC Ltd, above, show that both the level of activity (output) and the resources used were more than planned in the budget, but the workforce were slightly less efficient than the standard. As in variance analysis, the reasons for the level of efficiency could be investigated and they may include external factors such as problems with supply of materials, not necessarily the fault of the employees.

PERFORMANCE MEASUREMENT IN SERVICE ORGANISATIONS

It is more difficult to measure the performance of a service organisation or department than one which produces tangible goods. Services cannot be checked before being provided in the same way as products can be inspected for faults.

The usual financial measures and ratios can be used for profit-making service organisations. (Non-profit-making organisations are considered in the last section of this chapter.)

Non-financial and qualitative measures, discussed earlier in this chapter, are often applicable to services. For example:

- Average waiting times for customers can be calculated and compared to a target.
- The number of customer complaints indicates the level of customer satisfaction.
- Analysis of customer opinions can be collected through surveys. Aspects such as 'Are the staff are friendly and helpful?' can be judged in this way.
- Services can also be assessed by internal observation. Telephone services are monitored by supervisors listening to samples of calls, for example.

In central assessment tasks, you may be required to identify or discuss suitable performance indicators for a service organisation.

The appropriate performance indicators to use depend on the type of service being provided and what its aims must be. From the organisation's point of view, financial indicators are likely to be important. If you then consider what features of the service would be *important to customers*, you can see which items of data are available to measure those features.

For example, in a Further Education College, comparisons of costs and incomes with budgets measure financial aspects. Customers' views may be more dependent on non-financial indicators such as average class size and pass rates or qualitative measures relating to the teachers and the classroom environment.

The *financial* and *customer* aspects or perspectives discussed in this section form part of the 'Balanced Scorecard', which can be applied to any kind of profit-making organisation. (See page 188).

ASSESSING QUALITY

In Chapter 5 we saw that the quality of a product or service depends on its fitness for the customer's purpose.

Customers' expectations may include prestige value with some products and services, as well as value in use. From the point of view of the supplier, quality must be provided at a reasonable cost. Quality management means aiming at continuous improvement and eliminating mistakes. If Total Quality Management is introduced, it must involve all employees in the organisation, not just those who deal with the external customers. Employees must treat colleagues as 'internal customers', and the same principles apply when supplying products or services to internal customers.

From the definition of quality, it is clear that performance indicators will include measures of customer satisfaction. Examples are

- numbers of product units returned
- sales value of returns as a percentage of total sales
- numbers of warranty claims
- numbers of customer complaints

From the suppliers point of view, costs must be considered, for example:

- cost per unit of product or service
- cost of customer service department
- average cost of after-sales service per customer

Assessing the quality of tangible **products** is more straightforward than for services. Products can be inspected and compared to detailed product specifications. Samples can be tested to check their value in use. Quality can be measured by, for example:

- numbers of defects
- number of substandard goods as a percentage of units produced
- cost of reworking as a percentage of production cost

Performance measurement for **service** organisations has been discussed in the previous section. Assessing the quality of a service involves first deciding what customers expect from that service. There may be many aspects to this and these can be measured by, for example:

- customer opinions in response to surveys
- internal inspections or observations
- inspections or observations by external bodies
- non-financial indicators such as waiting times

CASE STUDY

A QUALITY POSTAL SERVICE: HERMES PLC

Hermes PLC is considering introducing a rival postal service in the UK. The company is carrying out market research into customer expectations

required
What would you consider to be the main features customers look for in a high quality postal service? How could the quality be measured?

solution
Suggestions of some of the features customers might want are:
- post to be delivered on time
- post to be delivered to correct address
- post to be undamaged
- postboxes to be conveniently placed

- post offices to be easily accessible
- short waiting times in post offices

Suggestions of ways these could be measured:
- percentages of letters delivered late
- numbers of returned letters or complaints (although mistakes may not be reported)
- numbers of damaged packets as percentage of total
- average distances between postboxes or numbers of postboxes per thousand households
- results of customer surveys or observations
- average post-office waiting times calculated from observations

As can be seen in this Case Study, quality cannot be assessed unless systems are in place to record and analyse the necessary data. The general principles of **comparability** must also apply. Comparison over time and trend analysis is necessary to measure improvements resulting from quality management. In the Balanced Scorecard, which is explained in the next section, measurement of quality is part of the internal perspective.

THE BALANCED SCORECARD

The Balanced Scorecard is a way of viewing the performance of a profit-making organisation from four *perspectives*, relating to profits, customers, quality and development, as follows:

- **the financial perspective** is concerned with satisfying the shareholders or owners of a business and relates to profits. Suitable indicators include ROCE and profit margin.

- **the customer perspective** is concerned with customer satisfaction and loyalty. It relates to customers' views of the business and suitable indicators include delivery times and numbers or amounts of orders from previous customers.

- **the internal perspective** is concerned with technical excellence and consumer needs, which relate to quality. Suitable indicators are those which assess quality and value.

- **the innovation and learning perspective** is concerned with the need for continual improvement of existing products and the ability to develop new products to meet customers' changing needs, so it is related to development. Suitable indicators may include the percentage of turnover attributable to new products or a measure of research and development expenditure.

In a given case, you may be asked to identify ways of measuring these four perspectives. You will need to look for data available in the case study which you can connect with each aspect of the business.

CASE STUDY

THE BALANCED SCORECARD: HSB LTD

You are employed by HSB Ltd, a company with several subsidiaries and you have been asked to apply the balanced scorecard to monitor the performance of the subsidiaries. The following information relates to Subsidiary H for the period ended 31 December 2000. You also have available the financial accounts of Subsidiary H for the same year. Extracts are given here.

	£000s
Sales	3,500
Less: returns	70
Turnover	3,430
Operating profit	825
Analysis of turnover by products:	
Sales of new products	1,350
Sales of existing products	2,080
Turnover as above	3,430
Analysis of turnover by customers:	
Sales to new customers	650
Sales to existing customers	2,780
Turnover as above	3,430
Value of orders placed for delivery during the year	4,250

required

Identify and calculate, from the available information, one performance indicator which you could use in monitoring each of the four perspectives in the balanced scorecard.

solution

Monitoring the balanced scorecard for subsidiary H for the year ended 31 December 2000:

- The *financial* perspective could be measured by operating profit margin, which is $(825 \div 3,430) \times 100\% = 24\%$.

- The *customer* perspective could be measured by repeat custom as a percentage of sales, which is $(2,780 \div 3,430) \times 100\% = 81\%$.

- An alternative would be the average delay in fulfilling orders. The unfulfilled orders amount to £4,250,000 – £3,430,000 = £820,000 and this could be used as a fraction of turnover to calculate $(820 \div 3,430) \times 365$ days, giving 87 days as the average delay.

- The *internal* perspective could be measured by the percentage of sales returns, which is $(70 \div 3,500) \times 100\% = 2\%$.

- The *innovation and learning* perspective could be measured by the percentage of sales derived from new products, which is $(1,350 \div 3,430) \times 100\% = 39\%$.

PERFORMANCE MEASUREMENT IN NON-PROFIT MAKING ORGANISATIONS

Non-profit making organisations include charities and clubs as well as some public sector organisations. Without the objective of profit, there may be no single aim by which 'success' can be measured.

Performance indicators need to be designed to measure how well the organisation has achieved its aims. Much of the section on service organisations above applies to non-profit making organisations, many of which do provide services. Instead of profit, *value for money* is the main financial criterion This is usually defined as:

- **economy**: controlling expenditure on costs

- **efficiency**: relating 'outputs' to inputs, meaning that obtaining more from the money spent shows greater efficiency

- **effectiveness**: relating 'outputs' to the aims of the organisation, so that achieving more of what it sets out to do shows greater effectiveness

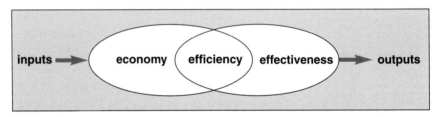

Economy can be measured in the same way as costs in businesses, by comparing with budgets and calculating variances for example.

A possible indicator for **efficiency** is the cost per unit, where units of output can be defined. For example, in a nursing home, the cost of a patient-day could be calculated.

Effectiveness may be measured by comparison with targets or with other similar organisations.

Some aspects of non-profit-making activities can only be assessed by qualitative measures: opinions and judgements of experts, users or those who provide the funding. Representatives of government agencies or funding bodies may carry out observations or inspections, as in schools for example.

The general principles of performance measurement apply to these organisations as well as to businesses:

- comparability – comparing like with like

- comparison with standards, budgets or targets

- comparison with similar organisations

- comparison over time, to look for trends

CHAPTER SUMMARY

- Data which is collected for performance measurement may be quantitative (numerical) data in terms of money or other units, or it may be qualitative data consisting of opinions or attitudes. A combination of quantitative and qualitative data can be used. Appraisal schemes often use qualitative data.

- Comparisons are more useful than single sets of data, provided the data being compared has been prepared on a consistent basis, to compare like with like.

- The performance of organisations is measured using performance indicators to make comparisons with
    - standards, budgets or targets
    - other periods of time
    - other similar organisations

- When making comparisons over time, index numbers are used to remove the effects of inflation from a series of data from different time periods.

- Value added is a financial indicator, which measures the difference in value between the outputs from an organisation and the inputs which come from external suppliers.

- Non-financial indicators are often in terms of time (such as machine hours or labour hours), but may be numbers of product units, transactions, errors and so on. They can be designed to measure specific aspects of performance in a particular organisation.

- Productivity and efficiency are both related to how much output is achieved from the inputs. Productivity generally refers to the quantity of output and efficiency to the value of output in relation to inputs.

- Unit cost is a financial indicator which can be applied to products or services, provided that units of output can be measured.

- Control ratios are based on direct labour hours and measure efficiency, capacity and activity in percentage terms.

- Non-financial and qualitative measures of performance are useful for service organisations, and should be designed to measure the aspects of the service which are important to customers.

- The quality of a product or service depends on its fitness for the customer's purpose and therefore suitable performance indicators include measures of customer satisfaction, which are often non-financial or qualitative measures.

- The 'balanced scorecard' looks at an organisation from the financial, customer, internal and innovation and learning perspectives and identifies ways of measuring each of these aspects of its performance.

- Financial performance measurement for non-profit making organisations is based on value for money, which is achieved through economy, efficiency and effectiveness.

• It is essential for fair and useful performance measurement that the indicators used are designed for the particular type of organisation, to measure how well it is achieving its aims and objectives. This must be planned in advance, as it can only be done if the necessary data is recorded during the period. The principle of consistency should be applied to both the collection and the analysis of data for performance measurement.

performance indicator	an individual measurement used to evaluate the performance of an organisation or part of an organisation
financial indicator	a performance indicator measured in money terms
non-financial indicator	a performance indicator measured in units other than money
quantitative data	data which can be measured in numerical terms, including financial and non-financial data
qualitative data	data which cannot be measured in numerical terms, such as opinions and attitudes
deflated series	a series of figures for different time periods from which the effect of inflation has been removed, to give comparison in 'real terms'
value added	turnover less the cost of materials and bought-in services
productivity	the aspect of the performance of an organisation which could be measured by the level of output
efficiency	the aspect of the performance of an organisation which could be measured by relating the value of the output to the inputs
unit cost	cost of inputs divided by the number of units of output
control ratios	the efficiency, activity and capacity ratios
efficiency ratio	$\frac{\text{standard hours for actual output}}{\text{actual hours worked}} \times 100\%$
activity (or production volume) ratio	$\frac{\text{standard hours for actual output}}{\text{budgeted hours}} \times 100\%$
capacity ratio	$\frac{\text{actual hours worked}}{\text{budgeted hours}} \times 100\%$
balanced scorecard	the concept of performance measurement from the point of view of four perspectives: financial, customer, internal and innovation and learning

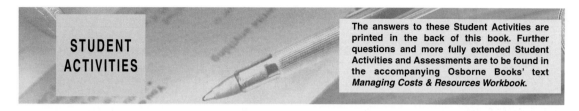

STUDENT ACTIVITIES

Note: some of these activities include topics from Chapter 6 as well as Chapter 7. Central Assessment tasks are often structured to cover various aspects of performance measurement in this way.

7.1 Give two examples of each of the following:

(a) Financial quantitative performance indicators

(b) Non-financial quantitative performance indicators

(c) Qualitative performance indicators

7.2 You have the following information relating to a small charity and also inflation index numbers:

	Year 1	Year 2	Year 3
Income (£)	260,000	305,000	400,000
Expenditure (£)	200,000	240,000	330,000
Surplus (£)	60,000	65,000	70,000
Inflation index	115	123	130

Required

Restate the figures for year 1 and year 2 in year 3 terms and state whether or not the income and surplus are growing in real terms.

7.3 The following information is given for Exe Ltd for the year 2000.

Turnover	£972,000
Output (product units)	67,500
Number of employees	54
Cost of materials used	£216,000
Total cost of bought-in services	£324,000
Total cost of inputs	£540,000

Required

Calculate for Exe Ltd for the year 2000:

(a) total value added

(b) value added per employee

(c) material cost per unit

(d) total cost of inputs per unit

7.4 Wessit Housing Association is considering offering a contract for double-glazing its properties to one of two suppliers, Staylite Ltd and Temeglass Ltd. The following information has been extracted from the most recent annual report and accounts of the two companies.

	Staylite Ltd £000s	Temeglass Ltd £000s
Sales	7,660	9,500
Gross Profit	3,467	4,522
Operating Profit	403	627
Interest charges	45	2
Fixed Assets (net book value)	600	800
Current assets	198	307
Stock included in current assets	82	120
Current liabilities	182	156
Debentures	450	0
Share capital and reserves	166	951
Average number of employees	16	18

Required

(a) Calculate the following ratios for each of the two companies:
- gross profit margin
- operating profit percentage
- return on capital employed
- current ratio
- quick ratio
- asset turnover
- sales per employee
- operating profit per employee

(b) Using the given information and the ratios you have calculated, comment on the profitability and financial position of the two suppliers.

(c) State which of the performance indicators you have calculated may be used to indicate how efficient the companies are.

(d) State which of the performance indicators you have calculated may be used to indicate the productivity of the companies.

(e) Explain the limitations of the above analysis, in particular from the point of view of Wessit Housing Association's decision about the contract.

(f) Suggest one further indicator which Wessit Housing Association should seek to obtain (not necessarily from the report and accounts) before making this decision.

7.5 CD Ltd makes a product which takes 6 hours per unit of direct labour time. In a given period it is planned (budgeted) that 14,700 direct labour hours will be worked.

During the period, the actual result is that 2,400 units of the product are made and the direct labour hours worked are 15,000 hours.

Calculate the Efficiency Ratio, the Capacity Ratio and the Activity Ratio for this period.

7.6 List and explain briefly the three aspects of 'value for money' which may be used as criteria in the performance measurement of non-profit making organisations.

7.7 Up-to-You Gym is a fitness centre, which obtains its sales income from membership fees, trainers' consultancy fees, sales of clothing and small items of equipment and sales of refreshments. During the year ended 30 September 20-2, there was considerable upgrading of the centre's equipment (fixed assets) and a drive to recruit more members by offering local firms group membership discounts for their employees. The following information is available for Up-to-You Gym for the years ended 30 September 20-1 and 20-2. (The total number of members in the year ended 30 September 20-0 was 580).

	30 Sept 20-2	30 Sept 20-1
Sales (£000s)	750	600
Costs (£000s)	520	430
Profit (£000s)	230	170
Number of new members	730	525
Number of returning members	470	175
Total number of members	1,200	700
Number of member visits	60,300	30,230
Number of employees	22	14
Total hours centre was open	4,368	3,698
Total days centre was open	364	360

Required

Using the above information, identify and calculate ONE appropriate indicator which may help to measure performance from EACH of the perspectives:

(a) The financial perspective

(b) The customer perspective

(c) The internal perspective

(d) The innovation and learning perspective

8 USING BUDGETS

this chapter covers . . .

In this chapter we examine:

* the purposes of budgets
* the initial steps in budget preparation
* the co-ordination of the main types of budget
* the responsibilities and timescales for budget setting
* the use of forecasting techniques
* the factors influencing forecasts
* the numerical practicalities of creating co-ordinated budgets

NVQ PERFORMANCE CRITERIA COVERED

unit 9: CONTRIBUTING TO THE PLANNING AND ALLOCATION OF RESOURCES

element 1

prepare forecasts of income and expenditure

● *relevant data for projecting forecasts is identified*

● *relevant individuals are given the opportunity to raise queries and to clarify forecasts*

element 2

produce draft budget proposals

● *draft budget proposals are presented to management in a clear and appropriate form and on schedule*

● *draft budget proposals are consistent with organisational objectives, have taken all relevant data into account and are agreed with budget holders*

● *annual budgets are broken down into periods in accordance with anticipated seasonal trends*

● *discussions with budget holders are conducted in a manner which maintains goodwill*

THE PURPOSES OF BUDGETS

A budget is a financial plan for an organisation, prepared in advance.

In any organisation the budget provides the mechanism by which the objectives of the organisation can be achieved. In this way it forms a link between the current position and the position that the organisation's managers are aiming for. By using a budget firstly to plan and then to monitor, the managers can ensure that the organisation's progress is co-ordinated to achieve the objectives of the organisation. The specific purposes and benefits of using budgets are as follows.

1 the budget compels planning

By formalising the agreed objectives of the organisation through a budget preparation system, an organisation can ensure that its plans are achievable. It will be able to decide what resources are required to produce the desired outputs, and to make sure that they will be available at the right time.

2 the budget communicates and co-ordinates

Because a budget will be agreed by an organisation, all the relevant personnel will be working towards the same ends. During the budget setting process any anticipated problems should be resolved and any areas of potential confusion clarified. All the organisation's departments should be in a position to play their part in achieving the overall goals. This objective of all parts of the organisation working towards the same ends is sometimes referred to as 'goal congruence'.

3 the budget can be used to monitor and control

An important reason for producing a budget is that management is able to monitor the actual results against the budget. This is so that action can be taken to modify the operation of the organisation as time passes, or possibly to change the budget if it becomes unachievable. This is similar to the way that standard costing is used to monitor and control costs, and can be used alongside that technique.

For organisations where control of activities is deemed to be a high priority the budget can be used as the primary tool to ensure conformity to agreed plans. Once the budget is agreed it can effectively become the authority to follow a particular course of action or spend a certain amount of money. Public sector organisations, with their necessary emphasis on strict accountability, will tend to take this approach, as will some commercial organisations that choose not to delegate too much authority.

4 the budget can be used to motivate

A budget can be part of the organisation's techniques for motivating managers and other staff to achieve the organisation's objectives. The extent to which this happens will depend on how the budget is agreed and set, and whether it is perceived as fair and achievable. The budget may also be linked to rewards (for example bonuses) where targets are met or exceeded.

THE INITIAL STEPS IN BUDGET PREPARATION

the aims of an organisation

Before a organisation's managers can begin to build a useful budget there are several initial steps that must be taken. These are based around the fundamental questions about the **aims** – the 'vision' – of the organisation:

'where do we want it to go?' and

'how do we get it there?'

These are essentially long-term issues, and once agreed upon would not tend to be changed very often.

objectives and strategy

For a budget to be of use to an organisation it must be a mechanism of helping the organisation achieve its **objectives**. The objectives are the targets that the managers of the organisation wish it to achieve. The way in which these objectives are expressed will depend upon the type of organisation and the way in which it operates. For example a pet food manufacturer may have the specific objective of obtaining sales penetration of 25% of the UK dog food market, whereas an independent TV production company may have the objective of achieving viewing ratings of over 25% on commercial UK TV.

The organisation must then develop a **strategy** for achieving those objectives. Several alternatives may need to be considered before the final strategy is decided upon. The pet food company mentioned in the above example may decide that it needs to develop and market a new food product for young dogs to help it to achieve its objective. The independent TV production company may have a strategy of producing pilots for ten new programmes each year from which it can then develop the most promising.

limiting factors – the 'key' budget factor

When an organisation prepares a budget, it must first analyse its **limiting factors** – the issues that determine the level of its output. For a commercial organisation these could include:

- the size of its market
- capacity of its premises
- availability of raw material
- amount of working capital
- availability of skilled workers

One of the factors will be the main one that affects the activity level of the organisation – the **key budget factor**. This is the factor (sometimes known as the 'principal budget factor') that all the aspects of the operation depend upon. For most manufacturing or trading operations the key budget factor is sales; the assumptions that are made about the level of sales in the budget will affect all the other parts of the budget. This is because the organisation will plan to support the budgeted sales level and build the budgets and assumptions around this one issue.

Although sales level is the most common key factor, some commercial organisations may decide that a different factor is the most important in their particular circumstances. For example, if a manufacturer can sell all that it produces, but has production restricted by lack of skilled labour then the assumed labour level would become the key budget factor. A similar situation would arise if there were production restrictions caused by shortages of raw materials, or limited machine capacity.

Non-commercial organisations will also need to identify their key budget factor, and build their budgets around their assumptions concerning it. Charities and government agencies may consider that there is a demand for their services that is virtually limitless; their principal budget (key) factor is the amount of money they receive to fund what they do. For example, the Government's healthcare provision is limited by the amount of funding it can get from the government spending allocation and from private enterprise. The demand for Oxfam's aid is very high, but its key budget factor is the amount of money it can expect to raise to fund that aid.

Later in the chapter (page 212) we will see the 'nuts and bolts' of how budgets are created.

the initial budgeting process

If we combine the ideas just discussed then the initial budget process for an established organisation would follow this pattern:

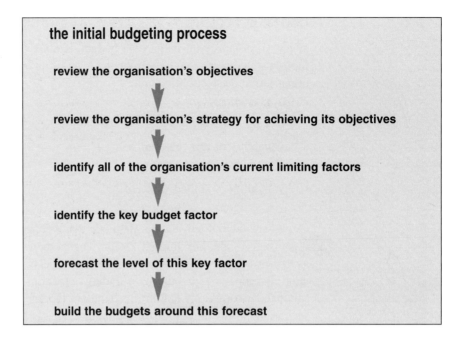

CO-ORDINATING THE MAIN TYPES OF BUDGET

Once the key factor has been determined, and an appropriate forecast developed, the budgets for the whole organisation can be generated. For a manufacturing organisation these would typically include:

sales budget   usually generated directly from the key factor – the forecast data

production budget   based on the sales budget together with the anticipated finished goods stock levels

materials usage budget based on the production budget

materials purchase budget based on the materials usage budget, together with the anticipated materials stock levels.

labour utilisation budget also based on the production budget

functional budgets   to support the operation (often based on departments), for example administration budget, finance budget; these may not be so dependent upon the sales level as other budgets that are linked more closely; zero base budgeting, as discussed in Chapter 10, can be used to develop this type of budget

capital expenditure budget this would also have to be developed in conjunction with the revenue budgets to ensure that the agreed spending on new or replacement equipment was in place

cash flow budget this would take account of all the other budgets and their effect on the organisation's liquidity (this budget is studied in the option unit 15)

master budget the calculations from all the revenue and capital budgets contribute to the **master budget** which takes the form of a budgeted profit and loss account and balance sheet

the effect of changing stock levels

You will have noticed several references in the list of budgets to **stock levels**. Where stock levels are to remain constant the situation is simple. For example the production budget will be identical to the sales budget if the finished goods stock level is to remain unchanged, ie the amount you will produce will be the amount you estimate you are going to sell. However if the stock level is to increase then the extra units of goods that will go into stock will need to be produced in addition to the units that are to be sold in the budget period. This is a concept that we will return to frequently, both in this chapter and in Chapter 9.

RESPONSIBILITIES AND TIMESCALES FOR BUDGET SETTING

the budget manual

For most organisations budget setting forms a vital part of the formal procedures: the organisation's method of budgeting will be set out in writing in its policy documents. These will include details of responsibilities and timetables. They may be combined into a **budget manual**.

The budget manual can be used to explain the 'why?' and the 'how?' of the organisation's approach to using budgets. It may include the following:

• the primary purposes of budgets for the organisation
• the types of budget that are to be produced
• what format is to be used for budgets
• how far in advance budgets are to be set

- who has responsibility for setting budgets
- who has responsibility for monitoring performance against budgets
- how often performance is to be monitored against budgets
- who has the authority to modify agreed budgets

the budget committee

The budget procedures may be the responsibility of a **budget committee**, chaired by the Managing Director or a person he/she has appointed. The composition of the committee may be set out in the budget manual, together with the committee's responsibilities. The budget committee may have the authority to modify the budget manual.

The committee will consist of senior representatives from all the departments of the organisation, so that there is full communication and co-ordination throughout the organisation. In this way there should be full understanding about the overall objectives of the organisation, and the part that each department must play in the total picture. It would not make sense for the marketing department to plan a promotion of a product that the production department could not supply in sufficient quantities. This concept of everyone working towards the same result is referred to as 'goal congruence'.

The committee will not only set and agree the budget, but it will also be responsible for monitoring the budget once it is in place. For example they may wish to monitor on a quarterly, monthly, or weekly basis, and will also want to decide on how quickly the information should be available and in what format.

budget timetables

There are two main types of budgets used by organisations:

- **strategic** budgets
- **operational** budgets.

They have different purposes, and are each based on different timescales. The budget committee will typically determine the way that these budgets are set and monitored, in line with the budget manual.

Strategic budgets will be produced well in advance of the period to which they relate. They are concerned with the long-term strategy of the organisation, and will therefore have the following features:

- they relate to long periods of time (typically five years)
- they are prepared a long time in advance of the budget periods
- they are limited to outline information and are not set out in great detail

- they are the responsibility of the senior management of the organisation

Some organisations may adopt a rolling programme of strategic budgets, perhaps five years ahead. Each year a further year would be incorporated into the far end of the budget.

Operational budgets will be produced for shorter periods of time – typically the next twelve months. They may be developed from the original strategic budgets for the budget period, but will take account of the fact that the business has information – facts and figures – about the immediate future. An operating budget will therefore have the following features:

- they relate to short periods of time (typically the forthcoming year, divided into manageable control periods)
- they are agreed a relatively short time in advance of the budget period (typically several months before the year starts)
- they are set up and agreed in considerable detail
- they are the responsibility of the middle managers that control the operations of the organisation

capital expenditure budgets

The overall strategic and operational budgets must include **capital expenditure budgets** as well as revenue budgets. Capital expenditure can range from straightforward replacement of equipment, to moving to new premises or acquiring whole businesses. The co-ordination of the capital expenditure budget is particularly important to ensure that:

- replacement equipment is acquired at the most cost-effective point for the organisation (before the old equipment becomes too costly to maintain, but not until the replacement is justified)
- planned production output that relies on capital expenditure is properly incorporated into both the appropriate revenue budgets and into the capital expenditure budget
- other resources are available to co-ordinate with the capital expenditure (for example installation, raw materials to cope with increased output)
- the labour requirements are available, and the workforce suitably trained
- suitable funding has been obtained to meet the capital expenditure
- appropriate planning has been carried out to phase in the use of the new fixed assets

We will look at the 'nuts and bolts' of creating budgets later in the chapter (page 212). Before an organisation can compile the budget figures, however, it will need to carry out some forecasting. This is not, as you will appreciate, an exact science.

USE OF FORECASTING TECHNIQUES

Forecasting is used in budget setting in two main ways.

1 The **key budget factor** will need to be forecast as accurately as possible to provide data that the various budgets can be built upon. This is often the sales level for a commercial organisation, but it could be other factors, as discussed previously in this chapter.

2 The **other data** in the various budgets may be subject to various forecasts. These could include forecasts of inflation that would affect all the budgets to some extent, along with other more specific forecasts, for example currency movements or interest rates.

The forecasting of the key (or principal) budget factor data is the most important part of the whole budgeting process, and yet is often the most difficult task to carry out. How does a business know, for example, how well its products will sell? Maybe a competitor will dent its sales, maybe the business will come up with an unexpected best-seller.

Techniques that can be used to assist in the forecasting process range from purely numerical methods like trend analysis using seasonal variations, to estimates that can amount to little more than informed guesses. In practice a combination of methods may be used.

For any technique that is based on using past data to produce useful forecasts of the future, the future must in some way depend upon the past. But there is always a danger of assuming that a trend will continue to travel in the same direction that it has done for the last few years. In reality there may be a massive change in direction about to happen caused by something that we did not know about or did not consider to be relevant.

The techniques used in sales forecasting include:

- trend analysis
- market research
- consulting experts

trend analysis

At its simplest trend analysis can mean assuming that sales will continue to move in the same direction and rate as they have in the recent past. Often seasonal variations are isolated from the historical data to produce 'deseasonalised' data that can be used as a basis for the forecast of the trend, before anticipated seasonal variations are added back in. This method cannot account for random movements in the data that may be a significant part of the data. The method also relies on there being suitable historical data available, so is not always appropriate.

market research

Market research may be an appropriate starting point, and is particularly suitable for new or revised products or services. Market research can make use of published statistics (eg economic and social trends) or it can involve a direct approach to the marketplace using techniques such as questionnaires and focus groups. Great care must be taken that the sampling system provides data that is as free from bias as practical. There will be costs and benefits applicable to methods ranging from postal or telephone questionnaires to focus groups and street interviews. A balance must be struck between the method used, the sample size, the accuracy required, and the cost involved. Users must be aware of the level of reliance that they can place on the data generated.

consulting experts

An organisation can build up a forecast by assessing the estimates of experts. Rather than making assumptions about overall sales levels, this method combines the estimates of those with local knowledge and experience. For example a business can ask individual sales representatives or sales outlets to forecast their expected sales levels, and then combine the results. This should have the advantage of utilising the knowledge of those aware of local conditions, but could be subject to personal bias and prejudices. Also, the experts providing the estimates may not be aware of wider economic issues that could affect the data. Major customers could also provide data by giving estimates of their requirements, or some form of questionnaire could be sent out to provide an estimate of all established customers' needs.

The Case Study that follows looks at a common example of the way in which sales can be forecast using seasonal trend figures.

CASE STUDY

FORECASTING SEASONAL SALES: WARMWEAR LIMITED

situation

Warmwear Limited manufactures a popular fleece which is branded the 'Arctic'.

The deseasonalised sales units for a single product during year 7 were:

Quarter 1	47,500 units
Quarter 2	51,010 units
Quarter 3	54,550 units
Quarter 4	58,000 units

The average seasonal variations are as follows:

Quarter 1	− 10,500 units
Quarter 2	− 2,500 units
Quarter 3	+ 6,200 units
Quarter 4	+ 6,800 units

required

Calculate the forecast sales units for quarters 3 and 4 of year 8, assuming the average trend movement during the last year was representative.

solution

The deseasonalised sales units represent the historical sales units after the seasonal variations have been excluded. We can therefore use these figures as the historical trend.

The average movement in the historical trend is:

$(58,000 - 47,500) \div 3 = +3,500$ units

because the trend moved from 47,500 units to 58,000 units in three changes of quarter.

Using this movement to extrapolate the trend shows that the trend would be:

$58,000 + (3 \times 3,500) = 68,500$ units by quarter 3 in year 8, and

$58,000 + (4 \times 3,500) = 72,000$ units by quarter 4 in year 8.

Incorporating the seasonal variations gives the forecasts of:

Quarter 3 year 8: $68,500 + 6,200 = 74,700$ units, and

Quarter 4 year 8: $72,000 + 6,800 = 78,800$ units.

USING SPREADSHEETS

You will be aware from your previous studies, and probably from your own experience that computer spreadsheet packages are an invaluable tool for manipulating a variety of numerical data. Spreadsheets can be used throughout the budgeting process, including when

- forecasting
- preparing budgets
- reporting results

The advantages of using spreadsheets include:

- the use of formats that can be copied or modified as required
- accurate calculations that can be carried out at great speed
- the ability to demonstrate 'what if' scenarios very easily
- the co-ordination of various budgets through linked spreadsheets

In an assessment you may be asked to comment on the use of spreadsheets, or be given a more practical task, as in the following Case Study.

CASE STUDY

USING A SPREADSHEET FOR FORECASTING: MICROCLIMATE LIMITED

situation

MicroClimate Limited manufactures and sells greenhouses, and cold frames through garden centres. It is currently developing a forecast for the sales of its new 'Victoriana' cold frame. The forecast is to be based on annual sales in the year of 40,000 units at a selling price of £50 each. It is to be assumed that sales will be subject to the following seasonal variations (as percentages of one quarter of the annual sales). This is in line with the company's experience of other similar products.

Quarter 1	- 30%
Quarter 2	+ 80%
Quarter 3	+ 40%
Quarter 4	- 90%

The following spreadsheet format is to be used to forecast the sales in units and value for the year.

	A	B	C	D	E
1	Unit selling price (£)	50			
2	Annual sales volume (units)	40000			
3	Seasonal variations (%)	-30%	80%	40%	-90%
4		Quarter 1	Quarter 2	Quarter 3	Quarter 4
5	Seasonal variations (units)				
6	Quarterly volume (units)				
7	Quarterly sales (£)				

required

1 Insert appropriate formulae in rows 5, 6, and 7 of the spreadsheet so that quarterly sales in both units and £ would be automatically calculated for any annual sales volume, and unit sales price.

2 Show the numerical information that would be produced by your formulae, based on the data given.

solution to Task 1

	A	B	C	D	E
1	Unit selling price (£)	50			
2	Annual sales volume (units)	40000			
3	Seasonal variations (%)	-30%	80%	40%	-90%
4		Quarter 1	Quarter 2	Quarter 3	Quarter 4
5	Seasonal variations (units)	=(B2/4)*B3	=(B2/4)*C3	=(B2/4)*D3	=(B2/4)*E3
6	Quarterly volume (units)	=(B2/4)+B5	=(B2/4)+C5	=(B2/4)+D5	=(B2/4)+E5
7	Quarterly sales (£)	=B1*B6	=B1*C6	=B1*D6	=B1*E6

solution to Task 2

	A	B	C	D	E
1	Unit selling price (£)	50			
2	Annual sales volume (units)	40000			
3	Seasonal variations (%)	-30%	80%	40%	-90%
4		Quarter 1	Quarter 2	Quarter 3	Quarter 4
5	Seasonal variations (units)	-3000	8000	4000	-9000
6	Quarterly volume (units)	7000	18000	14000	1000
7	Quarterly sales (£)	350000	900000	700000	50000

FACTORS INFLUENCING FORECASTS

Common sense tells us that there are events and developments going on locally, nationally and internationally which can affect our forecasts and should therefore be taken into account where possible.

the product life cycle

It is important when forecasting sales volumes to consider the effect of the product life cycle. Products typically go through a number of distinct stages between conception and finally being withdrawn from sale. The stages are:

- development
- launch
- growth
- maturity
- decline

These stages are shown on the following graph:

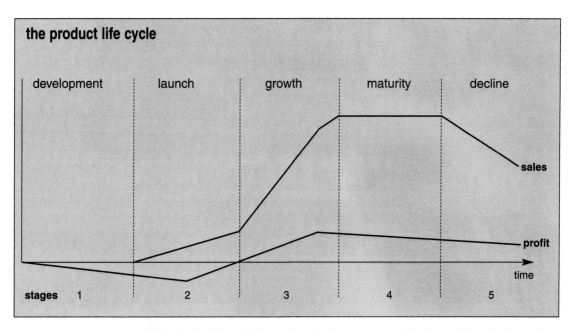

At the beginning of the cycle, development, production and marketing costs are high and so profit may even be negative. If the product is successful, a period of growth follows and sales accelerate up to the level of the maturity stage of the cycle. Here sales have reached a plateau, and demand may be sustained by making product improvements. After the market has become saturated, and virtually all potential buyers satisfied, sales of the product will go into decline. It may be wise to terminate production before all demand has been extinguished to avoid incurring losses, or alternatively repackage and revamp the product.

While some products may move quickly from start-up to decline, others may have a longer life cycle and become what are known as 'cash cows', providing the business with a steady cash flow and source of profitability. Baked beans, for example have been steady sellers for over 50 years!

It is clearly important to recognise the phases of the cycle, and to be able to identify what phase the products are in to improve forecasting. While a product during the mature phase may have a relatively steady sales level that should be easy to forecast, the approaching period of decline must not be ignored.

PEST analysis

PEST analysis examines

political

economic

social and

technological factors that affect the performance of a product.

- **political factors**

Governments have control over a variety of issues that can affect future activity levels. For example importing or exporting can be made more or less attractive by the use of trade tariffs, or joining or leaving exchange rate mechanisms or adopting the Euro. National and international laws affect issues from health & safety to minimum wage levels. Taxation policies will also be important: they affect competing companies and individuals who may be customers.

- **economic factors**

The forecast sales level of organisations must take account of the economy in the market place. If the general economic climate is good, then customers will be more confident about the future. Sales are likely to be higher when fewer people are unemployed, and more money circulates. When the economy deteriorates customers will be more restricted in their spending. The economy is, of course, influenced by political changes, and successive governments have attempted (with varying success) to minimise the large cyclical swings in the economy and promote sustainable growth. Inflation is also closely linked with the economy, and index numbers can be used to record and forecast inflation (see page 31).

- **social factors**

Patterns of individual behaviour, fashions, and perceptions of acceptability and political correctness can all impact on sales. In addition more fundamental changes in the structure of society like the size of the family, divorce levels and the average age at which people have children or retire are clearly important.

- **technological factors**

Technology can affect not only the way that a company manufactures its products, but also the market into which it is selling. A new product announced by a competitor can have a huge impact on sales levels, and the general effect of new technology is continually to shorten the product life cycle.

CASE STUDY

SENSIBLE FORECASTING: 'FOCUS'

situation

A new restaurant called 'Focus' is opened on 1 January. After running for 11 weeks it becomes clear that there is a regular pattern to the number of meals served on different days of the week. The daily variations seem to follow these percentages from the average daily meals sold in that week:

Mondays	- 70%
Tuesdays	- 50%
Wednesdays	- 20%
Thursdays	+30%
Fridays	+40%
Saturdays	+80%
Sundays	- 10%

The average number of meals per day served in week one was 20 per day. By week eleven the average had grown to 50 per day. The restaurant manager, Tom Hick, wants an idea of the likely number of meals eaten in twenty weeks' time. He asks you to carry out a number of forecasts but you are dubious about the value of all the methods he suggests and the data you are going to produce. However he is the boss and you have to do what he asks you to do.

required

(a) Using the data provided, forecast the average daily meals to be served in week 31, and the number of meals to be served on the Saturday in that week.

(b) State why you think his idea of a forecast may lack validity. Mention other forecasting factors which might be taken into account.

solution

(a) The average historical trend movement is

$(50 − 20) ÷ 10$ = + 3

(Meals per day). $11\ wks - 1 = 10$

ie a rise of 3 average daily meals each week.

Using this trend figure to forecast the average number of meals per day in week 31 results in:

$50 + ([31 − 11] \times 3)$ — figure above. = 110 average daily meals

This gives a forecast for the Saturday night of 110 + 80% of 110 = 198 meals.
(weeks)

(b) A new restaurant would be going through the start-up or growth phase of its life cycle during the weeks for which there is historical data. The trend movement is therefore not sustainable at this level indefinitely, and to assume it will continue for a further 20 weeks may be wildly optimistic.

There are other issues that do not seem to have been considered, including:

- the capacity of the restaurant
- the ability of the staff to maintain quality at higher output levels
- the effect on trade of seasonal variations
- the effect of holiday periods

CREATING BUDGETS

Earlier in this chapter we examined the methods and implications of creating budgets and using budgetary control. We will now look at the numerical work that is needed to produce a budget. This will involve co-ordinating the various budgets so that they are all based on the same assumptions and fit together in a logical sequence.

The procedure that we will need to follow when creating budgets is based on the system described in the earlier section on co-ordinated budgets (see page 200). Limiting factors need to be considered and the 'key' factor identified. For a manufacturing business sales volume is often the principal (key) budget factor. The system of budgets that will be created is shown in the diagram below and explained in the text that follows.

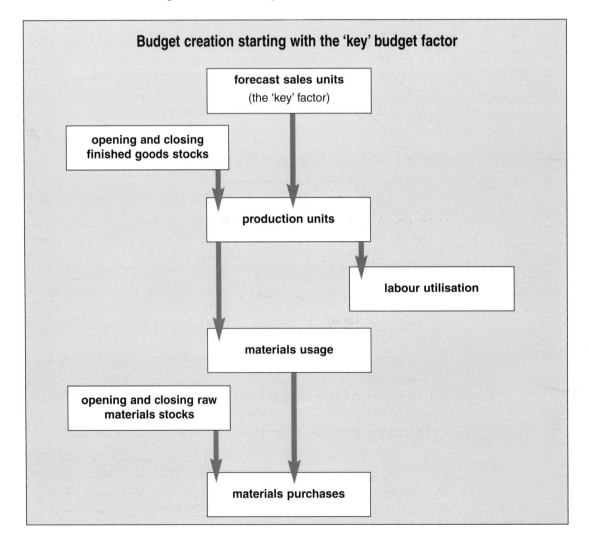

sales budget

The forecast of sales units will need to be developed first, as this is fundamental to the whole series of budgets. The level of actual production that is required will depend on two issues:

- the amount of finished goods the business plans to hold in stock ready to be sold
- whether any of these finished goods are likely to be rejected.

The complication of building in a provision for rejections will be dealt with in the next chapter, so we will now deal with the subject of planning production to allow for changes in the level of finished goods stock.

production budget

We will generally need to plan to produce the units that we intend to sell, but we can

- plan to reduce our production by the intended fall in the level of finished goods stock, or
- plan to increase our production to increase the level of our finished goods stock

The production budget in units for a period therefore equals:

Budgeted Sales Units

– Opening Stock of Finished Goods

+ Closing Stock of Finished Goods

This can be justified since:

- the **opening stock** of finished goods has already been produced, and can therefore be deducted from our calculation of what needs to be made, and
- the **closing stock** has yet to be made so needs to be added in to our total of goods to be produced.

In summary, the common-sense rule is:

- if stocks of finished goods are to increase, then production must be greater than sales
- if finished goods stocks are to remain constant production will be the same as sales
- if finished goods stocks are to fall production will be less than sales

materials usage and labour utilisation budgets

Once the production budget has been developed in units, we can calculate the quantity of material we need to use and the amount of labour time required. The **materials usage budget** is created to ascertain the amount of raw material that will be consumed in production. The **labour utilisation budget** is usually based on labour time in hours, but could be converted into full time equivalent employees. Any shortfall in the available number of personnel will become clear at this stage as will any anticipated requirement for overtime working. The use of both materials and labour can also be valued at this point if required. The data for these calculations may come from standard costing information, or some less formal estimates of the material and labour content of production units.

Indirect costs in the form of fixed and variable overheads can also be ascertained at this stage if required. If the absorption costing model is being followed these costs will need to be incorporated into the unit costs, whereas if a marginal costing procedure is adopted all fixed costs will be considered as relating to the time period rather than the production units.

materials purchases budget

The materials purchases budget can be created once the materials usage budget has been established. Here differences between the quantity of material to be consumed in production and the quantity to be purchased will be due to:

- the required movement in raw material goods stocks (adjusting for opening and closing stock)
- any wastage or loss of raw materials

We will examine how to account for wastage in the next chapter. At this point we will consider the adjustments needed for raw material stock movements.

The reasoning follows a similar pattern to the one described for sales, finished goods and production. If we already have raw materials in the opening stock this amount does not have to be purchased, but the quantity that we plan to have in stock at the end of the period must be purchased in addition to the amount that will be used in production.

The **quantity of material purchased** (as recorded in the material purchases budget) will therefore equal:

Quantity of material to be used (per materials usage budget)

– opening stock of raw materials,

+ closing stock of raw materials.

The rule is therefore:

- if stocks of raw materials are to increase, then purchases must be greater than materials usage
- if raw materials stocks are to remain constant purchases will be the same as materials usage
- if raw materials stocks are to fall purchases will be less than materials usage

One vital reason for creating a material purchases budget is that the information on the timing of purchases will feed into the cash budget which shows when the payments will need to be made.

BUDGETS FOR MATERIALS USED AND PURCHASED: FLUMEN LIMITED

situation

A manufacturing company, Flumen Limited, makes a single product, the Wye. The sales forecast for February is 5,900 units. Each unit of Wye uses 5 kilo of Monnow and 3 kilos of Lugg.

The anticipated stocks at the beginning of February are:

Finished Wyes	1,400 units
Unused Monnow	350 kilos
Unused Lugg	200 kilos

The required stocks levels at the end of February are:

Finished Wyes	1,800 units
Unused Monnow	250 kilos
Unused Lugg	450 kilos

required

Produce the following budget figures for the month of February:

(a)   Production of Wye (in units)

(b)   Materials usage of Monnow and Lugg (in kilos)

(c)   Materials purchases of Monnow and Lugg (in kilos)

solution

(a)   Production units =

Budgeted Sales Units	5,900	
– Opening Stock of Finished Goods	(1,400)	
+ Closing Stock of Finished Goods.	1,800	
Production units =	6,300	Wyes.

(b)   Materials Usage

Monnow: 6,300 x 5 kilos = 31,500 kilos

Lugg: 6,300 x 3 kilos = 18,900 kilos

(c) Materials purchases:

Monnow:

Quantity of material to be used	31,500 kilos
– opening stock of raw materials,	(350 kilos)
+ closing stock of raw materials.	250 kilos
Required purchases of Monnow	31,400 kilos

Lugg:

Quantity of material to be used	18,900 kilos
– opening stock of raw materials,	(200 kilos)
+ closing stock of raw materials.	450 kilos
Required purchases of Lugg	19,150 kilos

BUDGETS AND MANUFACTURING ACCOUNTS

The above case study was based on one period, the month of February. But the process is identical if we wish to generate a series of budgets for consecutive periods. Remember that the closing stock values for one period will be the same as the opening stocks for the next period, and so on. It is also a straightforward matter to incorporate values as well as quantities in the budgets if standard costs (or alternative estimates of value) are available. It is then also possible to summarise the budget information generated into a statement of the cost of production for the periods. This can be carried out in the format of a budgeted manufacturing account. You will probably be familiar with this format from your earlier Financial Accounting studies.

CASE STUDY

BUDGETED MANUFACTURING ACCOUNTS: COLLEY LIMITED

situation

Colley Limited produces a single product, the Colley. Each Colley has standard data as follows:

- 3 kilos raw material at £8.00 per kilo
- 2 hours labour at £6.00 per hour
- fixed overheads at £10.00 per unit.

The forecast sales level of Colleys for the first quarter of the next financial year is as follows:

January	11,800	units
February	12,400	units
March	12,100	units

The forecast stock levels on 1 January are:

Finished Units of Colley	5,800
Raw materials	8,000 kilos.

Colley Limited plans to reduce the raw material stock by 500 kilos in each month of the first quarter, and to increase the number of finished Colleys in stock by 2,000 each month in anticipation of a sales drive in the second quarter.

The fixed overheads absorption rate of £10 per unit is based on fixed overheads of £423,000, and production level of 42,300 units for the quarter.

required

1 Produce the following budgets for each of the months of January, February and March.

(a) Production of Colley (in units)

(b) Usage of Raw Material (in kilos and £)

(c) Purchases of Raw Material (in kilos and £)

(d) Labour Utilisation (in hours and £)

2 Using the information generated in task (1), produce a budgeted manufacturing account for the three months in total, and a budgeted cost of sales figure.

solution

Task 1

(a) Production Budget

	January	February	March
Forecast Sales Units	11,800	12,400	12,100
Less opening stock finished units	(5,800)	(7,800)	(9,800)
Add closing stock finished units	7,800	9,800	11,800
Production Units	13,800	14,400	14,100

The calculation could alternatively been carried out by adding each month's increase in finished goods stock to the sales forecast.

(b) Materials Usage Budget

	January	February	March
Production Units (per (a))	13,800	14,400	14,100
Usage Raw Materials (at 3 kilo per unit)	41,400 kg	43,200 kg	42,300 kg
Cost of Raw Materials Used (at £8.00 per kilo)	£331,200	£345,600	£338,400

(c) **Materials Purchases Budget**

	January	February	March
Usage Raw Materials (per (b))	41,400 kg	43,200 kg	42,300 kg
Less opening stock of Raw Materials	(8,000 kg)	(7,500 kg)	(7,000 kg)
Add closing stock of Raw Materials	7,500 kg	7,000 kg	6,500 kg
Raw Materials Purchases	40,900 kg	42,700 kg	41,800 kg
Cost of Raw Material Purchases (at £8.00 per kilo)	£327,200	£341,600	£334,400

(d) **Labour Utilisation Budget**

	January	February	March
Production Units (per (a))	13,800	14,400	14,100
Utilisation of Labour (at 2 hours per unit)	27,600 hrs	28,800 hrs	28,200 hrs
Cost of Labour (at £6.00 per hour)	£165,600	£172,800	£169,200

Task 2

Budgeted Manufacturing Account for 3 months to 31 March 2002

Raw Materials:		
Opening Stock (1 Jan)	8,000 kg	£64,000
Purchases (3 mths)	125,400 kg	£1,003,200
Less Closing Stock (31 Mar)	(6,500 kg)	(£52,000)
Usage	126,900 kg	£1,015,200
Direct Labour:		
Utilisation	84,600 hrs	£507,600
Direct Cost of Production		£1,522,800
Fixed Overheads (per budget)		£423,000
Total Cost of Production		£1,945,800

This total cost of production figure reconciles with the total number of units produced:
(13,800 + 14,400 + 14,100) = 42,300 units
at a unit cost of £46. (Materials £24 + Labour £12 + Fixed Overheads £10)
ie 42,300 x £46 = £1,945,800.

The manufacturing account format restates the same information that appears in the budget, but presents the working for materials in the opposite direction. It is therefore fully compatible with the calculations that we have carried out. The cost of production can then be used as part of a budgeted trading account in conjunction with the finished goods stocks to form the cost of sales, as follows:

Budgeted Cost of Sales (Budgeted Trading Account [extract])

Opening Stock of Finished Goods	5,800 units	£266,800
Cost of Production (from Man'f a/c)	42,300 units	£1,945,800
Less Closing Stock Finished Goods	(11,800 units)	(£542,800)
Cost of Sales		£1,669,800

(Stocks are valued at £46 per unit, as per working above)

The cost of sales figure reconciles with the forecast sales units of
(11,800 + 12,400 + 12,100) = 36,300 units x £46 = £1,669,800.

CHAPTER SUMMARY

- Budgets can be used to compel planning, to communicate and co-ordinate ideas, and to monitor and control outcomes. They may also be used to help motivate managers and employees.

- Budgets must be in line with the objectives of the organisation, and the organisation's chosen strategy to achieve those objectives. Before starting to create a budget, the key budget factor must be recognised, and its numerical impact forecast. For most commercial organisations this factor is the sales level, but it could be based on specific resources or factors.

- Budgets that are prepared for manufacturing organisations typically include Sales, Production, Material Usage, Material Purchases, and Labour Utilisation, together with other budgets including various functional (including departmental) budgets, capital expenditure budgets and cash flow budgets. These are co-ordinated and amalgamated to form a set of Master Budgets.

- The way in which budgets are used in an organisation is often laid down in the budget manual. In many organisations the responsibility for budget setting and control will rest with the Budget Committee. This will incorporate senior representatives of all major parts of the organisation to ensure full co-ordination.

- Techniques to assist with forecasting include numerical techniques like trend analysis and index numbers, together with market research and technical estimates. Forecasts should consider the effects of the product life cycle, and political, economic, social and technological factors.

- Budgets for manufacturing organisations can be created by working from the forecast sales data to the production level by using anticipated finished goods stock levels. From the production budget the materials usage can be ascertained, and by incorporating the anticipated materials stock levels the materials purchases can be calculated. Other budgets can also be created from the production budget. Budgeted manufacturing accounts can also be generated and will link with the budgets.

budget	A financial plan for an organisation, prepared before the period starts.
goal congruence	The concept of each part of the organisation working towards a common set of objectives.
key (or principal) budget factor	The main factor (whether internal or external) that determines the planned activity level of the organisation.
budget committee	A committee charged with the responsibility of setting and monitoring the budget. It will include senior representatives from all parts of the organisation.
budget manual	A document containing information about how an organisation's policy on budgeting is implemented.
strategic budget	A long-term budget produced in outline only.
operational budget	A short-term budget produced in detail.
trend analysis	A numerical technique for analysing historical data so that it can be used for forecasting future data. It involves identifying and separating seasonal and other variations so that the underlying trend can be ascertained.
deseasonalised data	Data that has had the effects of seasonal variations stripped away.
sampling	A series of techniques whereby a small number of items within the whole population are analysed so that data about the whole population may be estimated.
market research	Techniques involving compiling data from published statistics or from representatives of the existing or potential market for a product or service. Techniques include using various forms of questionnaire, as well as focus groups and personal interviews.
product life cycle	The natural cycle of stages that a commercial product undergoes between introduction to the market and ultimate withdrawal. The stages include development, launch, growth, maturity, and decline.

STUDENT ACTIVITIES

8.1 (i) At which stage in a product life cycle is trend analysis with seasonal variations likely to produce the best forecast?

   (a) Start-up

   (b) Growth

   (c) Maturity ✓

   (d) Decline

(ii) Which of the following have an effect on the reliability of a forecast which has been based on sampling?

   (a) The size of the sample

   (b) Whether the sample was random or non-random

   (c) The size of the population from which the sample was drawn

   (d) Whether the sample was quasi-random or quota based

   (e) All of the above ✓

(iii) Which of the following constitute good guidelines for the use of price index numbers for budgeting?

   (a) Use as general an index as possible

   (b) Extrapolate past index numbers only when future prices are believed to follow past trends

   (c) Choose index numbers that are as specific to the circumstances as possible ✓

   (d) Never attempt to use index numbers for budgeting prices

8.2 Suggest the key (or principal) budget factors for the following organisations:

   (a) A partnership of two craftsmen who make high quality violins for leading musicians. The work is labour intensive and highly skilled. They are able to easily sell all they produce.

   (b) A transport company that has a contract to work only for a major supplier of turkeys. The turkey supplier is currently expanding, but there is an agreement in place for all their transport requirements to be met by this one company for the next 12 months.

   (c) A company whose team of engineers has a contract to maintain the Metro in Manchester. They have no plans to seek other contracts.

   (d) A company that has opened a new baked potato outlet on a busy business park. The firm has the sole rights to supply potatoes to the 3,000 staff on the site, and has the capacity to cook and sell 100 baked potatoes per day.

8.3 An insurance company has analysed its sales of travel insurance over the last two years, and produced the following information:

Year	Quarter	Trend (Policies)	Seasonal Variation (Policies)
1	1	5,800	- 430
	2	5,870	- 350
	3	5,935	+880
	4	6,010	- 100
2	1	6,090	- 430
	2	6,165	- 350
	3	6,220	+880
	4	6,290	- 100

Required

(a) Calculate the average trend movement per quarter over the last two years.

(b) Use the average trend movement to forecast the expected sales (in numbers of policies) in quarters 3 and 4 of year 3.

8.4 A manufacturing company that makes kitchen chairs is planning its activities for month 5 in the current year. The following data is available:

Sales in month 5 are forecast at 1,800 units.

Each completed unit requires 4 kilos of raw material.

Planned stock levels are:

	Raw Materials	Finished Goods
At end of month 4	1,200 kilos	500 units
At end of month 5	1,500 kilos	400 units

Required

Calculate the following budgets for month 5:

- production budget (in units),
- raw materials usage (in kilos)
- raw materials purchases (in kilos).

8.5 A company that manufactures a single product (the Zapp) is planning for the next six months. Each unit of Zapp produced uses 2 litres of Woo and 3 litres of Koo.

Each unit of Zapp takes 0.5 hours of direct labour to produce.

The anticipated demand for Zapp is as follows:

January	5,000	units
February	4,000	units
March	6,500	units
April	5,000	units
May	6,500	units
June	5,000	units,

after which the demand can be assumed to stabilise at 5,000 units per month.

It will be company policy to maintain raw material stocks at a level of 100% of the following month's usage, and to maintain finished goods stocks at a level to satisfy half of the following month's estimated sales. Stocks held on 31 December were 3,000 finished Zapps, and 8,000 litres of Woo and 16,000 litres of Koo.

Required

(a) Calculate the following budgets for each month and in total:

- Production of Zapps (in units)

- Materials Usage (in litres of Woo and Koo)

- Materials Purchase (in litres of Woo and Koo)

- Direct Labour (in hours)

(b) The Zapp is sold for £70 per unit, and Woo costs £3.00 per litre and Koo £11.00 per litre. Direct labour costs £6.00 per hour. Fixed production overheads are estimated at £100,000 per month. Stocks are valued at direct costs only.

Complete the Sales and Cost of Sales Budgets (both in £) for the six months in total, and calculate the budgeted gross profit.

9 PRACTICAL ASPECTS OF BUDGET PREPARATION

this chapter covers . . .

This chapter examines the practical aspects of budget preparation and deals with the problems of:

- *the rejection of finished goods*
- *inefficient working*
- *wastage of raw materials before or during production*
- *dealing with limited materials*
- *dealing with limited labour*
- *dealing with limited production capacity*

NVQ PERFORMANCE CRITERIA COVERED

unit 9: CONTRIBUTING TO THE PLANNING AND ALLOCATION OF RESOURCES

element 2

produce draft budget proposals

- *draft budget proposals are presented to management in a clear and appropriate format and on schedule*

- *draft budget proposals are consistent with organisational objectives, have taken all relevant data into account and are agreed with budget holders*

- *discussions with budget holders are conducted in a manner which maintains goodwill*

BUDGETS – ACCOUNTING FOR RESOURCES

When creating budgets for manufacturing organisations we must be aware that there may be situations when not all our resources are translated into saleable products. This may occur at various stages in the manufacturing process, and must be accounted for accurately when budgets are being prepared.

the problems

The range of problems that we must be able to deal with include:

- **producing finished goods that are not up to standard**

  Depending on the production process and the quality control system, some finished goods that are not up to standard may be only detected once they have been manufactured. This means that we must plan to produce more than we need so that the expected number of rejects is allowed for. An example of the type of product where rejection may occur after completion is electronic components that would undergo a final quality test.

- **a labour force that is not operating at a standard efficiency level**

  When standard efficiency levels are used to plan for the amount of direct labour time to produce the required output, problems will arise if the workforce is significantly slower (or faster) than expected. When this difference can be anticipated the budgets can be modified to take account of the different efficiency level. This could occur (for example) if a workforce was undergoing training to use new equipment.

- **wastage of raw materials**

  In some situations the amount of raw materials that are contained in the finished product may be less than the amount that must be purchased. This can be due to a variety of situations occurring before or during manufacture, including deterioration, spillage, or evaporation. It can also occur due to the raw materials naturally including unusable parts. An example of this could be timber that needs to have the bark removed before being cut to size.

how to deal with the problems

The issues that we face when preparing budgets incorporating these situations are:

- In which budget should we account for the situation?
- How do we accurately account for the situation?

The following diagram summarises the first of these issues. It is based on the budget preparation diagram shown in the last chapter.

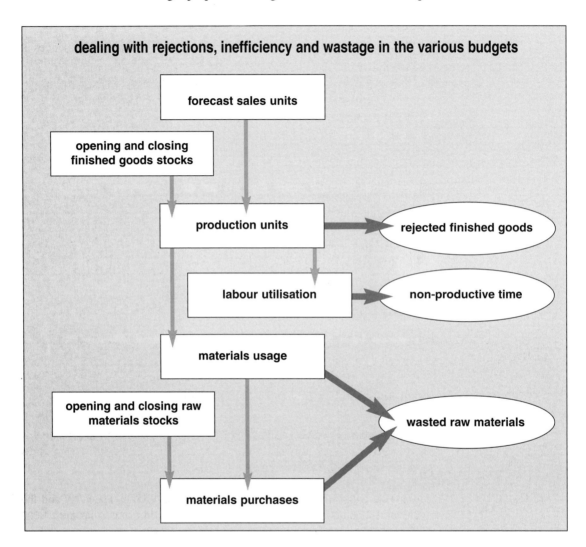

dealing with rejections, inefficiency and wastage in the various budgets

forecast sales units

opening and closing finished goods stocks

production units → rejected finished goods

labour utilisation → non-productive time

materials usage

opening and closing raw materials stocks

wasted raw materials

materials purchases

The problems described earlier are dealt with at the following points in the overall budgeting process:

- Anticipated **rejections** of finished goods are built into the **production budget**. We therefore plan to produce enough so that when some output has been scrapped there is still enough to sell and account for changes in finished goods stock levels.

- **Non-productive time** is built into the **labour utilisation budget**. We plan for sufficient time to be available so that the productive part is enough to satisfy the needs of the production budget.

- **Wastage of materials during production** is accounted for when determining the **materials usage budget**. A higher level of usage is planned for so that the materials will still be sufficient, despite wastage during production.

- **Wastage of materials before the production process** commences is taken account of when the **materials purchases budget** is prepared. In this way sufficient materials are acquired to deal with wastage, the amount needed for the materials usage budget, and the required changes in raw materials stock levels.

REJECTION OF FINISHED GOODS

The approach to take when dealing with a situation where finished goods are scrapped after a final inspection is to work back from the number of perfect products that we need to make. This is illustrated in the following case study.

CASE STUDY

OSBORNE ELECTRICAL COMPONENTS: REJECTION OF FINISHED GOODS

An electrical component manufacturer's system involves a quality control check of all the completed components. The records show that on average 6% of completed components will fail this check and will need to be scrapped.

The forecast sales volume for the month of March is 5,200 components, and the production budget is to incorporate an increase in finished goods stock from 1,000 components to 1,440 components, as well as the typical failure rate.

required

Calculate the production budget (in numbers of components) for March.

solution

Both the sales forecast and the finished goods stock increase must be based on 'good' components. It would not make sense to sell or place into stock any units that had failed the quality inspection.

The number of 'good' components required is therefore:

Budgeted Sales Units	5,200
– Opening Stock of Finished Goods	(1,000)
+ Closing Stock of Finished Goods.	1,440
= production of 'good' components	5,640

But actual production must be greater than this amount to account for rejects. Since the rejection rate is assumed to be 6%, the 5,640 'good' units must equal 94% of the required production level, as demonstrated in this diagram.

reject units	6% of production
'good' units (5,640)	94% of production

The production budget must therefore equal 5,640 x 100 ÷ 94 = 6,000 units.

You should be careful to note that the calculation does not involve simply adding 6% to the good production, but is effectively adding 6/94, because the good production is 94% of the total production. This technique is often assessed, and is a frequent source of confusion amongst students.

NON-PRODUCTIVE TIME

When a lack of efficiency results in non-productive time, the problem should be dealt with at the time the labour utilisation budget is being drawn up. By definition, non-productive time cannot be used to produce output, and so the amount of time that can be effectively used in production is less than the time that must be allowed for in total (and paid for).

If, on the other hand, it is anticipated that the efficiency level will be more than 100% (ie the work is to be carried out more quickly than the standard) this would also be accounted for at the same point in the process.

These two possibilities – inefficiency and a high level of efficiency – are dealt with in the Case Studies that follow.

CASE STUDY

PERFECT PATIOS:
LOW LABOUR EFFICIENCY

A company that manufactures paving slabs has traditionally used standard labour times to build up the labour utilisation budget. Output is measured in hundreds of slabs, and the standard direct labour time to manufacture 100 type A slabs is 3.6 hours, and 100 type B slabs is 4.2 hours.

Recent legislation means that additional break times need to be accounted for in the labour utilisation budget. It is estimated that break times will in future account for 12% of the direct labour time allocated to production work, This has not been accounted for in the standard times quoted.

The production budget for January is for 24,000 type A slabs and 58,000 type B slabs.

required

Calculate the labour utilisation budget (in total direct labour hours) for January.

solution

The productive time (excluding breaks) is as follows:

Type A slabs:
      240 (hundreds of slabs) x 3.6 hours =   864 hours
Type B slabs:
      580 (hundreds of slabs) x 4.2 hours =   2,436 hours

Total productive time   **3,300 hours**

This productive time will equal 88% of the total paid time due to the 12% allowance for breaks, as shown here.

break times	12%
productive time (3,300 hours)	88%

The total paid time will therefore equal 3,300 hours x 100 ÷ 88 = 3,750 hours, and 3,750 direct labour hours will form the labour utilisation budget.

CASE STUDY

SLICK PERFORMERS LTD: HIGH LABOUR EFFICIENCY

A small pottery that makes rustic crockery by hand set its standards some time ago, when the potters were relatively inexperienced. These standards included a time of 8 hours to create a 48-piece dinner service using a potter's wheel. Since that time all the potters have become more proficient, and can now produce work of the same standard more quickly. It is estimated that they are currently working at a 120% efficiency level based on the old standards. During the coming month of April the pottery needs to fulfil orders for 32 dinner services, and also increase its stock level from 3 dinner services to 7 dinner services.

required

Calculate the labour utilisation budget for creating dinner services (in total direct labour hours) for April.

solution

The production required for April will be:

32	dinner services (for current orders), *plus*
4	dinner services (for stock increase)
36	dinner services

At standard time of 8 hours per dinner service, this would take 288 standard hours. Since the potters are working at 120% efficiency they will take less time than standard. This is calculated as:

288 hours x 100 ÷ 120 = <u>240 hours</u>.

The logic can be checked by working back from the solution as follows:

At standard rate (of 8 hours per set) in 240 hours they could make
240 ÷ 8 = 30 dinner services.
Operating at 120% efficiency they can produce 20% more output, i.e.
30 x 120% = 36 dinner services.

MATERIAL WASTAGE DURING PRODUCTION

Wastage during manufacture is a common problem, and occurs in industries as diverse as food production and house building. There can also be situations where one material incurs wastage, while another adds to the weight of the finished product. The next case study examines this problem.

CASE STUDY

COOL CHIP COMPANY:
MATERIAL WASTAGE

A frozen potato chip manufacturer purchases whole potatoes with skins. These are then peeled, any imperfections are removed, and the potatoes are sliced into chips and fried before freezing. The average wastage that occurs during peeling and imperfection removal is 20% of the weight of the whole potatoes.

No further wastage occurs during slicing, but frying oil is absorbed during cooking which amounts to an increase in weight of 5% of the uncooked chips.

The production budget for July is for 105,000 kilos of frozen chips, based on their weight immediately prior to freezing.

required

Calculate the materials usage budget (in kilos) for July for

(a)   Whole raw potatoes, and

(b)   Frying oil.

solution

In order to calculate the usage we must work back from the production budget:

1   Firstly, to produce 105,000 kilos of chips we will need slightly less than this weight of uncooked chips, due to the absorption of oil. Note that in this example the weight of the oil absorbed is 5% of the weight of the uncooked chips, so the cooked chips are 105% of the weight of the uncooked chips.

Therefore 105,000 kilos of cooked chips will be made from 105,000 x 100 ÷ 105 = 100,000 kilos of uncooked chips plus 5,000 kilos of frying oil.

2   Secondly to produce 100,000 kilos of uncooked chips we need to start with a larger weight of whole potatoes. The uncooked chips represent 80% of the weight of the whole potatoes, since 20% is lost as skin and imperfections.

Therefore whole potatoes will equal 100,000 x 100 ÷ 80 = 125,000 kilos.

3   The materials utilisation budget will therefore be:

125,000 kilos whole potatoes, and

5,000 kilos frying oil.

4   It is worth double-checking our calculation, especially with a complicated example like this one. This can be done as follows:

125,000 kilos whole potatoes used, less 20% wastage at the peeling stage, leaving 100,000 (80%) uncooked chips.

The 100,000 uncooked chips absorb 5% of their weight in frying oil (i.e. 5,000 kilos) making a cooked weight of 105,000 kilos.

MATERIAL WASTAGE BEFORE PRODUCTION

The final type of situation that you may need to deal with involves wastage occurring while the material is being stored, prior to production. In the next case study this idea has been combined with the technique from the last case study to show how to deal with wastage when it occurs at two points; one before production starts and the other during production.

<table><tr><td>**CASE STUDY**</td><td>

WALVERN WATER LIMITED

A manufacturer uses large quantities of distilled water in its production process. It buys the water in bulk and keeps it in large storage tanks. Due to the temperature in the vicinity of the factory, it is estimated that 3% of the distilled water will have evaporated between being purchased and being drawn from the storage tanks. A further 5% of the distilled water that is used in the process evaporates during production.

The final product has a distilled water content that is 89% of its volume.

The production budget for June shows that 390,000 litres of the finished product is required.

The distilled water stock is estimated at 50,000 litres at the start of June, and 80,000 litres at the end of June (both figures assume that the initial evaporation in storage has taken place).

required

Calculate the following data for the distilled water for June:
1   the volume to be input into the production process, and
2   the volume to be purchased
Carry out calculations to the nearest litre.

solution

As in the other case studies, we need to work back from the required output.
1   The finished goods will contain (390,000 litres x 89%) = 347,100 litres of distilled water.

Evaporation during the production process means that this figure is equal to 95% of the distilled water input into the process.

The volume to be input is therefore (347,100 x 100 ÷ 95) = 365,368 litres
</td></tr></table>

2   We therefore need to purchase sufficient distilled water to allow for:

the evaporation in storage, *plus*

the required increase in distilled water stocks, *plus*

the volume to be input into the production process.

The following diagram illustrates the amount of water that will need to be purchased:

evaporation during storage
increase in stock level
input into production

As calculated in part 1, 365,368 litres needs to be input into production. A further 30,000 litres are needed to increase the stock level (from 50,000 litres to 80,000 litres).

This means that (365,368 + 30,000) = 395,368 litres are needed after evaporation in storage.

Since the evaporation in storage is estimated at 3% of the amount initially acquired, the above amount that we need must represent 97% of the amount that we must purchase.

We therefore need to purchase (395,368 x 100 ÷ 97) = 407,596 litres

COMPREHENSIVE PROBLEMS

The techniques examined so far may arise in combination to create a more complex situation. This is not more difficult − it just means that you will need to deal with each complexity separately, checking your logic as you go, and re-working the problem in the opposite direction as necessary. The next Case Study involves several of the problems that we have dealt with previously, combined into one situation.

CASE STUDY

FOOD IN FOIL LIMITED:
A COMPREHENSIVE PROBLEM

Food in Foil Limited processes pears that are sold in foil packs to the catering industry. The process starts with the purchase of whole fresh pears that are peeled and cored before cooking. The cooked pears are then sealed into foil packs.

During peeling and coring 25% of the weight of the whole pears is lost, and a further 10% of the weight of the uncooked pears (after peeling and coring) is lost during the cooking due to evaporation. The foil packs are inspected after production, and it is estimated that 1% will be rejected due to splits or inadequate seals.

The forecast sales level for October is 180,000 kilos of finished product. Stocks of finished goods are budgeted at 30,000 kilos at 30 September and 50,475 kilos at 31 October.

Stocks of raw pears are budgeted at 5,000 kilos at 30 September and 1,000 kilos at 31 October.

Each 1,000 kilos of finished product was originally expected to take 6 direct labour hours to produce. However, the company is currently employing inexperienced workers, and they are working more slowly than the original standards predicted. They are now expected to work at 81% efficiency during October (i.e. they will only produce 81% of the standard output during their working time).

Raw pears are expected to cost £1 per kilo, and the rate of pay for direct labour is £5 per hour.

required

Calculate the following budgets for October:

1   Production in kilos of the finished product.

2   Material usage in kilos of raw pears and £.

3   Materials purchases in kilos of raw pears and £.

4   Labour utilisation in hours and £.

solution

1   Production in kilos of the finished product

The amount of finished production that passes the quality control check will need to be:

Budgeted Sales (kilos)	180,000
– Opening Stock of Finished Product	(30,000)
+ Closing Stock of Finished Product	50,475
= production of 'good' finished product	200,475 kilos

This amount will equal 99% of the total production to allow for the rejection of 1%. The total production must therefore be:

200,475 x 100 ÷ 99 = 202,500 kilos of finished product

2 Material usage in kilos of raw pears and £

To calculate the amount of pears that are to be used in production, we must work back from the amount of finished product, stage by stage.

The 202,500 kilos calculated in 1 (above) will be after:
- the evaporation of 10% of the cored and peeled pears
- the wastage of 25% of the raw pears

Dealing with the evaporation, the input of cored and peeled pears must be:

202,500 x 100 ÷ 90 = 225,000 kilos

The coring and peeling will also need to be accounted for. The input of raw pears (i.e. the materials utilisation) must be:

225,000 x 100 ÷ 75 = 300,000 kilos

At £1 per kilo this will cost £300,000

3 Materials purchases in kilos of raw pears and £

The materials purchases budget will allow for the changing stocks of raw pears.

Materials Usage (kilos raw pears)	300,000
– Opening Stock of raw pears	(5,000)
+ Closing Stock of raw pears	1,000
= Raw pears to be purchased	296,000 kilos.

At £1 per kilo this will cost £296,000.

4 Labour utilisation in hours and £

The amount of labour needed is based on the production budget. At normal efficiency the requirement would be:

202,500 kilos x 6 hours ÷ 1,000 = 1,215 hours.

Since they are working at 81% efficiency, the actual input of direct labour hours (the labour utilisation budget) will be:
1,215 x 100 ÷ 81 = 1,500 hours
These will cost 1,500 x £5 = £7,500

DEALING WITH LIMITED MATERIALS

Sometimes an organisation finds that it cannot obtain the amount of materials that it had planned to purchase. This could be due to a worldwide shortage, or to a more localised problem, perhaps just with the organisation's usual supplier. The problems with supplies could be simply temporary, or relate to a longer-term situation that is developing.

The range of tactics that can be used to overcome or lessen the effect of such problems include the following, which can be used individually or in combination:

- **Utilising raw material stocks.** The planned production can sometimes be maintained by simply running down raw material stocks. This will only work in the short term, and will depend on the current raw material stock level.

- **Utilising finished goods stocks.** If production needs to be reduced due to limited raw materials, sales may still be maintained if there are sufficient finished goods in stock. This can also only be effective as a temporary measure.

- **Finding an alternative supplier.** This may be an obvious solution, although there may be cost implications, as well as quality considerations.

- **Substituting an alternative material.** Although some products can only be made from one material, for others there may be alternatives that could be used. Implications may include material cost and quality, as well as usage levels, including wastage. The labour force may also work less efficiently, and the suitability of current machinery and equipment would need to be considered.

- **Reformulating the product.** Changing the formula for manufacture can be carried out so that less of the raw material that is in short supply will be used. Clearly the quality of the finished item would have to be carefully considered, and the customers would need to accept the revised specification. This may involve using more of other raw materials to compensate.

- **Buying in finished goods.** This may be a possibility, although it begs the question of where the supplier of those goods obtained their raw materials. This solution would imply reducing in-house production, and losing profit. The organisation's manufacturing facilities would be under utilised, and the labour force may need to be laid off unless an alternative product could be made on the premises.

- **Manufacturing an alternative product using different materials.** This may involve major changes in the whole production process. If it is to be a substitute for the previous product the new product must be designed and marketed to meet the same need, and customers will have to be persuaded of its merits.

CASE STUDY

THE ZEDFIN COMPANY:
DECISIONS OVER MATERIALS

A company currently manufactures its product 'Zedfin' entirely from a raw material 'Xeraw'. The material has a standard cost of £9.00 per kilo, and there is 10% wastage in the production process. After this wastage is accounted for, every completed kilo of Zedfin contains one kilo of Zeraw.

The sales budget for April is for 150,000 kilos of Zedfin, and the original planned stock levels are as follows:

	Xeraw	Zedfin
Stock 31 March	20,000 kilos	42,000 kilos
Stock 30 April	15,000 kilos	35,000 kilos

The company has been notified that there will be no Xeraw available from their usual supplier during April. The decision has therefore been made to satisfy as many expected sales as possible by running down the stocks of both Xeraw and Zedfin to zero. There are then two alternatives for satisfying the remaining demand:

- Purchase Xeraw from an alternative supplier at £11.70 per kilo, *or*

- Purchase an alternative material 'Wyeraw' at £10.80 per kilo.
  This will not affect the quality of Zedfin, but the raw material wastage is expected to be higher at 20%.

required

1 Calculate the sales (in kilos) that could be achieved by running down all stocks to zero, and work out the sales shortfall that remains.

2 Calculate which is the most cost effective of the two alternatives for making further Zedfin.

3 Calculate the quantity of raw material to be purchased, based on your answer to 2, assuming all closing stocks remain at zero.

4 Calculate the additional cost that the company will incur for raw materials due to the shortage if your advice is followed.

solution

1 Sales and shortfall calculation (kilos of Zedfin)

Sales are expected to be 150,000 kilos Zedfin

This can be partly satisfied by:

- Using existing Zedfin stocks providing 42,000 kilos Zedfin.
- We could use the opening stock of Xeraw to produce (20,000 x 90%)

  = 18,000 kilos of Zedfin.

This leaves a shortfall of 90,000 kilos Zedfin

2 Which alternative for producing Zedfin is the more cost-effective?

Using Xeraw from alternative supplier, the cost would be:

£11.70 x 100 ÷ 90 = £13.00 per kilo of Zedfin
(allowing for 10% wastage)

Using the alternative Wyeraw, the cost would be:

£10.80 x 100 ÷ 80 = £13.50 per kilo of Zedfin
(allowing for 20% wastage)

These calculations take account of the fact that we would need to buy additional material to take account of wastage. The costs are expressed in cost per kilo of finished product to make comparison easier.

Using Xeraw from the alternative supplier is the cheaper of the two options based on the information given.

3 Extra raw materials needed

To manufacture sufficient Zedfin to make up the shortfall in sales calculated in part 1 (above) we would need:

(90,000 x 100 ÷ 90) = 100,000 kilos of Xeraw from the alternative supplier.

4 Cost of extra raw materials

The additional cost would be:

100,000 kilos Xeraw x (£11.70 – £9.00 per kilo) = £270,000.

DEALING WITH LIMITED LABOUR

Where labour is in limited supply a range of alternative solutions are possible. Appropriate labour can usually be obtained eventually, even if it means paying a high rate and/or investing substantial amounts in training. Because of this, labour shortage problems are typically short-term ones. The range of ways to deal with a labour shortage include:

- **Overtime working.** Although this probably involves paying a premium rate it is a logical way to tackle a temporary problem.

- **Utilising finished goods stocks.** If production needs to be reduced due to limited availability of labour, sales may still be maintained if there are sufficient finished goods in stock. In the same way as dealing with a stock shortage, this can also only be effective as a temporary measure.

- **Using sub-contractors.** This could include self-employed or agency staff within the factory, or possibly sub-contracting parts of the production process to another organisation and location. The latter may be a major decision with other implications. Any use of sub-contractors will have cost implications, although the responsibility for work quality may also lie with the sub-contractor, which may offset some of the disadvantages.

- **Buying-in finished goods.** This would be a major decision, and would have to be carefully costed. The loss of control over the production process would have to be considered, including quality issues and reliability of supply. It may also leave the organisation's own premises under-utilised.

- **Improving labour efficiency.** Although probably only a very limited change could be made in the short term, in the longer term training or better equipment may improve efficiency. Internal or external experts may be able to direct the organisation as to the best way to maximise the output of its labour force.

DEALING WITH LIMITED PRODUCTION CAPACITY

When demand for an organisation's products is likely to outstrip its capacity to supply then the likely solutions will depend on whether the problem is believed to be permanent or temporary.

permanent inability to supply

Permanent inability to supply sufficient goods to customers can be solved by the organisation:

- increasing capacity by expanding premises or relocating

- increasing selling prices to reduce demand (and increase profit)
- sub-contracting or buying-in finished goods

temporary inability to supply

There may be temporary capacity problems caused either by:

- unexpected demand, or
- regular seasonal variations in demand

These factors can be dealt with by application of the following techniques:

- **Manipulating finished goods stock levels.** The most logical technique is to utilise spare capacity when it exists to build up stock to deal with higher demand. The stock can be used as a contingency against unexpected demand, or in anticipation of seasonal peaks. The cost of holding excess stocks should not be overlooked.

- **Shift working.** This will have the effect of spreading the fixed overheads over a greater production level, and therefore reducing the indirect cost per unit. The direct labour cost may increase through shift premium payments, and the net effect on costs would have to be calculated carefully.

- **Renting temporary premises or additional equipment.** There may be additional costs in these approaches that would need to be considered.

- **Sub-contracting, or buying in finished goods, or improving efficiency.** The implications are as discussed previously when examining materials and labour shortages (pages 236 and 239).

CASE STUDY

THE CAPACITY COMPANY: DEALING WITH CAPACITY PROBLEMS

The Capacity Company has a maximum production capacity of 50,000 units per month. This is based on its direct labour employees working 8-hour days, five days per week, and fully utilising all the current equipment during that time.

The estimated demand for the product over the next three months is:

January	45,000 units
February	42,000 units
March	60,000 units.

There will be no finished goods stocks at the beginning of January.
Each completed unit requires 0.5 hour of direct labour. Labour cost is normally £6 per hour.

Three options are being examined to overcome the capacity problem in March:

1 Produce additional finished goods during the earlier two months.
  This will incur additional financing costs of £1 per unit for each month that the production is brought forward.

2   Pay the direct labour force overtime to complete the additional production in March. Overtime is paid at a rate of time and one half.

3   Bring in agency workers to work alongside the normal labour force during March. The agency rate is £8.50 per hour, but additional equipment will also need to be hired for £500 for the month.

required

Calculate the additional cost of producing the units required in comparison with the normal production cost, based on each of the three options, and identify the cheapest solution.

solution

Option 1 – producing additional goods in earlier months

Due to the nature of the financing cost, it will be cheapest to bring forward production by the least amount. Therefore February production should be increased to capacity first, followed by January.

This means that:

February production will increase by 8,000 units, Costing an additional 8,000 x 1 month x £1	= £8,000
January production will increase by 2,000 units Costing an additional 2,000 x 2 months x £1	= £4,000
Total additional cost for the 10,000 units in comparison with normal production costs.	= £12,000

Option 2 – paying overtime in March

Additional cost of overtime premium payment is: 10,000 units x 0.5 hours x £6.00 x 1/2	= £15,000

Option 3 – bringing in agency workers in March

Agency workers time required (10,000 units x 0.5 hour) = 5,000 hours	
Additional Cost = 5,000 x (£8.50 - £6.00)	£12,500
Additional Cost of Equipment Hire	£500
Total additional cost	£13,000

conclusion

The cheapest and recommended solution is to use Option 1, producing

45,000 + 2,000 =	47,000 units in January,
42,000 + 8,000 =	50,000 units in February,
and	50,000 units in March.

**CHAPTER
SUMMARY**

- When preparing budgets we must accurately account for rejection of finished goods, a labour force that is not operating at 100% efficiency, or wastage of materials that occurs during or before production. In each situation care must be taken to allow for the correct quantity of unusable resources.

- The expected level of rejection of finished goods that are not up to standard is allowed for when the production budget is prepared. An additional amount of production is planned so that once goods have been scrapped there is still sufficient to sell and place in stock.

- Any expected over or under efficiency of the direct labour force is built into the labour utilisation budget so that the amount of productive working will be sufficient to meet the needs of the production budget.

- Planned wastage of raw materials during production is built into the materials utilisation budget. In this way the plan is modified to input additional materials to allow for the situation. Where the wastage is expected to occur before production, the materials purchases budget must be modified so that there will be enough materials to be used in production, once wastage and stock movements have taken place.

- Situations may develop where an organisation cannot obtain sufficient resources to produce the level of output that it requires. This may involve shortages of materials or labour, or a limitation on production capacity. The situation may be perceived to short or longer term and this will influence the choice of tactic adopted. The possible solutions range from changing production schedules to buying in completed goods, but all alternatives would need to be carefully evaluated before a choice was made.

**KEY
TERMS**

production budget	A budget that plans how much should be produced in a particular period, to allow for anticipated sales, stock movements of finished goods, and rejections due to poor quality.
labour utilisation budget	A budget that details the labour input required to meet the needs of the production budget.
materials usage budget	A budget that plans the amount of materials that is required to satisfy the production budget, after allowing for wastage during production.

materials purchases budget	A budget that plans for the level of purchases needed to meet the demands of the materials utilisation budget, as well as allowing for wastage before production and changing stock levels.
production capacity	The maximum that can be produced based on the current resources and working practices.

STUDENT
ACTIVITIES

The answers to these Student Activities are printed in the back of this book. Further questions and more fully extended Student Activities and Assessments are to be found in the accompanying Osborne Books' text *Managing Costs & Resources Workbook.*

9.1 State which budget should be used to take account of each of the following anticipated situations.

(a)   Reduction in finished goods stocks.

(b)   Deterioration of raw materials whilst in storage.

(c)   Rejection of finished goods at final inspection.

(d)   Spillage of raw materials during production.

(e)   Direct Labour working at 80% standard efficiency level.

(f)   Increased demand for finished goods.

(g)   Increase in raw material stocks.

9.2 The Super Soup Company needs 50 kg of prepared carrots as an ingredient in a one tonne batch of soup. During preparation 20% of the weight of the raw unprepared carrots is lost in peel and imperfections. What should the unprepared carrots utilisation budget be (in kilos) for week 15, when 30 tonnes of soup are to be made?

(a)   7,500 kg

(b)   1,800 kg

(c)   1,875 kg

(d)   1,200 kg

9.3 The sales budget for A B Wainwright Limited's product is 13,000 units in April, 15,000 units in May, and 20,000 units in June. The company policy is to plan for month end finished goods stocks of half of the following month's sales demand. All goods are inspected upon completion, and at this point an estimated 12.5% of finished goods are scrapped due to faults.

Required

Calculate the production budget for May in numbers of units.

9.4 The Auto Protection Company makes car bumpers using plastic pellets that are heated and mounded. Each completed bumper contains 4 kilos of plastic.

The sales requirement for week 9 is for 37,500 bumpers, and the finished goods stock is planned at 10,000 at the start of week 9, and 2,425 at the end of week 9.

All bumpers are inspected for defects at the end of the production process, and an estimated 5% of production are scrapped at that point, and immediately sold to the pellet manufacturer for recycling.

There is 10% wastage of plastic during the production process, and the stocks of plastic pellets are planned as 20,000 kilos at the start of week 9 and 30,000 kilos at the end of week 9.

Required

Calculate the following budgets for week 9:

(a)   Production (in numbers of bumpers)

(b)   Bumper rejects for sale to pellet manufacturer (in numbers)

(c)   Plastic pellet usage (in kilos)

(d)   Plastic pellet purchases (in kilos).

9.5 The Pie in the Sky Company buys in raw whole apples to use in its apple pies. Each cooked pie must contain 0.4 kilos of apple. Demand in October is forecast at 150,000 pies. Raw whole apples are expected to cost £0.60 per kilo.

The process operates as follows:

Raw whole apples are taken from the stores and peeled, cored and any blemishes removed. This involves a loss of 20% of the weight of the whole apples.

The apples are put into the raw pies and cooked. The heat causes a loss of 25% of the weight of the uncooked prepared apples.

There are not expected to be any rejected pies following cooking.

Stocks are planned at the following levels:

	Raw Whole Apples	Cooked Pies
30 September	10,000 kg	10,000 pies
31 October	15,000 kg	2,500 pies

Required

Calculate the following budgets for October.

(a)   Apple pie production (numbers of pies)

(b)   Raw whole apple usage (in kilos and £)

(c)   Raw whole apple purchases (in kilos and £).

9.6 A manufacturer has a temporary shortage of direct labour. Consideration is being given to either using overtime working of the remaining staff, or sub contracting part of the manufacturing process to another organisation.

Suggest possible advantages and disadvantages of each approach.

9.7 The Mindup Manufacturing Company has a normal production level of 65,000 units per week. However it can exceed this level by paying the direct labour force at overtime rates for additional output up to a maximum capacity of 80,000 units per week. Each direct labour hour costs £8 (based on normal working), and produces 20 units of output. The overtime premium payable is 50% of the usual rate.

Normally production is carried out in the same week as the units are sold, but if production is carried out in advance of sales there is an additional financing cost of £150 per thousand units for each week that production is brought forward. This cost applies proportionally to volumes of less than one thousand.

The sales demand for weeks 10 – 14 is forecast as follows:

Week 10	60,000 units
Week 11	65,000 units
Week 12	62,000 units
Week 13	70,000 units
Week 14	75,000 units

Required

(a) Calculate the additional cost per unit of:

    (i) producing the unit at overtime rates, or

    (ii) producing the unit one week before it is to be sold.

(b) Use the information produced in (a) to calculate

    (i) an optimal production schedule for each week in numbers of units, and

    (ii) the total additional cost that will be incurred by using that schedule, compared to normal production costs.

10 APPLICATIONS OF BUDGETING METHODS

NVQ PERFORMANCE CRITERIA COVERED

unit 9: CONTRIBUTING TO THE PLANNING AND ALLOCATION OF RESOURCES

element 2: prepare forecasts of income and expenditure

- *relevant individuals are given the opportunity to raise queries and to clarify forecasts*
- *forecasts are produced in a clear format with explanations of assumptions, projections and adjustments*
- *the validity of forecasts is reviewed in the light of any significant anticipated changes*

element 2: produce draft budget proposals

- *draft budget proposals are presented to management in a clear and appropriate format and on schedule*
- *draft budget proposals are consistent with organisational objectives, have taken all relevant data into account and are agreed with budget holders*
- *discussions with budget holders are conducted in a manner which maintains goodwill*

element 3: monitor the performance of responsibility centres against budgets

● *budget figures are checked and reconciled on an ongoing basis*

● *actual cost and revenue data are correctly coded and allocated to responsibility centres*

● *variances are clearly identified and reported to management in routine reports*

● *significant variances are discussed with managers and assistance is given to managers to take remedial action*

APPLICATIONS OF BUDGETING

In Chapter 8, we considered the purposes of budgeting and the steps involved in budget preparation. The calculations in Chapter 8 show how budgets can be prepared for the main activities of an organisation, starting from forecasts for sales and allowing for limitations imposed by the key budget factor.

Chapter 9 developed further the calculations for production budgets, and hence for materials usage, purchases and labour utilisation budgets.

In this chapter, we examine various methods which can be used as the basis for the preparation of budgets, either as the principles on which all budgets are based, or particularly for functional budgets such as the administration budget. Functional departments which support the main operations of the organisation may not be so dependent on sales levels. Budgeting in non-profit-making organisations also requires a different approach, as starting from forecasts of demand may not be appropriate.

The methods to be considered are:

• incremental budgeting

• zero base budgeting

• programme based budgeting

INCREMENTAL BUDGETING

Incremental budgeting is a traditional method, widely used in commercial organisations and in the public sector. Incremental budgeting means

basing the budget for a department or function on that of the previous period, usually adjusting for inflation by a percentage increase.

Specific changes, such as a planned expansion or reduction in activities, would also be allowed for. In some cases the previous year's actual costs may be used as a starting point, rather than the budget, particularly if the actual costs were lower.

practical example

Quenchit Ltd is a water bottling company. Transport costs for last year amounted to £120,000. Planned expansion is expected to result in £10,000 additional transport costs (estimated at current prices). Inflation is expected to be 3%.

The transport budget for the next year could be based on:

£120,000 + £10,000 = £130,000 to allow for expansion,

then £130,000 x 103% = £133,900 to allow for inflation.

advantages of incremental budgeting

The **advantages** of the incremental budgeting method are:

- the budget is stable and change is gradual and planned
- managers can operate their departments on a consistent basis
- the system is relatively simple to operate and easy to understand
- conflicts should be avoided if departments can be seen to be treated similarly, and coordination between budgets is easier to achieve
- the impact of change can be seen quickly

disadvantages of incremental budgeting

There are, however, a number of **criticisms** of this method:

- incremental budgeting assumes activities and methods of working will continue in the same way, giving no incentive for developing new ideas
- there is no incentive to try to reduce costs – on the contrary, spending up to the budget is encouraged by this method, so that next year the level of budget is maintained
- the budgets may become out of date, and no longer relate to the level of activity or the type of work being carried out
- the priority for resources may have changed since the budgets were set originally
- there may be 'budgetary slack' built in to the budgets, which is never reviewed – this means that managers have overestimated their requirements in the past, in order to obtain a budget which is easier to work to, and which will allow them to achieve favourable results

For example . . . a city council using incremental budgeting would continue to budget at the same level, increased for inflation, for hospitality and catering relating to meetings, visitors and so on. This would encourage staff to spend up to the budget, even if the number and timing of meetings or visits changed. There would be no incentive to review catering provision or to look for more cost-effective ways of providing suitable hospitality.

Because of these problems, which can occur in a similar way throughout an organisation, the incremental approach may not lead to the best use of its resources. A department which has had a large share of the total funds available over a number of years may no longer be as important to the organisation, whereas newer departments which are gradually increasing in importance will need a greater share.

ZERO BASE BUDGETING (ZBB)

Zero base budgeting is a method which was developed in the 1970s with a view to eliminating some of the problems of incremental budgeting. It takes the opposite view: instead of assuming everything will continue as before, the focus is on achieving the organisation's objectives in the most efficient way. Zero Base Budgeting means

The budget for each budget centre starts from a base of zero for each period. Budgets for proposed activities are then put forward, assessed and prioritised (in relation to the organisation's objectives) and allocated funds in order of priority.

The stages in the process are as follows:

- the functions of the organisation are analysed to identify the structure of departments to be used as budget centres
- the work of each department (budget centre) is then analysed to identify the activities actually carried out
- starting from a base of zero, budgets are prepared in each budget centre, showing the costs and benefits of the work of the department; these budgets show the expected results at several different levels of activity and are called 'decision packages'
- the decision packages must then be judged by managers and put in order according to how efficiently they contribute towards the organisation's objectives
- the total funds available are allocated to decision packages in order of priority, thus deciding which activities are to be carried out and at what level – if a particular activity is obsolete or contributing nothing, it will receive no funds and will be discontinued.

advantages of zero base budgeting

The advantages of the zero base budgeting method are:

- this system focuses the use of resources on achieving the organisation's objectives
- budget centre managers have to re-evaluate in detail the cost-effectiveness of the working methods and results achieved in their departments
- new projects are compared with existing work, so that innovation is encouraged, rather than assuming existing activities must continue
- allocation of resources is linked to the achievement of results
- wastage and budgetary slack should be eliminated, because budgets which are not cost-effective will not be given funds
- planning and budgeting is combined into a single process when the decision packages to be funded are chosen

disadvantages of zero base budgeting

Zero base budgeting is also criticised, because:

- the process itself is very complex and therefore costly to operate
- by separating different activities, links between them may not be allowed for, leading to an uncoordinated approach
- short-term benefits may be emphasised in the decision packages, to the detriment of long-term planning
- the process of judging and prioritising the decision packages may be extremely difficult and it may be affected by the internal politics of the organisation, so that it is not really objective

Zero base budgeting can only be applied where different levels of a particular type of work are possible and where the costs and benefits can be identified. Therefore it is more likely to be appropriate for service departments or service organisations and for non-profit-making organisations than for direct cost budgets in manufacturing. As we have seen in Chapter 8, direct cost budgets are more dependent on forecasts of demand for products and can be justified on that basis. Priorities may change, however, between service departments, making a review starting from a base of zero a useful tool.

For example, maintenance of machinery will need a greater share of funds when an organisation is highly automated, and if there is a corresponding reduction in the workforce, it will reduce the necessity for a large personnel department.

Zero base budgeting can be applied to **'discretionary' costs**, where the level of expenditure and the methods to be used can be decided by managers.

For example:

- training costs: decisions can be made between 'packages' detailing the costs and benefits of in-house training, computer-based training, day release and block release, at different levels
- advertising: decisions can be made between 'packages' detailing the expected benefits from different levels of expenditure, using various methods of advertising, particularly where new opportunities such as websites become available and older methods may become less effective
- credit control: decisions can be made between 'packages' detailing the costs of different levels of activity – increasing the activity would mean more frequent checks and chasing of debtors and hence better control – for each control level, the financial benefits in terms of reducing finance costs and avoiding bad debts would be estimated and compared with the costs

PROGRAMME BASED BUDGETING

Programme based budgeting is a method which is applicable to non-profit-making organisations. Programme based budgeting means

breaking down the work of the organisation into 'programmes' designed towards achieving its various objectives.

Several departments within the organisation may contribute towards a single programme. The total funds available are shared between the programmes, rather than being split into budgets for departments.

It is usually the case that insufficient funds are available to achieve all the desired objectives, and decisions have to be made as to which programmes are to be carried out and what level of work can be supported. The choice of programmes should ensure that cost-effective methods are used, to achieve as much as possible (in terms of the organisation's objectives) with the total funds available.

practical examples

A **local authority** may decide to allocate funds to a programme designed to improve services to elderly people. This may include work from the housing department on security and insulation, an allocation of funding towards increased transport subsidies, input from the social services department to improve day care, and so on. It would be necessary to prepare a budget for the programme as a whole, broken down into budgets for costs of each aspect of the programme.

A **charity** may have money donated to help alleviate famine in a particular area. Decisions may be made between immediate relief programmes and longer-term programmes to provide clean water, support for agriculture and education.

COST BEHAVIOUR AND BUDGETS

When setting budgets it is essential to take into account how costs behave in relation to the amount of work which is to be carried out. It is impossible to prepare a realistic budget for a particular amount of work unless it is known whether, for example, costs remain fixed, increase steadily or go up in steps as the amount of work increases. The measurement of an amount of work is usually referred to as the 'level of activity' and it must be measured in appropriate cost units for the type of work involved.

In manufacturing, numbers of units produced can be used as a measure of level of activity. In other types of organisation, the cost units used must relate to the work being done, for example miles travelled in a transport business, or occupied room-days in a hotel.

fixed and flexed budgets

When the level of activity changes, it is expected that the total of all costs (and the total income) will change. Information about how each type of cost behaves will enable budgets to be adjusted for different levels of activity. A budget for one specific level of activity is referred to as 'fixed'. A budget adjusted for a change in level of activity is called a 'flexed' or 'flexible' budget. If actual results are to be compared with budgets for the purposes of performance measurement, such adjustments would be necessary to ensure that the comparison is of 'like with like', as emphasised in Chapter 6.

In variance analysis, studied in Chapters 2, 3 and 4, we compare the actual results with the standard cost of actual output, which is a flexed budget where standard costing is being used.

practical example

If a budget is set in a manufacturing business for production of 10,000 units of a product, then it will not be applicable if production changes to 11,000 units or to 9,000 units. With information about how each part of the cost may change (or not) in relation to production, new adjusted budgets can be prepared for 11,000 units and 9,000 units. These are the 'flexed' or 'flexible' budgets as opposed to a single level 'fixed' budget.

A manager of a department which produced 11,000 units of a product would not expect the costs to be measured against those for making 10,000 units. Fair comparison would be with the flexed budget for 11,000 units. This is the principle of comparing 'like with like' as discussed in Chapter 6.

If standard costing and variance analysis were being used in this business, variances would be calculated as the difference between the total actual costs and the total standard costs for the 11,000 units of actual output.

Cost behaviour is examined in Chapter 1 for the purposes of marginal costing. Marginal costing depends on being able to split costs into their fixed and variable parts. In marginal costing, the cost of each unit of output is based on variable costs only, the fixed costs being regarded as time based and linked to the accounting period.

The main types of cost behaviour which you will be expected to apply in preparing flexed budgets are:

- variable costs
- fixed costs
- step costs
- semi-variable costs

variable costs

A cost is described as variable if the total cost varies in direct proportion to the level of activity. In other words, it depends on the number of cost units, the amount per unit being constant.

Total variable cost = variable cost per unit x number of units

For example:

Quenchit Ltd is a water bottling company. The cost to the company of the bottles used is £0.08 each. The total cost of bottles varies in proportion to the number of bottles used and is therefore a variable cost.

Total cost of bottles = £0.08 x number of bottles used.

A graph showing the behaviour of the total cost against level of activity is shown below.

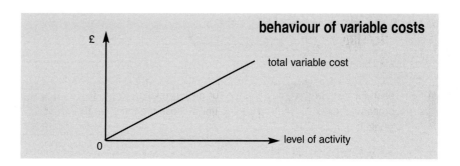

In some cases, the cost per unit may remain constant only within a certain relevant range of levels of activity. Large changes in the number of units produced may alter the cost per unit and hence the behaviour of the total cost. For example, the cost per unit of direct materials may be reduced by bulk purchase discounts when larger amounts are required.

**CASE
STUDY**

KANN LIMITED:
VARIABLE COSTS

Kann Ltd manufactures metal boxes. The total cost of direct materials is £42,000 for making 350,000 boxes and £51,600 for making 430,000 boxes.

required

1   Calculate Kann Ltd's direct material cost per unit at each of the given levels of output and hence determine whether it behaves as a variable cost.

2   Calculate the total cost of direct materials for making 400,000 boxes.

solution

1   £42,000 for 350,000 boxes: £42,000 ÷ 350,000   =   £0.12 per box

£51,600 for 430,000 boxes: £51,600 ÷ 430,000   =   £0.12 per box

Therefore direct material cost is a constant amount per unit and hence behaves as a variable cost. We can assume it is £0.12 per box for output between 350,000 boxes and 430,000 boxes.

2   Output of 400,000 boxes is within this range.

Total variable cost = variable cost per unit x number of units

For 400,000 boxes:

Total direct material cost = £0.12 x 400,000 = £48,000.

fixed costs

A cost is described as fixed if the total cost does not change when the level of activity changes.

The fixed nature of the cost will only apply when the level of activity changes within a certain relevant range. If major changes occur, such as doubling production or ceasing to make a product, then all costs are likely to change.

Rent is an example of a fixed cost, because once rent is paid to have space available, changes in the amount of work carried out in that space will not affect the total rent. The relevant range would cover the amounts of work possible within the space available. The rent would change if the amount of work increased beyond this capacity.

Notice that in defining fixed costs, we are not referring to costs remaining unchanged from one time period to another. All costs will eventually change over periods of time. A graph showing the behaviour of the total cost against level of activity for a fixed cost is shown below.

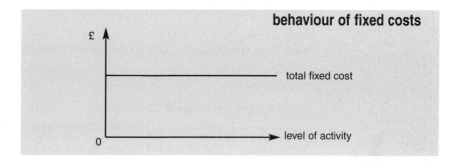

behaviour of fixed costs

step costs

A cost is described as a step cost if its total changes in steps at certain levels of activity, remaining unchanged in between.

The name clearly corresponds to the graph showing the behaviour of the total cost against level of activity for a step cost – see below.

Costs which behave as step costs are often related to machines or people who can deal with any number of units of work, up to a maximum number. When the maximum is reached, an additional machine or person is required.

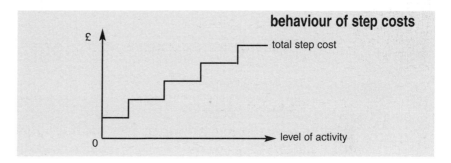

behaviour of step costs

practical examples

A **pre-school nursery** requires one carer for every six children. For more than six and up to twelve children, two carers are required. For thirteen, another carer must be employed, and so on. The total cost of carers' wages will behave as a step cost.

The **reprographics department** of a large organisation uses photocopiers which are leased. Each machine can produce 10,000 copies in a given period. If the organisation's requirements go above 10,000 for the period, another machine will be leased. The total cost of leasing photocopiers will behave as a step cost.

semi-variable costs

A cost is described as semi-variable (or sometimes semi-fixed) if the total cost is made up of a variable part and a fixed part.

Any cost which consists of a fixed charge plus an amount per unit is a semi-variable cost. Telephone bills may be of this form: a fixed line rental plus a variable amount dependent on the number of minutes of call time, for example.

Total semi-variable cost =

Fixed cost + (variable cost per unit x number of units)

The graph showing the behaviour of the total cost against level of activity for a semi-variable cost is shown in the graph below. The calculation is illustrated in the Case Study on the next page.

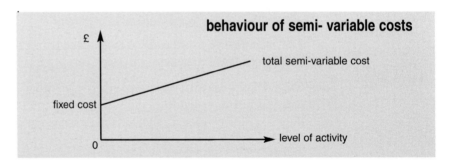

limitations of cost behaviour analysis

The four kinds of cost behaviour described above are not the only possible cost behaviour patterns. In some cases, the actual behaviour of the cost may only approximate to one of these patterns, but useful information can still be obtained using the approximation. Also, a particular pattern of behaviour may only be applicable within a certain relevant range of levels of activity, but again useful information can be obtained within that range.

Using a pattern of behaviour to calculate costs for a level of activity within a given range is called 'interpolation'. Calculations for levels outside the range involve 'extrapolation' and careful consideration must be given to the usefulness of the information obtained in this case, because it may not be realistic to assume that the pattern of behaviour will continue beyond the given range.

The assumption underlying marginal costing is that all costs behave as fixed, variable or semi-variable costs, so that the total of all costs of an organisation can be split into fixed and variable parts. Provided that this assumption is realistic over a relevant range of levels of activity, then useful information can be obtained.

CASE STUDY

MILLIE LIMITED: SEMI-VARIABLE COSTS

Production overheads in a manufacturing company have been identified as semi-variable. They consist of fixed costs of £120,000 plus £2.80 per unit produced, for a range of levels of production from 15,000 units to 30,000 units for the period.

required

Calculate the total production overheads for

1   20,000 units

2   24,500 units

Why would the same calculation be inappropriate for 40,000 units?

solution

1   Total production overheads for 20,000 units would be:

   £120,000 + (£2.80 x 20,000)

   =   £120,000 + £56,000

   =   £176,000

2   Total production overheads for 24,500 units would be:

   £120,000 + (£2.80 x 24,500)

   = £120,000 + £68,600

   = £188,600

The part of the calculation in brackets is the variable part of the cost, which depends on the number of units.

It would not be realistic to use this data and this method to calculate the total production overheads for 40,000 units, because that level of activity is beyond the relevant range. We cannot assume the same cost behaviour outside the range.

The following graph illustrates the behaviour of the total cost in this Case Study.

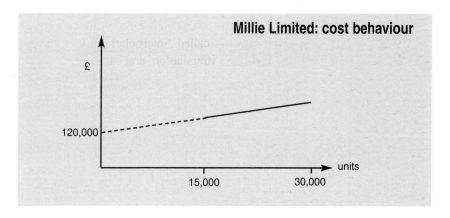

the high-low method

It is important to be able to split a semi-variable cost into its fixed and variable parts in order to prepare a flexible budget. The fixed part will remain unchanged and the variable part can be calculated for a different level of activity. The method you will be expected to use to analyse a semi-variable cost is the 'High-Low' method, which may be familiar to you from your earlier studies.

The high-low method can be used where the total of a semi-variable cost is known for at least two different activity levels. If the total is known for more than two levels, then the highest and lowest are chosen for the calculation.

The Case Study that follows illustrates the high-low method.

**CASE
STUDY**

HILO PRODUCTS
THE HIGH LOW METHOD

Hilo Products makes ladders. We are given the total of a semi-variable cost at four different levels of activity, as follows:

Level of activity (units)	400	650	800	900
Total cost (£)	6,200	6,950	7,400	7,700

First we identify the lowest and highest totals, which are:

£6,200 for 400 units and £7,700 for 900 units.

To calculate the variable cost per unit, we use the fact that the extra cost has been caused by the variable cost of the extra units. That is:

	Cost		Units	
High	£7,700		900	
Low	£6,200		400	
Difference	£1,500	÷	500	= £3 per unit

Using £3 per unit, we then calculate the variable part of the cost for 400 units:

£3 x 400 = £1,200

But the total cost for 400 units is £6,200

Therefore the fixed part (which is the same for any number of units)

= £6,200 – £1,200 = £5,000

We can now check the solution by calculating the total cost for 900 units, using our answers:

Total cost = Fixed cost + (variable cost per unit x number of units)

= £5,000 + (£3 x 900)

= £5,000 + £2,700

= £7,700 which agrees with the original data.

The following graph illustrates the behaviour of the total cost in this Case Study. The variable cost per unit determines the gradient (slope) of the line, and the fixed cost is shown where the line cuts the vertical axis. The total costs for 650 units and 800 units lie exactly on the line, but in some cases the points between the high and low may not fit exactly. The high-low method still gives useful information provided that the cost behaviour is approximately semi-variable – that is provided that all the points are approximately in a straight line.

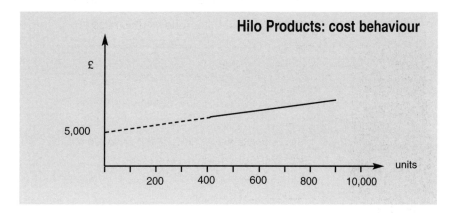

Now check your understanding of this subject by reading through the summary below and following through the practical example on the next page.

high-low method summary

1   identify the highest and lowest cost totals and their levels of activity

2   calculate the difference between the two cost totals

3   calculate the difference in cost units between the two levels of activity

4   divide the difference in cost by the difference in units: this gives the variable cost per unit

5   use the variable cost per unit to calculate the variable part of one of the cost totals

6   deduct the variable part from the cost total to obtain the fixed part

7   check the answers by using them to calculate the other cost total, which should agree with the given data

practical worked example

required

Calculate the fixed and variable parts of the semi-variable cost which behaves as follows:

Total cost for 6,400 units is £136,000

Total cost for 9,900 units is £162,250

solution

- Only two levels are given, high and low
- Difference in total cost = £162,250 - £136,000 = £26,250
- Difference in number of units = 9,900 – 6,400 = 3,500
- Variable cost per unit = £26,250 ÷ 3,500 = £7.50
- Variable part for 6,400 units = £7.50 x 6,400 = £48,000
- Fixed part = £136,000 - £48,000 = £88,000
- Check your answer £88,000 + (£7.50 x 9,900) = £162,250

The high-low method is used in the preparation of flexed budgets, because once the fixed cost and the variable cost per unit have been calculated, the total semi-variable cost for any level of activity (within a suitable range) can be found.

For example, if we require the total cost for 7,300 units in the worked example above, it is calculated as:

Total cost = fixed cost + (variable cost per unit x number of units)

$$= £88,000 + (£7.50 \text{ x } 7,300)$$

$$= £88,000 + £54,750$$

$$= £142,750$$

We will now look at a Case Study which shows how a cost can be analysed to see if it is variable or semi-variable.

CASE STUDY

CHOCO LIMITED
VARIABLE OR SEMI-VARIABLE COSTS?

Choco Ltd is a chocolate manufacturer. The original budget for Choco Ltd's boxes of chocolates was set at a sales volume of 25,000 boxes. There is to be no change in the level of stock of finished goods, and therefore production is also planned to be 25,000 units.

After the original budget was prepared, a revised forecast of demand showed that

20,000 boxes were likely to be sold. A revised budget for 20,000 boxes to be produced and sold was therefore prepared. The following is an extract from the two budgets:

Budget	Original	Revised
Number of boxes	25,000	20,000
Direct Materials (£)	26,250	21,000
Direct Labour (£)	90,000	81,000

required

Given that the direct costs are either variable or semi-variable, calculate for each type of cost:

- the variable cost per box
- the fixed part of the cost, if any

solution

■ Since two budgets have been prepared, we can establish whether the direct costs are strictly variable.

For **Direct Materials**, we calculate the cost per unit in the original budget:

£26,250 ÷ 25,000 = £1.05

If it is a variable cost, then the revised budget should show the same unit cost:

£21,000 ÷ 20,000 = £1.05

Alternatively: test that the total cost varies in line with production by checking that £26,250 x 20,000 ÷ 25,000 gives £21,000.

Direct materials is therefore a variable cost. The amount per unit is constant and the total varies in line with production.

Direct materials cost is £1.05 per box.

■ For **Direct Labour Cost**

£90,000 ÷ 25,000 (from the original budget) is not the same as

£81,000 ÷ 20,000 (from the revised budget).

Alternatively: £90,000 x 20,000 ÷ 25,000 does *not* give £81,000.

Direct Labour does *not* vary in line with production and it is *not* a variable cost. From the given information, Direct Labour cost is therefore semi-variable.

■ Using the **high-low method**:

	Cost		Boxes	
High	£90,000		25,000	
Low	£81,000		20,000	
Difference	£9,000	÷	5,000	= £1.80 per box

Variable cost per box   = £9,000 ÷ 5,000   = £1.80 per box

Variable cost for 20,000 boxes   = £1.80 x 20,000   = £36,000

Fixed cost = total cost for 20,000 boxes minus variable cost for 20,000 boxes
                                         = £81,000 - £36,000   = £45,000

Check for 25,000 boxes: £45,000 + (1.80 x 25,000)   = £90,000.

Therefore the cost of Direct Labour in Choco Ltd's budgets is made up of £45,000 of fixed costs, plus a variable cost of £1.80 per box.

PREPARATION OF FLEXED OR FLEXIBLE BUDGETS

The Case Studies in this chapter so far have shown how we can analyse and use information about how costs behave. This will enable budgets to be adjusted for different levels of activity. A budget for one specific level of activity is referred to as 'fixed'.

A budget adjusted for a change in level of activity is called a 'flexed' or 'flexible' budget, which is more suitable if actual results are to be compared with budgets for the purposes of performance measurement, because it would mean that the comparison is of 'like with like'.

In order to prepare a flexible budget for costs, we need sufficient information to be able to calculate, for each element of cost:

• the variable cost per unit of activity

• the total fixed part of the cost

Some costs may be entirely variable or entirely fixed. For those which are semi-variable, the high-low method can be used if we have enough data. Once the costs have been analysed in this way, a budget can be prepared for any level of activity.

The cost behaviour identified may only apply within a relevant range, however, and therefore it may not be realistic to 'flex' the budget for very large changes in level of activity.

A flexed budget is useful for preparing a performance report, where the actual costs and income are compared with the flexed budget applicable to the actual level of activity. Differences are shown in a 'variance' column, labelled as adverse or favourable.

preparing a flexible budget

To produce a flexible budget for the required level of activity, the total for each element of cost is calculated using:

- total variable cost = variable cost per unit x number of units
- total fixed cost remains unchanged
- total semi-variable cost =

  Fixed part of cost + variable cost per unit x number of units
- if, in a given case, there are any additional fixed costs which are incurred at certain levels of activity, or any step costs, these must be set at the correct level for the activity level of the flexed budget

CASE STUDY

MAC LIMITED: BUDGETED COSTS

Mac Ltd manufactures a single product – a raincoat – using automated processes. The costs of production are budgeted, as shown in the table below, for output of 20,000 units per year and for 30,000 units per year.

Direct Labour consists of machine operatives' wages and the total wages behave as a step cost:

Output	Total Direct Labour
Up to 15,000 units	£20,000
Over 15,000 and up to 25,000 units	£35,000
Over 25,000 and up to 35,000 units	£50,000

Mac Limited: Budgeted Production Costs			
Output (units)	20,000	27,000	30,000
	£000s	£000s	£000s
Direct Material	140		210
Direct Labour	35		50
Machine running costs	90		110
Other production overheads	100		100
Total Production Cost	365		470

required

Complete the Budgeted Production Costs table by calculating the budgeted costs for Mac Ltd for output of 27,000 units. Note that Direct Labour is the only step cost.

solution

Mac Limited: Budgeted Production Costs			
Output (units)	20,000	27,000	30,000
	£000s	£000s	£000s
Direct Material ^{W1}	140	189	210
Direct Labour ^{W2}	35	50	50
Machine running costs ^{W3}	90	104	110
Other production overheads ^{W4}	100	100	100
Total Production Cost	365	443	470

working notes

(see working note references in the table above)

W1 Direct Material is a variable cost:

£140,000 ÷ 20,000 = £210,000 ÷ 30,000 = £7

Therefore Direct Material = £7 per unit and £7 x 27,000 = £189,000.

W2 Direct Labour is a step cost, as given, and for 27,000 units it would be at the level of £50,000.

W3 Machine running costs are semi-variable, because they do not change in line with output. Using the high-low method:

	Cost		Units	
High	£110,000		30,000	
Low	£90,000		20,000	
Difference	£20,000	÷	10,000	= £2 per unit

Fixed cost = £90,000 – (£2 x 20,000) = £50,000

Total cost for 27,000 units = £50,000 + (£2 x 27,000) = £104,000

W4 Other production overheads are fixed at £100,000.

The purpose of a flexed budget is shown in the Case Study which follows. This Case Study is similar to a central assessment task. A performance report which compares actual results with a fixed budget is given, and this has to be revised to compare the actual results with a flexible budget for the actual output. The revised version is a better report because it compares like with like.

CASE STUDY

PP PLC: A FLEXED BUDGET

PP plc is a manufacturer of photocopying machines, and one of its divisions (Casings Division) makes the outer casings for the machines. The casings are not sold to external customers, only transferred at cost to another division of PP plc, where they are fitted to the machines. The demand for casings therefore depends on the total production of photocopiers in PP plc.

Last year, Casings Division prepared two provisional budgets because there was uncertainty about how many casings would be required. These two budgets are shown below. They have been prepared on a consistent basis which would apply to any level of demand from 11,500 to 15,000 casings.

Casings Division provisional budgets: 12 months to 30 September 2001

Volume (number of casings)	12,000	15,000
	£	£
Material	138,000	172,500
Labour	76,000	85,000
Power and Maintenance	32,400	36,000
Rent, Insurance and Depreciation	70,000	70,000
Total cost	316,400	363,500

After these budgets were prepared, Casings Division was told that 12,000 casings would be required, so the first budget above was used as the budget for the year.

During the year ended 30 September 2001, PP plc actually required only 11,800 casings from Casings Division and a performance statement for the year for the division was then produced, as shown below. It shows the differences between budgeted total costs and actual total costs in the 'variance' column.

Casings Division performance statement: 12 months to 30 Sept 2001

	Budget	Actual	Variance	
Volume (number of casings)	12,000	11,800		
	£	£	£	
Material	138,000	136,500	1,500	F
Labour	76,000	74,000	2,000	F
Power and Maintenance	32,400	32,400	zero	-
Rent, Insurance and Depreciation	70,000	70,500	500	A
Total cost	316,400	313,400	3,000	F

Note: F=Favourable, A=Adverse

required

Task 1 Using the data given in the two provisional budgets, calculate the fixed and variable cost elements for each of the four types of cost.

Task 2 Using your answers to Task 1, prepare an amended performance statement based on flexible budgeting. Show a flexed budget compared with the actual results to give the (revised) variances.

solution

Task 1

Initial analysis of the two provisional budgets shows that Materials cost is variable, Labour is semi-variable, Power and Maintenance is semi-variable, and Rent, Insurance and Depreciation cost is fixed. (The instruction to calculate the fixed and variable cost elements implies that each cost is assumed to have one of these cost behaviour patterns).

workings

- **Material** (variable)

  £138,000 ÷ 12,000   = £172,500 ÷ 15,000   = £11.50 per casing

- **Labour** (semi-variable), using the high-low method:

Difference in cost	= £85,000 − £76,000	= £9,000
Difference in units	= 15,000 − 12,000	= 3,000
Variable cost	= £9,000 ÷ 3,000	= £3.00 per casing

  Fixed cost = Total in first budget − Variable cost of 12,000 casings

  = £76,000 − (£3.00 x 12,000)

  = £76,000 − £36,000

  = £40,000

- **Power and Maintenance** (semi-variable), using the high-low method:

Difference in cost	= £36,000 − £32,400	= £3,600
Difference in units	= 15,000 − 12,000	= 3,000
Variable cost	= £3,600 ÷ 3,000	= £1.20 per casing

  Fixed cost = Total in first budget − Variable cost of 12,000 casings

  = £32,400 - (£1.20 x 12,000)

  = £32,400 - £14,400

  = £18,000

- **Rent, Insurance and Depreciation** (fixed), does not change with the level of activity and remains as £70,000.

Note that the calculations for the semi-variable costs can be set out in a table. (This form of table may be required in solutions to central assessment tasks and can be expanded to include costs which are entirely variable or entirely fixed. It could be set up as a spreadsheet – see Chapter 8).

Casings Division: analysis of semi-variable costs

	1st budget (low)	2nd budget (high)	Difference	Unit variable cost	Total variable cost (1st budget)	Fixed cost
Volume	12,000	15,000	3,000			
	£	£	£	£	£	£
Labour	76,000	85,000	9,000	3.00	36,000	40,000
Power & Maintenance	32,400	36,000	3,600	1.20	14,400	18,000

Task 2 - solution

The solution can be set out in table format, firstly to calculate the flexed budget and then to present the report. (The budget can be flexed to 11,800 casings as this is within the relevant range).

Calculation of flexed budget for 11,800 casings

	Unit variable cost £	*Total variable cost £	Fixed cost £	**Flexed budget £
Material	11.50	135,700	-	135,700
Labour	3.00	35,400	40,000	75,400
Power & Maintenance	1.20	14,160	18,000	32,160
Rent, Insurance & Depreciation	-	-	70,000	70,000
Total	15.70	185,260	128,000	313,260

Note that, for each type of cost:

* Total variable cost = Unit variable cost x 11,800

** Flexed budget = Total Cost = Total Variable Cost + Fixed Cost

Casings Division performance statement: 12 months to 30 September 2001
Comparison with flexed budget for 11,800 casings

	Flexed budget £	Actual cost £	Variance £	
Material	135,700	136,500	800	A
Labour	75,400	74,000	1,400	F
Power & Maintenance	32,160	32,400	240	A
Rent, Insurance & Depreciation	70,000	70,500	500	A
Total	313,260	313,400	140	A

Note: A = Adverse, F = Favourable

flexible budgets in marginal costing

The format of marginal costing operating statements is shown in Chapter 1. As flexible budgets involve separating the fixed and variable parts of costs, they can easily be shown in marginal costing format if required. The variable costs are listed first (including variable overheads) and the fixed costs (which may include direct costs) are then grouped together. The Case Study that follows demonstrates this and is similar to part of a Central Assessment task. The high-low method is not used because the information is given in a different way.

CASE STUDY

TT LIMITED: MARGINAL COSTING

TT Ltd produces a single chemical product, TCH, which cannot be stored as work-in-progress or finished goods for technical reasons. For the year ended 31 August 2001, the budget was for 10,000 litres of TCH to be produced and sold, but the actual production and sales for the period amounted to 11,000 litres. An operating results statement, with attached notes, is shown below.

TT Ltd Operating results for the year ended 31 August 2001

		Budget			Actual
Volume (litres of TCH)		10,000			11,000
	£	£		£	£
Turnover		450,000			489,500
Direct costs:					
Material	80,000			90,200	
Production labour	95,000			98,000	
Power	46,500			45,700	
	221,500			233,900	
Fixed overheads	130,000			126,400	
Cost of sales		351,500			360,300
Operating profit		98,500			129,200

Notes

1   There are no opening or closing work-in-progress or finished goods.

2   The cost of direct material is a variable cost.

3   The cost of direct production labour is a fixed cost, because the employees are paid a fixed wage. The employees available are sufficient to produce up to 12,000 litres of TCH

4 The cost of power is semi-variable and the fixed part of the cost allowed for in the budget is £30,000. However, the fixed part of the actual cost is £27,660, due to re-negotiation of the contract with the power company.

required

Calculate the following:

1 the budgeted unit selling price
2 the budgeted material cost per litre of TCH
3 the budgeted marginal cost (variable cost) of power
4 the actual marginal cost of power
5 prepare a marginal costing operating results statement, comparing the actual results with a flexible budget for 11,000 litres and showing the variances
6 explain briefly why the revised operating results statement is different from the original one, and state one advantage of flexible budgeting

solution

1 The budgeted unit selling price is £450,000 ÷ 10,000 = £45 per litre.
2 The budgeted material cost per litre is £80,000 ÷ 10,000 = £8
3 The total budgeted cost of power is £46,500, of which £30,000 is fixed (note 4). Therefore the variable part of the cost is £16,500 for 10,000 litres.

   The budgeted marginal cost of power is therefore £16,500÷10,000 = £1.65 per litre of TCH.
4 The total actual cost of power is £45,700, of which £27,660 is fixed. Therefore the actual marginal cost of power is £(45,700 − 27,660) ÷ 11,000 = £1.64 per litre of TCH.
5 The answer is shown in the following table, using the above answers to calculate the variable costs for 11,000 litres. Marginal costing format is used.

TT Ltd Flexible budgeting results statement for the year ended 31 August 2001

	Flexible budget		Actual results		Variance	
Litres of TCH	11,000		11,000		-	
	£	£	£	£	£	
Turnover W1		495,000		489,500	5,500	A
Marginal costs:						
Material W2	88,000		90,200		2,200	A
Power W3	18,150		18,040		110	F
Total marginal costs		106,150		108,240	2,090	A
Contribution		388,850		381,260	7,590	A
Fixed costs						
Direct Labour	95,000		98,000		3,000	A
Power W4	30,000		27,660		2,340	F
Overheads	130,000		126,400		3,600	F
Total fixed costs		255,000		252,060	2,940	F
Operating Profit		133,850		129,200	4,650	A

workings notes to the table

Note these use answers 1 to 4:

W1 Budget = £45 x 11,000 and actual is as given. (Note that the sales variance is Adverse when actual turnover is less than budget).

W2 Budget = £8 x 11,000 and actual is as given.

W3 Budget = £1.65 x 11,000 and actual is £45,700 - £27,660 or £1.64 x 11,000

W4 Fixed part of the power costs are as given. Fixed overheads are also given.

solution (continued)

6   The revised operating results statement is different from the original one because the costs have been separated into their fixed and variable parts. A flexed budget for 11,000 litres can then be prepared, to show what the results should have been for this level of output and sales. This is not the same as the original budget because the budgeted turnover and some of the budgeted costs depend on the number of litres. This is emphasised by the marginal costing layout. The budgeted profit is higher than the original one, because there are more litres of TCH to contribute to the fixed costs and profit.

The revised statement has the advantage that the comparison is more meaningful when we compare like with like, i.e. both budget and actual figures are applicable to 11,000 litres of TCH.

comparison of marginal and absorption costing

In the last Case Study, there were no opening or closing stocks of finished goods, so that the units of production and units sold were equal. In the next Case Study below, we have the situation that sales volume is less than production volume. Hence, there is an increase in the level of finished goods stocks over the period. As has been seen in Chapter 1, this will mean that the methods of absorption costing and marginal costing will report different profit figures in this period. A combination of flexible budgeting with marginal and absorption costing and changes in stock levels has been used in the Central Assessment.

CASE STUDY

LIDDEAN LIMITED: FLEXIBLE BUDGETING

Liddean Ltd makes and sells a single product, the Lidd. The original budget for Liddean Ltd for the 6 months ended 30 September 2001 planned for production and sales volumes to be equal, both being 12,500 Lidds. The actual results for the period were that 12,000 Lidds were produced and only 10,000 sold. Opening stock of Lidds was zero and therefore the closing stock was 2,000 Lidds. The budgeted and actual figures are given below, together with attached notes.

Liddean Ltd: Operating results for 6 months ending 30 September 2001

	Budget	Actual
Sales volume (Lidds)	12,500	10,000
Production volume (Lidds)	12,500	12,000
	£	£
Sales	312,500	260,000
Less: Cost of Sales:		
Direct costs:		
Materials	62,500	72,000
Labour	81,250	75,000
Overheads:		
Production overheads	58,000	52,000
Total production cost of sales	201,750	199,000
Selling overheads	42,500	20,000
Total cost of sales	244,250	219,000
Profit	68,250	41,000

Notes

▦ Direct materials and direct labour are both variable costs.

▦ Production overheads are semi-variable. For the fixed part, the budget is based on £8,000 for this level of activity. However, for production volume below 12,200 Lidds, the budgeted fixed production overhead would be £6,000. The actual fixed production overhead was in line with the budget.

▦ Selling overheads are semi-variable. The budget for the fixed part is £5,000. The remainder varies in relation to sales volume. The actual fixed selling overhead was in line with the budget.

▦ There were no stocks of work-in-progress and no opening stocks of finished goods.

▦ To calculate the actual cost of sales in the statement above, the closing stocks were valued at actual production cost. The number of Lidds was used to apportion the actual production costs between the cost of sales and the closing stock. Using this policy, the composition of the production cost of sales and closing stock was:

	Closing Stock	Cost of Sales	Cost of Production
Number of units (Lidds)	2,000	10,000	12,000
	£	£	£
Direct material	14,400	72,000	86,400
Direct labour	15,000	75,000	90,000
Production overhead	10,400	52,000	62,400
Production cost	39,800	199,000	238,800

required

1 Calculate the following:

(a) the budgeted selling price per Lidd

(b) the budgeted direct material cost per Lidd

(c) the budgeted direct labour cost per Lidd

(d) the budgeted marginal cost of production overhead

(e) the actual marginal cost of production overhead

(f) the budgeted marginal cost of selling overhead

(g) the actual marginal cost of selling overhead

2 Prepare a flexible budget statement for the operating results of Liddean Ltd for the 6 months to 30 September 2001, using marginal costing. Identify the fixed costs for the period and show any variances.

3 Write a brief memo to the production manager of Liddean Ltd, explaining:

- why the revised operating statement which you have prepared shows different results from the original statement

- why the revised operating statement may be an improvement on the original statement for the purpose of measuring performance.

solution:

1 The calculations are as follows:

(a) budgeted selling price = £312,500 ÷ 12,500 = £25 per Lidd.

(b) budgeted direct material cost = £62,500 ÷ 12,500 = £5 per Lidd.

(c) budgeted direct labour cost = £81,250 ÷ 12,500 = £6.50 per Lidd.

(d) budgeted marginal (variable) cost of production overhead =

£(58,000 – 8,000) ÷ 12,500 = £4 per Lidd.

The £8,000 budgeted fixed part is deducted before dividing by the number of units.

(e) actual marginal cost of production overhead =

£(62,400 – 6,000) ÷ 12,000 = £4.70 per Lidd.

Notice that this is using the cost of production and the number of Lidds produced. Nb. also the reduced fixed part for reduced production (see notes)

(f) Budgeted marginal cost of selling overhead

= £(42,500 – 5,000) ÷ 12,500 = £3 per Lidd.

(g) Actual marginal cost of selling overhead

= £(20,000 – 5,000) ÷ 10,000 = £1.50 per Lidd sold.

Notice that the number of Lidds sold is used because the variable part of selling overhead depends on sales volume (see notes)

2 Using marginal costing, and the answers calculated above, we can then present the results as shown in the table on the next page.

Liddean Ltd: Flexible budgeting results statement for 6 months to 30 Sept. 2001						
	Flexible budget		Actual results		Variance	
Lidds sold	10,000		10,000		-	
	£	£	£	£	£	
Sales^{W1}		250,000		260,000	10,000	F
Marginal costs:						
Material^{W2}	50,000		72,000		22,000	A
Labour ^{W3}	65,000		75,000		10,000	A
Production overhead^{W4}	40,000		47,000		7,000	A
Variable production cost of sales	155,000		194,000		39,000	A
Variable selling overhead^{W5}	30,000		15,000		15,000	F
Total variable costs		185,000		209,000	24,000	A
Contribution		65,000		51,000	14,000	A
Fixed costs^{W6}						
Production overhead		6,000		6,000	- -	
Selling overhead		5,000		5,000	- -	
Operating profit		54,000		40,000	14,000	A

Working notes to the table

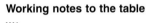

^{W1} Budget = £25 x 10,000 and actual is as given

^{W2} Budget = £5 x 10,000 and actual is as given in table in notes (variable cost)

^{W3} Budget = £6.50 x 10,000 and actual is as given in table (variable cost)

^{W4} Budget = £4 x 10,000 and actual = £4.70 x 10,000, using answers 1(d) and 1(e)

^{W5} Budget = £3 x 10,000 and actual = £1.50 x 10,000, using answers 1(f) and 1(g))

^{W6} Fixed costs are in line with budget and the budget for fixed production overhead has been reduced because production is below 12,200 Lidds.

3   MEMO

To: Production Manager

From: Cost accountant

Date: 14 October 2001

Subject: Operating results for the 6 months to 30 September 2001.

Comparison of the attached operating results statements shows that there are differences between the way the actual profit is reported and the variances calculated. The reasons for the differences are:

- In the original statement, results for sales of 10,000 Lidds and closing stock of 2,000 Lidds were compared with a budget for sales of 12,500 Lidds and zero closing stock

- In the original statement the cost of sales had been calculated by using average cost of production to value the closing stock. This included an element of fixed production overhead. In the revised statement closing stock has been valued at variable cost of production only and fixed costs for the period have been kept separate.

- There is a difference of £1,000 between the reported actual profit of £41,000 in the original statement and the reported actual profit of £40,000 in the revised statement. This amount is due to the fixed cost element which was included in the closing stock in the original statement and which would be carried forward rather than charged against the period. This can be calculated as £6,000÷12,000 = £0.50 per Lidd, for 2,000 Lidds.

  £0.50 x 2,000 = £1,000, the difference in reported profit.

- The reason why the revised statement is preferable for performance measurement is as explained in the first point above. Comparison of like with like gives more meaningful results. Also, marginal costing emphasises which costs change when the level of activity changes, and which remain fixed. Fixed costs are often related to time periods and marginal costing charges them to the time period.

ACTIVITY BASED BUDGETING

The process of preparing budgets can be carried out using any costing method. The last two Case Studies have compared the use of marginal costing with absorption costing.

Activity Based Budgeting means that

budgets are prepared using the principles of Activity Based Costing.

Activity Based Costing is described in Chapter 1 (see page 12). It involves identifying activities which are being carried out in the organisation, and, for each activity, the cost driver. If Activity Based Budgeting is to be used, decisions need to be made, as part of the planning process, as to the amount of each activity that will be required, and the funds to be allocated to it.

The analysis of cost behaviour here is just as important as in marginal and absorption costing. In Activity Based Budgeting and Costing, the behaviour of costs is defined in terms of the cost drivers, because these are the factors which cause costs to change. The Case Studies on pages 14 and 15 of Chapter 1 show calculations of budgeted costs using Activity Based Costing and you may find it useful to review these now that you have studied methods of budgeting in more detail.

MANAGEMENT REPORTING ASPECTS OF BUDGETING

monitoring of budgets

The last three Case Studies in this chapter show how variances can be calculated by comparing the actual results of an organisation with its budget, usually flexed to give a budget for the actual level of activity. This is an important aspect of a budgetary system. The preparation of budgets is part of the planning process, the comparison with actual results is part of the control process, as shown in the diagram below. (Compare the 'planning' part of this diagram with 'The initial process' in Chapter 8 [page 199] and the 'control' part with 'Interpreting Variances' in Chapter 4 [page 97]).

budgetary planning and control

- the organisation's objectives
- strategy for achieving objectives
- short-term aims
- key budget factor
- forecast level of key budget factor
- budgets

forecast budgeted results in line with short-term aims?

yes	no
implement budget	revise budget and/or aims
monitor budget	

actual results in line with budget?

yes	no

investigate and take control action

PLANNING

CONTROL

'**Monitoring**' the budget involves regular comparisons of actual results with budget, so that control action can be taken if necessary. The **budget period**, which is the period of time for which the budget is prepared, is usually six months or a year, but monitoring should take place more frequently than this. Waiting until the end of the budget period would give out-of-date information, too late for action.

The '**control period**' is the part of a budget period after which budgeted and actual results are compared. The control period could be a week or a month, for example, depending on the type of work.

If standard costing is being used, the variances would be analysed further into parts which indicate their causes, such as materials price and usage variances as studied in chapters 2, 3 and 4. The 'variance' column in the performance reports shown in this chapter shows the sales variance and each of the total cost variances.

feedback

Feedback is information obtained and reported after comparing the budgeted and actual results for a control period.

Feedback is used to determine the necessary control action if results are significantly different from the budget. What is meant by 'significantly different'? This would have to be decided in advance. It could be defined in terms of absolute amounts or percentages of the budget, that is, 'control limits' would be set (see also Chapter 4).

Only when the feedback shows variances going beyond the control limits would they be reported for action to be taken by the appropriate person. This is called 'exception reporting', which has the advantage that only the 'significant' differences are brought to the attention of management, thus saving time and avoiding the risk of important figures being lost among a mass of data.

It would be useful to refer back to the section on Interpreting Variances in Chapter 4, where these principles are explained in detail (see page 97).

favourable variances

It is often thought that only adverse variances are significant, but **favourable** variances which are **beyond the control limits** are equally important and may require action to be taken.

The word 'favourable' is perhaps misleading because it suggests something good. Favourable variances may indeed indicate some advantageous situation which it would be useful to investigate to see if it can be continued, for example efficiency improvements. However, large favourable variances may not be desirable in some cases, for example favourable materials variances may result from using the wrong material or using insufficient material to maintain the quality of a product.

control action

The control action to be taken on receipt of feedback from the monitoring of budgets depends on the situation. The section on Interpreting Variances in Chapter 4 is relevant again here (see page 97).

If the reason for the variance can be identified it may be possible to correct it, in order to bring the actual results for the next control period back in line with (or at least closer to) the budget. The **feedback loop** is shown in the diagram on the next page (this is an extended version of the diagram on page 275). The feedback loop is an important part of the Budgetary Control process.

Sometimes it is not possible to bring the actual results back in line with the budget, because there has been a permanent change in costs which is not controllable by the managers of the organisation. This could be due to external factors, such as national wage agreements or permanent price changes (increases or reductions). The action to be taken then involves adjusting the budget to plan for realistic costs, so that the feedback from the next control period is more meaningful. This brings us to the idea of feeding forward information.

feedforward

Feedforward is information about the current performance of an organisation and its environment which is used in budgeting for the future.

The budgeting process, introduced in Chapter 8, starts from identifying the organisation's objectives and translating these into desired results for the budget period. For example, if the long-term objective is to achieve a particular level of market share, the short term aim can be expressed in terms of budgeted sales volume.

In a feedforward system, the initial budget is considered by looking at the results it is expected to achieve in comparison with the desired results. This process uses information about the current performance of the organisation (feedback) and information about the economic environment, together with the budget.

If the forecast results, according to the budget, are significantly different from the desired results, then the budget may be amended to eliminate the differences. However, the organisation's aims and objectives may have to be re-considered and brought closer to what is achievable. In either case, a revised budget and/or revised objectives should help to ensure that future results do meet the organisation's objectives.

The feedforward loop is shown on the diagram below. Notice that the feedforward loop takes information to the Budgetary Planning process for the next period.

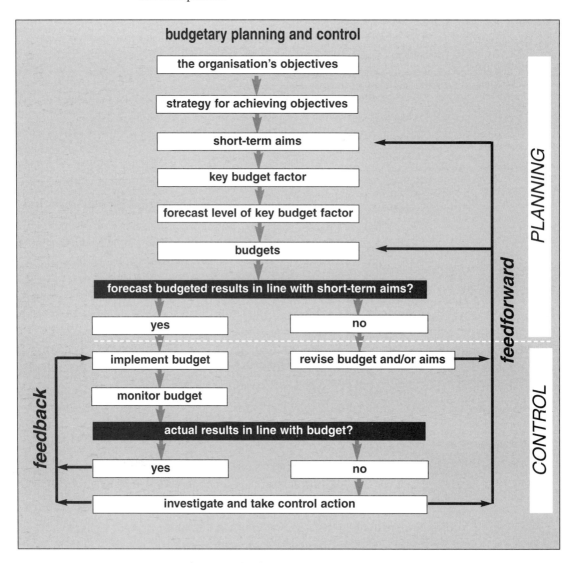

performance reports

Performance reports based on budgets should be produced regularly to show the results of each control period, possibly together with accumulated figures for 'the year to date'. The case studies in this chapter illustrate some formats of performance reports.

Reports which compare budgeted and actual results usually give variances. The original fixed budget may be shown as well as a flexible budget, the flexible budget being used for the calculation of variances. If control limits are known, then the variances which should be investigated can be highlighted.

CASE STUDY

TT LIMITED:
PERFORMANCE REPORTING

required

In the results statement for TT Ltd shown below, identify which variances should be investigated if:

(a) control limits are set as ± £2,500, *or*

(b) control limits are set as ± 3% of budget

TT Ltd Flexible budgeting results statement for the year ended 31 August 2001

	Flexible budget		Actual results		Variance
Litres of TCH	11,000		11,000		-
	£	£	£	£	£
Turnover		495,000		489,500	5,500 A
Marginal costs:					
Material	88,000		90,200		2,200 A
Power	18,150		18,040		110 F
Total marginal costs		106,150		108,240	2,090 A
Contribution		388,850		381,260	7,590 A
Fixed costs					
Direct Labour	95,000		98,000		3,000 A
Power	30,000		27,660		2,340 F
Overheads	130,000		126,400		3,600 F
Total fixed costs		255,000		252,060	2,940 F
Operating Profit		133,850		129,200	4,650 A

solution:

(a) The variances which are greater than ± £2,500 are:

- the sales variance (adverse)
- the contribution variance (adverse), partly due to the sales variance
- the direct labour variance (adverse)
- the fixed overhead variance (favourable)
- the operating profit variance (adverse), which results from the other variances

Reasons for the difference in profit should be identified by investigating the most significant sales and cost variances.

(b) The variances which are greater than 3% of budget (using the flexible budget), are:

- the direct labour variance (3.2% of budget, adverse)

- the fixed cost power variance (7.8% of budget, favourable)

- the operating profit variance (3.5%, adverse), which results from the other variances

Reasons for the difference in profit should be identified by investigating the most significant sales and cost variances.

format of reports

It is essential that any report is designed to give **useful information to management**, (see also Chapter 1), and therefore the particular lay-out and headings used will depend on the **information requirements** of managers. They will also depend on the method of costing being used, whether it is absorption costing, marginal costing or activity based costing, and whether detailed standard costs are set.

In Chapter 4, detailed variance reports have been prepared, and in this chapter performance statements comparing actual results with flexible budgets have been produced. These are examples of performance reports.

In Central Assessment Case Studies you may be expected to comment on the headings and groupings of costs and income which you consider would give the most useful information in a performance report for a particular manager in a given organisation. This involves identifying what should be highlighted in the report in relation to the organisation's objectives, taking into account the area of responsibility of the manager. Whatever the format of a report showing performance against budget, the principle of comparing like with like applies and the variances must be reported to the person who is in a position to take the required remedial action.

If you are asked to design an improved report format, try to answer the question: 'What does this manager need to know?' The aspects to bear in mind include:

- ensure that the report shows useful information (as in Chapter 1) and is relevant to the organisation's objectives

- present numerical data logically in the form of a table, labelling rows and columns clearly

- ensure consistency in the preparation of information when comparisons are being made

- group costs or incomes together according to functions, activities or products, depending on the type of work and the manager's area of responsibility

- avoid unnecessary detail or irrelevant workings

- show information for suitable time periods, so that timely control action can be taken
- show cumulative figures, for the 'year to date', if considered to be relevant and useful
- consider seasonal variations when using short time periods
- use flexed budgets for comparison with actual results
- show clearly whether variances are adverse or favourable and highlight significant variances
- as well as financial information, show useful non-financial information, such as numbers of employees, units of output and so on.

Chapter 11 includes discussion of the levels of authority and responsibility of managers and what is meant by 'controllability' of costs and incomes. We will then return to the question of how to design or improve the format of a report in order to show useful, relevant information as required by managers.

CHAPTER SUMMARY

- Three methods of budgeting which can be applied in different situations are incremental budgeting, zero base budgeting (ZBB) and programme based budgeting.

- For budgeting, it is important to have information about how costs behave in relation to levels of activity. This is particularly relevant to the preparation of flexible budgets. A fixed budget is one which is prepared for a specific level of activity, whereas a flexed or flexible budget is one which allows for a change in the level of activity.

- The types of cost behaviour studied for the purposes of preparing flexed budgets are variable costs, fixed costs, step costs and semi-variable costs.

- To calculate semi-variable costs for different levels of activity, we analyse them into their fixed and variable parts using the high-low method.

- After splitting all the costs into their fixed and variable parts, a flexible budget can be prepared by calculating the costs and income at the required level of activity.

- A budget which is flexed to the actual level of activity is suitable to use for comparison with actual costs and income, because it compares like with like. The comparison, giving the variances, is shown in a 'performance report' or 'operating results statement'.

- Budgets, operating statements and performance reports can be presented using any method of cost accounting, in particular marginal and absorption costing.

- Marginal and absorption costing may report different profit figures in a given period when there is a difference between the levels of opening and closing stocks of finished goods. Absorption costing reports a higher profit in a period when stocks are built up, because fixed costs absorbed into the stock increase are carried forward into the next period.

- Activity Based Budgeting refers to budgeting using the principles of Activity Based Costing (see Chapter 1).

- After a budget has been prepared and implemented, it is used for control purposes by comparing the actual results with the budget, investigating significant differences and taking appropriate control action. The information being used in this process is called feedback.

- Budgets are used to make detailed plans which should be in line with the organisation's objectives. If the forecast results from the initial budget differ from the desired results, either the budget or the objectives may be amended. The information being used is called feedforward.

- The use of budgets for performance reporting (the control aspect of budgeting) leads to a consideration of features which should be included in the format of performance reports in order to ensure that they provide useful information for managers (see also Chapter 1 and Chapter 11).

KEY TERMS

incremental budgeting	a method of budgeting in which budgets are based on the previous period's budgets, updated for developments and inflation
zero base budgeting	a method of budgeting in which budgets are set to zero at the start of each period – budgets for proposed activities are then judged and prioritised in relation to the organisation's objectives, and funds allocated accordingly
programme based budgeting	a method of budgeting applicable to non-profit-making organisations, in which funds are allocated to programmes designed to achieve the organisation's objectives, up to the highest level possible with funds available.
fixed budget	a budget which is set for a particular level of activity
flexed (or flexible) budget	a budget which is adjusted to allow for changes in costs (and income) resulting from a change in the level of activity

variable cost

a cost which behaves such that its total varies in proportion to the level of activity

Total variable cost = (cost per unit x number of units)

fixed cost

a cost which behaves such that its total remains unchanged when the level of activity changes (within a relevant range)

relevant range

the range of levels of activity within which a certain pattern of cost behaviour applies

step cost

a cost which behaves such that its total changes in steps as the level of activity reaches certain points, remaining unchanged between these points

semi-variable cost

a cost which is such that its total is made up of a part which is variable and a part which is fixed.

Total semi-variable cost = Fixed cost + (variable cost per unit x number of units)

marginal costing

a costing system which uses a cost for each unit of output based purely on the variable (or 'marginal') costs – all fixed costs are regarded as time based and are therefore linked to accounting periods rather than units of output

budget period

the period of time for which a budget is prepared

control period

the part of a budget period after which budgeted and actual results are compared

feedback

information obtained and reported after comparing the budgeted and actual results for a control period – feedback is used to determine necessary control action if results show significant differences from the budget

feedforward

information about the current performance of an organisation and its environment which is used in budgeting for the future – a feedforward system attempts to ensure that future results will meet the organisation's objectives

10.1   Which one of the following is a feature of an incremental budget?

(a)   all budgets are initially set at zero

(b)   it is based on the previous year's budget initially ✓

(c)   it remains fixed and is not updated for inflation

(d)   it is based on specific organisational programmes

10.2   The following graphs show total costs against level of activity. Identify the type of cost behaviour illustrated by each graph.

(a)

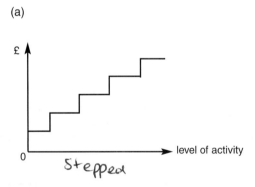

Stepped

(b)

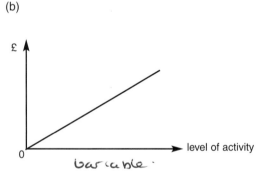

variable.

(c)

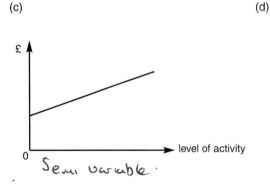

Semi variable.

(d)

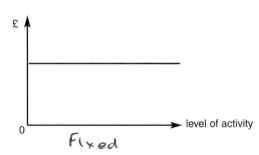

Fixed

10.3 For this task, assume that the cost of power is a semi-variable cost.

    (a)   Using the high-low method, calculate the fixed cost and the variable cost per unit for power from the following data:

Month	Total cost of power	Level of activity
1	£51,000	90,000 units produced
2	£43,000	70,000 units produced
3	£59,000	110,000 units produced

    (b)   Using your answers to (a), calculate the expected total cost of power if 80,000 units are produced.

10.4 Budgets are prepared for the transport costs of the fleet of vehicles run by a local authority. The level of activity is measured on mileage and the original budget for the year to 31 March 2001 was set on the basis of an annual mileage of 350,000 miles. Due to uncertainty about the number of contracts to be serviced by the transport fleet, it was then decided to prepare two further budgets, for 250,000 miles and 300,000 miles respectively. Each element of cost is assumed to behave in one of three ways:

- Entirely fixed
- Entirely variable
- Semi-variable

Required

Complete each of the two tables given below. The first table gives the original budget and one of the flexed budgets. The other flexed budget is to be prepared. The second table gives the actual results for the actual mileage of 300,000 miles. The appropriate flexed budget figures are to be inserted and the variances calculated.

Transport Fleet Flexible Budgets for the year to 31 March 2001			
Budgeted annual mileage	250,000	300,000	350,000
	£000s	£000s	£000s
Running costs	37.5		52.5 ✔
Maintenance of vehicles	29.0		39.0 ✔
Vehicle licences	24.0	—	24.0
Insurance	10.0		10.0
Garaging	12.5		12.5
Depreciation	40.0	—	40.0
Total costs	153.0		178.0
Cost per mile (to nearest 1p)	£0.61		£0.51

Transport Fleet Operating Results for the year to 31 March 2001			
	Budget	**Actual**	**Variance**
Annual mileage		300,000	
	£000s	£000s	£000s
Running costs		51.5	
Maintenance of vehicles		33.0	
Vehicle licences		24.0	
Insurance		11.0	
Garaging		12.3	
Depreciation		40.0	
Total costs		171.8	
Cost per mile (to nearest 1p)		£0.57	

10.5 A photographer acquired the rights to reproduce, frame and sell a set of historic prints. It was decided to budget for this new activity and record the results separately from the remainder of the business.

The forecast costs for the first year were:

Copying costs: £5.00 per print.

Mounting and framing costs: £22.00 per print.

Power costs are expected to be semi-variable and by comparison with similar existing processes are expected to be:

£175 per month if 300 prints per month are produced

£225 per month if 500 prints per month are produced.

Power costs are to be included in Production Cost.

Other costs related to this activity are expected to be fixed at:

• £1,000 per month for administration

• £2,500 per month for advertising.

The selling price per print has been set at £50.

The forecast for sales and production of prints in the first year is 400 prints per month. Opening stocks of finished prints are zero and the planned closing stock at the year end is also zero.

Required

Task 1

(The workings and answers for this task, together with further information, will be used for Task 2 below).

Using the forecast of 400 prints per month, prepare two alternative formats of the budget for the first year of the historic print activity, on:

(a)   an absorption cost basis

(b)   marginal cost basis

Further information

The actual results for the first year were as follows:

- Opening stock of finished prints was zero

- Closing stock of finished prints was 500 prints

- 4,000 prints were produced in the year

- 3,500 prints were sold in the year

- Actual sales revenue = £157,500

- Actual costs of production were:

  - Copying costs = £20,000

  - Mounting and framing costs = £84,000

  - Power costs = £1,700 (the fixed part was as budgeted).

- Actual administration costs were £1,300 per month

- Actual advertising costs were £2,000 per month.

Task 2

Using your answers to task 1 and the actual results, prepare two alternative performance statements comparing the actual results for the year with a flexed budget, on

(a)   An absorption cost basis, where closing stock (in both the flexed budget and the calculation of actual profit) is valued on the basis of the average budgeted production cost per print.

(b)   A marginal cost basis where closing stock (in both the flexed budget and the calculation of actual profit) is valued on the basis of variable budgeted production cost.

Hint: care must be taken when you are given a mixture of monthly and yearly data.

11 MANAGEMENT ISSUES IN RELATION TO BUDGETING

this chapter covers . . .

Tutorial note

This chapter extends the discussion of certain issues relating to budgeting, which have been referred to in earlier chapters as part of the background to the budgetary process. These are discussion topics, of which a basic knowledge and understanding is required, in order to be able to make recommendations regarding methods of budgeting and the use of budgets for control and for performance evaluation.

In this chapter we examine:

- *organisational goals in relation to budgeting*
- *authority and responsibility*
- *budget centres as areas of responsibility*
- *controllable costs and incomes*
- *reporting to management*
- *motivational aspects of budgets*
- *participation in budget preparation*
- *performance related pay*
- *goal congruence*

NVQ PERFORMANCE CRITERIA COVERED

unit 9: CONTRIBUTING TO THE PLANNING AND ALLOCATION OF RESOURCES

element 2: produce draft budget proposals

- *draft budget proposals are consistent with organisational objectives, have taken all relevant data into account and are agreed with budget holders*

- *discussions with budget holders are conducted in a manner which maintains goodwill*

MANAGEMENT ISSUES IN RELATION TO BUDGETING

uses of management accounting information

Budgets and performance statements (which we have discussed in chapter 10) are examples of **management accounting information**. Chapter 1 examined the characteristics necessary for information to be of value and these should be borne in mind whenever the usefulness of information for any particular purpose is discussed.

Management Accounting information must be of value to managers and in general it is expected to be useful for:

- **reporting results** (sometimes referred to as 'score-keeping')
- **highlighting problems** that need action (sometimes referred to as 'attention directing')
- **assisting with decision-making**: showing the likely effects of different alternative actions

In particular, a budgetary system can give information to assist in all three of these functions. Examples and Case Studies in chapter 10 included:

- **reporting results**: actual results are compared with flexed budgets and variances reported
- **highlighting problems** that need action: by identifying the significant variances (using control limits and exception reporting)
- **assisting with decision-making**: flexible budgets using patterns of cost behaviour show the expected results from different levels of activity

importance of management accounting information

Management accounting information becomes increasingly important to managers the more complex an organisation becomes.

The owner-manager of a small business can maintain close contact with all parts of the business, but the senior managers of a large company are further detached from day-to-day operations and require **good information** of the three types listed above to help them in their work as managers.

The work of a manager in controlling an organisation can be seen as steering it in the desired direction through a continuously changing environment, and in order for this to be possible the manager needs:

- to know what the desired direction is – in other words the goal or objective must be known
- to be able to tell whether the organisation is heading in the right direction or not – in other words some form of performance measurement must be

possible. (Chapters 6, 7 and 10 include many examples of possible methods)

- to understand how the direction will change if certain actions are taken – in other words to understand the effects of possible control action
- to be able to steer the organisation – in other words to have the authority and the resources to take the control action necessary. In modern businesses it is particularly important to be able to respond quickly to external influences, such as changes in the economic environment

The first of these requirements – knowing the goal or objective – is the starting point for all planning and decision-making and we saw, in Chapter 8 and Chapter 10, that it is the first step in the budgetary process.

The diagram on page 275 starts with the steps:

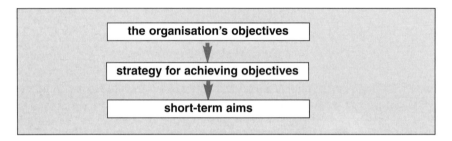

There may be several main objectives, for each of which a number of strategies can be mapped out. As a result there will be numerous short-term aims for different activities or functions within the organisation.

We will now consider these processes in more detail and illustrate them with Case Studies.

ORGANISATIONAL GOALS IN RELATION TO BUDGETING

profit-making organisations

For **profit-making organisations** it is often stated that the objective is to maximise profit. If the organisation is a limited company, the same idea may be put forward as 'maximisation of share-holder wealth'. It is not possible, however, for every part of a large organisation to work to a single general objective like this in every time period.

Profit-making organisations clearly do aim to make profits, but they are likely to have a number of other goals, which are linked to this.

For example:

- to develop new technologies

- to expand into new markets
- to improve the quality of the product range, and so on

In some time periods, profit maximisation may be secondary to such other goals if a long-term view is taken.

Expansion into new markets may reduce profits temporarily, but eventually generate higher profits.

Spending on improving quality (Chapter 5) will increase some costs and some of the expected benefits may not be seen until a later time period. For instance, inspection costs incurred in order to avoid selling substandard goods are expected to result in an enhanced reputation for quality and higher sales, but this will not happen immediately.

non-profit-making organisations

Non-profit-making organisations do not state their objectives in terms of profit. They will have goals which are expressed in terms of the work that they have been set up to do. Financial goals may be related to achieving a surplus of income over expenditure, but the main objectives are more likely to be expressed in terms of the quality or range of services which the organisation should offer.

Public bodies, such as local government authorities, may have goals set for them, for example by the Government. The Local Government Act 1999 places a duty on local government authorities to provide certain services to the public on the basis of 'best value'. This means that the public funds must be used in an effective, economic and efficient way to provide services giving the best possible value to the users. There must be regular reviews to check performance against stated targets. (See 'Performance measurement in service organisations' in Chapter 7.)

The main, long-term goals of the whole organisation are determined by those with the authority to make strategic decisions. Whatever they identify as the main goals of the whole organisation, these will not be reached without the organisation being steered in the right direction. The overall goals will have to be translated into what is to be done, by whom and to what timescale. This is the process of budgeting – making detailed plans for a given time period.

The plans eventually agreed will be based on achieving, by the end of the budget period, a position which is at least a step in the required direction. We have seen in Chapter 10 that a feedforward system attempts to ensure that the budget will lead to the required position. If projections show that it will not, then it may have to be amended, or a revised version of the steps to be taken will have to be worked out.

The budgetary process therefore involves breaking down the long-term goals of the organisation into short-term aims and working out a detailed financial plan (budget) designed to achieve those aims.

Working from long-term goals to short-term detailed plans can be a very complex process, in which information about the past, present and future and about both the internal and external environment of the organisation will be needed. The two Case Studies on the next page illustrate this process, which may be summarised as follows:

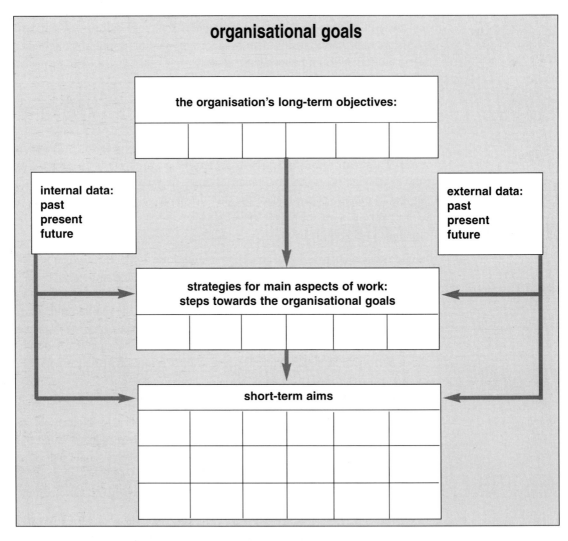

The setting of objectives for parts of the organisation may involve consultation, negotiation and compromise. The manager of a department or division may put forward sufficiently strong arguments for review of the plan, and revised objectives may be agreed.

WYVERN COLLEGE OF FURTHER EDUCATION: ORGANISATIONAL GOALS

In a college such as Wyvern College, the organisational goals may include improving the cost-effectiveness of expenditure on academic staff salaries. Departments may be given the objective of running only those courses which achieve a minimum class size. A head of department may be able to argue in favour of retaining some courses with smaller classes, if it can be shown that they feed into other, more cost-effective courses and therefore provide an overall benefit.

WYVERN COUNTY COUNCIL WASTE DISPOSAL: ORGANISATIONAL GOALS

A county council's organisational goal is to provide 'best value' in its service to the community.

The work of the council is very varied and therefore separate goals are needed for each of the services provided, which include:

- Education
- Social services
- Transport and strategic planning
- Culture and life-long learning
- Safer communities
- Economic development
- Sustainable development and environment

The last category includes **waste disposal** and **waste planning**, as well as conservation and the countryside.

The goal for this aspect of the council's work is to maintain and enhance a sustainable environment.

This very general goal would have to be set down in terms of what actually could be done: increasing the recycling of waste, for example, could be one of a number of ways of achieving the goal.

For waste recycling, short-term aims could then be set out, for example to increase the percentage of waste which is recycled by a certain percentage per year, so that in 5 years' time the maximum is achieved. The budget for recycling initiatives would then be worked out in detail, including decisions about how the improvements would be made: for example, in the next year, should they concentrate on waste paper collections, or some other kind of waste?

The data needed from internal and external sources would include

- past costs of disposal or recycling of different types of waste
- present levels of waste recycling
- present levels of waste paper collected
- currently available land-fill sites for waste disposal
- future prices expected to be obtainable for recycled waste, and so on.

This aspect of the Case Study can be illustrated using the diagram we have seen already on page 292 expanded to show the example at each level:

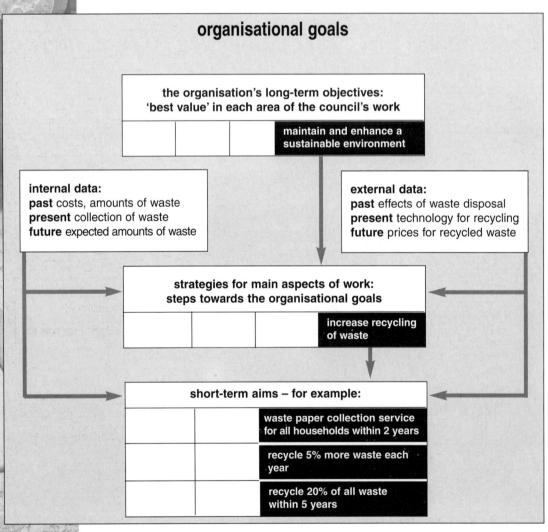

CASE STUDY

TAX COLLECTION: ORGANISATIONAL GOALS

The main goal of organisations such as Inland Revenue and HM Customs and Excise is to collect taxes for the Government. A related goal, which it is expected will assist in the collection of the correct amount of tax from tax-payers, is 'to serve the needs of tax-payers well'.

The Inland Revenue service commitment, for example, states its aims in a number of areas relating to dealing with tax-payers. Annual reviews of how well these aims are being achieved are published.

The diagram below shows the aims of a typical tax collecting organisation. These will, of course, have to be incorporated in the budgeting process.

LONG-TERM OBJECTIVES

- **to collect taxes**
- **to serve tax-payers' needs well**

to act fairly and impartially	to communicate effectively	to provide good quality service	to take responsibility for service

STRATEGIES FOR MAIN ASPECTS OF WORK
steps towards the organisational goals

strict confidentiality accuracy	clear and simple forms accurate and complete information helpfulness	prompt and accurate accessible courteous professional serving special needs	annual reviews published advice on how to complain

EXAMPLES OF SHORT-TERM AIMS

Review design of all forms according to specified timetable

Introduce big print and Braille versions of all forms within one year

Check 'customer care' training of all staff who deal directly with the public

Ensure all main offices have wheel-chair access by specified date

Three Case Studies on the previous pages illustrate how there must be a step-by-step process to get from the overall long-term goals of the organisation to aims, and hence budgets, for given time periods and for small parts of the organisation.

AUTHORITY AND RESPONSIBILITY

The term '**responsibility accounting**' is used to describe a way of looking at an organisation in terms of areas of responsibility, which could be departments, activities or functions. Such areas of responsibility are called **responsibility centres**.

An individual manager can then be held accountable for certain aspects of the performance of the particular department, activity or function for which he or she is responsible.

Which aspects of performance should a particular manager have to account for? Clearly, in a fair system, these would be those aspects which they can actually do something about, or over which they have some influence. This brings us to the concept of **controllability**, which is explained in more detail later in this chapter.

In order to be able to influence the outcomes of a responsibility centre, the manager must have the authority to take the necessary actions. Within a large organisation, there will be various levels of management from the senior executives to supervisors of small departments, each with an appropriate level of authority.

For example, the chief executive may have the authority to sign a contract for a major capital investment project, whereas a production manager has the authority to organise the week's production scheduling.

The extent of a person's authority is clearly linked to the area for which they can be held responsible. There are three categories of responsibility centre which are linked to different levels of authority:

- A **cost centre** (or expense centre) is a responsibility centre where the manager has responsibility for costs. The manager has the authority to take certain actions in relation to the control of costs.

  For example, an office manager can authorise the purchase of stationery and introduce controls to reduce wastage of paper.

- A **profit centre** is a responsibility centre where the manager has responsibility for both costs and income, and hence profit. The manager has the authority to take action relating to income as well as costs.

  For example, the manager of a branch office of an estate agent may have the authority to negotiate levels of commission with clients (perhaps within a specified range), as well as deciding on advertising expenditure.

- An **investment centre** is a responsibility centre where the manager has responsibility for costs, income and some investments. The manager's authority is as for a profit centre, with the additional authority to buy and sell assets, up to certain limits. The manager therefore has some influence over the capital employed in this section of the organisation and Return on Capital Employed could be used as a measure of management performance.

For example, the manager of a division which makes some of the products of a large manufacturing company may have the authority to buy and sell machinery up to a given value.

budget centres as areas of responsibility

A **budget centre** is a department, activity or function for which a budget is prepared and the person who is responsible for implementing that budget is the **budget holder**.

In order to implement a budget, the budget holder must have sufficient authority to take the necessary actions, and can then be held responsible for the performance of the budget centre in comparison with the budget. Each budget centre is therefore a responsibility centre and may be any of three types of centre described above:

- a budget centre which is a cost (or expense) centre would have a budget for costs (or expenses) only
- a budget centre which is a profit centre would have a budget for both costs and incomes
- a budget centre which is an investment centre would have a budget for costs, incomes and capital expenditure

When the performance of a department, activity or function is measured against the budget, it is important to apply the principle of comparing like with like (as we have seen in calculations with flexed budgets in Chapter 10), and also to measure only those aspects of performance which the budget holder is able do something about. These are the aspects which are described as controllable for that person, as explained below.

CONTROLLABLE COSTS AND INCOMES

A particular cost or income is described as 'controllable' by a particular person if that person is in a position to influence it. It does not necessarily mean that the person has absolute control over it.

For example, the total cost of wages in a department can be said to be controllable by the manager of the department if he (or she) has the authority to decide how many staff of each grade to employ. However, the manager may not have absolute control over the total wage bill, because the rates of pay may be set at levels which he cannot change. The manager can influence the total wages and therefore it can be considered as being within his area of responsibility.

Whether something is controllable or not depends on the individual manager being considered, in terms of the post which they occupy and the level of responsibility that goes with it. Every cost or income can be influenced by someone in the organisation with a sufficiently high level of authority. Factors such as bank interest rates, foreign exchange, inflation and so on are not controllable, but the costs affected by these factors can be influenced by management decisions.

For example, the cost of borrowing money is affected by interest rates, but decisions relating to amounts of borrowing and sources of finance can influence the total cost.

Controllability of costs or incomes is important for performance measurement, because clearly it would be unfair and demotivating to measure people's performance on something over which they have no influence.

Controllability of costs or incomes links to the idea of responsibility accounting: if managers have clearly defined areas of responsibility, where they can influence the costs or incomes or both, then they can be held responsible for those costs or incomes and their performance can be measured on the results.

The fairest ways of measuring performance would therefore be:

- On **controllable costs** in a cost centre – a possible measure with which you are familiar is variance analysis. The cost centre manager should not have to account for variances on costs which he cannot influence, for example apportionments of fixed overheads

- On **controllable profit** in a profit centre – profit margin or contribution : sales ratio, as well as variance analysis, could be used for measurement, again applying the principle of excluding items which cannot be influenced by the manager, if possible. Difficulties arise because the exact boundaries between what can and cannot be influenced are not always completely clearcut: for example, by how much does a quality improvement affect sales volumes?

- On **return on capital employed** in an investment centre. Here, the calculation of profit and of capital employed may be based where possible on controllable items. However, capital provided by the organisation as a whole and which is not controllable by the centre manager may be taken into account. This allows measurement of how well the total capital employed has been used by the manager to generate profits.

We have seen in Chapters 6 and 7 that there are many other possible measures of performance which could be used as well as those mentioned above, and we have emphasised there the importance of comparability. Whatever measure is used, it must be calculated on the same basis each time for the purposes of comparison. If, for example, 'controllable profit' is being used for comparison, it must include the same items as being controllable each time.

CASE STUDY

CC LIMITED: CONTROLLABILITY

The following information relates to the production departments A and B of CC Ltd.

Department	A		B	
		£000s		£000s
Sales Revenue		450		680
Direct Costs	100		220	
Production overheads	310		280	
General overheads (apportioned)	80		120	
Total costs		490		620
Net (loss)/profit		(40)		60

Department A manufactures a product which is supplied to a single customer on a long-term contract, which is negotiated by a senior manager of CC Ltd.

The product manufactured in **Department B** is sold in bulk to a number of customers and the departmental manager has the authority to negotiate prices with customers, depending on the quantities ordered.

required

Comment briefly on the suitability of profitability as a measure of performance for the managers of Department A and Department B.

solution

The performance of the two departmental managers should not be measured on the same basis, because the situation is not the same in each department.

In Department A, the manager cannot influence the sales revenue, because the sales price and quantity are negotiated by a senior manager.

In Department B the manager can influence the sales revenue by negotiating prices with customers.

The information given implies that **Department A is a cost centre** and **Department B is a profit centre**.

Appropriate performance measures are therefore related to costs in A and profit in B.

When considering costs in both departments, we can assume that the apportioned general overheads are not controllable by the departmental managers and should therefore be excluded from the calculations. We would require more detailed information about the controllability of the production overheads. These may include depreciation of plant and machinery, for example, which the departmental managers may not be able influence.

The 'bottom line' profit or loss figure from the above statement does not provide a measure of departmental management performance in this case.

In Department A, variances for controllable costs would be more appropriate and in Department B, controllable profit (that is, sales revenue less controllable costs) would be suitable.

REPORTING TO MANAGEMENT

In the introduction to this chapter, we saw that useful management information is essential for managers. This holds for any level of manager in an organisation. Different levels of authority and responsibility would make a difference to the type of information which would be useful and the format of reporting required.

For example, in the last Case Study, the manager of Department A can control some of the costs: regular reporting of significant cost variances would be useful. Comparison of accumulated costs and production volumes for the 'year to date' with the budget may also assist this manager. The manager of Department B requires similar cost information, but would also find it useful to have a breakdown of monthly sales by customer, details of outstanding orders, aged debtors and so on. This manager deals directly with customers and requires useful information about them.

In Chapter 10, we showed that a budgetary system can give useful information to assist managers. The last section of chapter 10 includes a summary of aspects to bear in mind when designing the format of a report. You may find it helpful to refer back to that section at this point. One of the points listed is:

'Group costs or incomes together according to functions, activities or products, depending on the type of work and the manager's area of responsibility.'

Discussion relevant to the meaning of 'the manager's area of responsibility' is in this chapter, in the sections:

- authority and responsibility (page 296)
- budget centres as areas of responsibility (page 297)
- controllable costs and incomes (page 297)

In order to design or improve methods for reporting to management, it is necessary to take these ideas into account, for a particular case study scenario.

You may be asked to point out how a performance report can be misleading – in particular:

- how apparent changes in performance can occur without the manager taking any action – for example, sales of some products are affected by the weather
- why the performance measures chosen are unsuitable because the manager cannot take action to change them – for example, measuring sales (and hence profit) is unsuitable for the manager of department A in the last Case Study

The Case Study that follows illustrates some of these ideas. It is essential, for Central Assessment tasks, to read the detail of the situation carefully and prepare or design a report which will present useful information clearly. The principles involved have appeared in many different contexts throughout this book.

CASE STUDY

SUPREME HOTELS: PERFORMANCE REPORTING

Supreme Hotels is a chain of 15 luxury hotels in major towns and cities in the UK. In October 2001, Jo Grant has just been appointed as Manager of one of the Supreme Hotels. Budgets are prepared for each hotel in the chain and the hotel managers have responsibility for implementing the budget. Hotel managers have the authority to appoint all grades of staff, to plan the use of rooms for meetings and conferences, and to authorise revenue expenditure for the running of the hotel. Prices of the various services are common to all hotels in the chain and are determined by central management, and so is depreciation policy. Individual hotel managers are responsible for maintaining the quality of service to customers.

Jo Grant has been given a file of management accounting information relating to the current financial year. She is disappointed to find that the reporting of results does not appear to be very useful to her in her job as manager, and also it may give an unfair picture of her management performance.

The hotel is divided into three profit centres: Guest Accommodation, Catering and Conferences. There are two service cost centres: Administration and Cleaning. The report is set out as follows:

6 months to 30 September 2001: Actual

	Guest accomm.	Catering	Conferences	Total Actual
Income				
Direct consumables				
Direct wages				
Direct expenses				
Admin. apportioned				
Cleaning apportioned				
Premises costs* apportioned				
Total costs				
Net Profit				

6 months to 30 September 2001: Performance Report

	Annual budget	6 months' budget (50% of annual)	Total actual (from above)	Variance
Income				
Direct consumables				
Direct wages				
Direct expenses				
Admin. apportioned				
Cleaning apportioned				
Premises costs* apportioned				
Total costs				
Net Profit				

*   Premises costs include rent and rates, heating and lighting, insurance, depreciation, maintenance of buildings.

required

1   Comment briefly on Jo Grant's concerns regarding the performance report format.

2   Suggest three further items of information which would be useful to Jo Grant.

3   Suggest three or more additional columns which would improve the second table for the purpose of assisting Jo Grant with her job as hotel manager.

(It may be useful to refer back to the list of points relating to the format of reports in chapter 10).

solution

1 For management purposes, the report lacks detail and the apportionment of administration and cleaning is not helpful. These cost centres could be kept separate in the management accounts, so that their costs can be controlled. The apportionment of premises costs is also unhelpful, especially as it seems that some of these costs (such as rent, rates and depreciation) are not controllable by the hotel manager. This point relates to the performance measurement aspect as well – only costs and income which Jo Grant can influence should be taken into account.

The second table can also be improved. Account should be taken of possible seasonal variations. The 6 months to 30 September may include the hotel's busiest period of the year and therefore more than half the annual income and costs. 50% of the annual budget may not therefore be a fair comparison.

2 You may have suggested some of the following:

- numbers of staff hours in each department
- numbers of guests staying in the hotel by week/month
- proportion of customers who book return visits
- numbers and type of customer complaints
- numbers of visitors on conferences split into resident/non-resident
- summaries of previous years' sales or visitor numbers for the purposes of analysing seasonal variations
- more detail of direct costs in each department
- a breakdown of cleaning costs in terms of work done for the other departments
- or other useful financial or non-financial data

3 You may have suggested additional columns which show budgets and variances for the three main activities of the hotel.

Alternatively you may have suggested additional columns for shorter time periods. Taking into account that there may be seasonal variations, the budget could be split into appropriate monthly amounts. Columns for 'Actual this month', 'Budget this month' and 'Variance this month' could therefore be added. Another possible extra column would be to show 'Budget remaining'.

Another alternative would be to consider flexing the budget. Jo Grant cannot change the prices charged by the hotel, but has some influence over the use of rooms for conferences. Incomes and some of the costs would be related to visitor numbers and more detailed information would be needed to prepare a flexible budget. You may have suggested including a column (or three columns for the three activities) for flexed budgeting.

Other suggested column headings may be equally valid.

MOTIVATIONAL ASPECTS OF BUDGETS

The main purpose of budgeting is to produce a detailed plan for a given period. The budget is not usually designed specifically to motivate employees, but the process of budgeting and the budget itself can affect the behaviour of employees. The effect may be to motivate or to demotivate under different circumstances.

When studying standard costing in Chapter 2, we have seen that standards may be set at an ideal or attainable level and that the latter is more useful for variance analysis. It is also more likely to motivate employees than a standard which they dismiss as impossible and are therefore quite likely to ignore. The same principle applies to budgeting. A budget will help to motivate employees if they accept that it is achievable. If it is too easy to achieve, it will not be sufficient motivation, and if it is too difficult it will not be accepted. If a budget which employees see as impossible is imposed upon them, they may be demotivated to the extent of setting out to prove that the budget is wrong, which would lead to completely the opposite effect than that which is intended.

There have been a number of research projects carried out to investigate the effects of budgeting on people's behaviour, and to a certain extent the results appear to give conflicting views. However, there seems to be general agreement that employees are motivated to work towards a target or budget:

- only if they accept it as their personal goal
- if it is sufficiently high a target to be challenging
- if, although it is a challenge, they see it as achievable

Some research has looked at the effect of involving people in the budget setting process (participation), to see whether this results in a greater likelihood of the budget being accepted in this way.

participation in budget preparation

A participative budget system means that those who will have to work to a particular budget are involved in its preparation. They are consulted throughout the process, so that they can input their specialised knowledge of the work involved and contribute to the planning process involved in budgeting. This is sometimes described as a 'bottom up' style of budgeting, as opposed to 'top down', which would refer to the situation where the budget is imposed on people by higher levels of management.

The main advantages of the method of participative budgeting are:

- the budget takes account of information from those with specialised knowledge

- those involved will have improved awareness of organisational goals
- those involved will accept the budget and be motivated to work to it
- coordination and cooperation between those involved will improve
- participating in budget preparation broadens their experience and develops new skills
- participation in budget setting gives those involved a more positive attitude towards the organisation and this leads to better performance.

It should be borne in mind, however, that these advantages depend on the participation being genuine: if people are consulted, but their opinions later appear to be ignored, the effects will be the opposite of those listed above. (This is sometimes referred to as 'pseudo-participation').

Supporters of the idea of participation in budgeting may point to apparent improvements in performance as 'proof' of its motivating effect. It should be borne in mind that coincidences can occur, and the improvement may have happened for some other reason: favourable cost variances can result from suppliers reducing their prices, for example, or sales volumes might increase because of purely external factors like changes in the weather.

Another reason for favourable results may be the introduction of **budgetary slack**. This means that managers have succeeded in obtaining a budget based on an over-estimation of costs or an under-estimation of income. They are then more likely to be able to achieve a good level of performance when measured against the budget. An argument against participation could be that it increases the risk of managers being able to introduce budgetary slack.

Research projects relating to participation in budgeting do not seem to have provided any firm conclusions about its motivational effects. It is not surprising that the effects seem to depend on the attitudes of the individuals involved, and different people react in different ways. Some employees may not want to spend time on budgeting, or may feel they do not have the necessary skills, so that participation would be seen as added pressure on them rather than an opportunity. They may feel that it is not part of their job, or that they have not been trained to carry out the task. Therefore, under some circumstances, an imposed ('top down') method of budgeting may be preferred.

Imposing a budget is also likely to be quicker than a consultation process, and sometimes the timescale will mean that a participative approach is impossible. We have seen earlier in this chapter that managers must be able to respond quickly to changing circumstances and maintain the progress of their organisation in the required direction. Part of this response may be to revise budgets at short notice.

performance related pay

Performance related pay is a method of rewarding employees in the form of bonuses, options to buy shares or other incentives, with a view to motivating them to improve their own performance or, in the case of managers, the performance of the part of the organisation which they manage.

Our earlier discussions of authority, responsibility and motivation are all relevant here. The principles of performance measurement from Chapter 10 are also relevant, as no scheme for performance related pay would be possible without some way of measuring performance. There must be some standard or target against which to measure the actual results, and this is most likely to be in the form of a budget.

Taking all these aspects into account, the conditions necessary for performance related pay to be an effective way of motivating people can be summarised as follows. Those involved will need:

- to understand the organisational goals

- to want to work towards achieving those goals

- to have budgets which they accept as consistent with achieving those goals

- to feel that the budgets are challenging, but achievable

- to have the appropriate skills to achieve improved performance

- to feel that they can influence the performance outcomes

- to see the measurement of performance outcomes as fair

- to be motivated by the level and type of rewards in the scheme

The scheme itself must have:

- clear definitions as to what performance outcomes will be rewarded

- an organisational structure which allows performance to be linked to authority and responsibility

- a method for measuring the relevant performance outcomes

- information systems which collect the data necessary to measure these outcomes

- rewards for improved performance which are at a suitable level and of a type which will motivate employees

goal congruence

We have seen earlier in this chapter that the overall goals of the organisation have to be translated into subsidiary goals for parts of the organisation and then, through budgetary planning and control, the organisation should make progress towards its goals. This describes the ideal situation, but the complexities of these processes and the effects on the behaviour of individuals within the organisation may mean that the ideal is not achieved.

In practice, when we look at a particular department, for example, we may find that its manager has different goals, which are not actually in line with those of the whole. Typical examples are sometimes described as 'empire-building' – increasing production of one product for example, or employing more staff, or alternatively cutting costs to achieve favourable variances. These strategies to enhance the manager's own situation and performance may not be in the best interests of the organisation as a whole, and may be contrary to its stated goals. This is called **dysfunctional** decision-making or behaviour.

The term 'goal congruence' is used if the ideal situation does exist, and the goals of parts of the organisation are in line with those of the whole. The complex process of breaking down the long-term goals of the whole organisation into shorter-term aims for its parts may have involved negotiation and compromise. These planning and budgeting activities are never 'finished', as information is continuously fed back and fed forward so that action can be taken to steer the organisation in the required direction. To keep the organisation on track, a well designed budgetary control system, which leads to goal congruence, is a very important factor.

CHAPTER SUMMARY

- Managers need useful information which reports results, highlights problems that need action and assists with decision-making.

- Budgets and performance statements are examples of management accounting information and therefore the usual principles for presenting useful information (see Chapter 1) apply.

- Organisational goals are the starting point for planning and budgeting. These may be stated in financial terms relating to profits or costs, or in non-financial terms relating to quality, market share, range of products or services and so on.

- Non-profit making organisations may state their goals in terms of economy, efficiency and effectiveness, which may come under the heading of 'best value' for local government authorities.

- Strategies are identified for achieving the organisational goals, and these are then translated into short-term aims on which to base detailed budgets.

- Managers at different levels have different levels of authority and areas of responsibility, which may be defined in terms of the costs, incomes and investments in assets for which they are responsible.

- An area of responsibility may be termed a cost centre, profit centre or investment centre, depending on the level of authority of the manager.

- Responsibility for costs or incomes is related to controllability, which is defined in terms of whether the particular manager responsible can influence that cost or income.

- The controllability of income and costs has implications for performance measurement, because managers should not be held accountable for items over which they have no influence.

- Reports should be designed to assist managers (at any level) in their work, by presenting useful information with a suitable amount of detail, consistently prepared. The report format should be related to the level of authority and the area of responsibility of the manager, so that any problems are highlighted and control action can be taken.

- Budgets are most likely to have a motivational effect on employees if the budgets are seen as challenging, but achievable.

- Participation in the budgeting process by those to whom the budget will apply may increase the likelihood of their acceptance of the budget. Improvements in results may however result from factors other than the motivational effects of participation.

- Under certain conditions performance related pay can be an effective way of motivating employees.

- Goal congruence is the ideal situation, when the parts of an organisation are all working towards goals which are in line with those of the whole.

- Dysfunctional decision-making results in parts of an organisation developing alternative goals, usually related to the personal aspirations of individuals and not contributing to the progress of the organisation as a whole.

KEY TERMS

responsibility accounting	management accounting based on departments, activities or functions, each of which is the area of responsibility of an individual
responsibility centre	a department, activity or function which is defined to be the area of responsibility of an individual: it may be a cost centre, profit centre or investment centre

cost (or expense) centre

a responsibility centre where the manager is accountable for costs

profit centre

a responsibility centre where the manager is accountable for both costs and income, and hence profit

investment centre

a responsibility centre where the manager is accountable for costs, income and the purchase and sale of some of the assets – the manager can therefore influence both profits and capital investment

budget centre

a department, activity or function for which a budget is prepared: it may be a cost, profit or investment centre as defined above

budget holder

the manager of a budget centre, who is responsible for implementing the budget in that centre

controllable cost or income

for an individual manager, a cost or income is said to be controllable if that person has some influence over it

participation in budgeting

a system of budgeting where managers of budget centres and others are consulted and involved in the preparation of their budgets

goal congruence

the situation in which the goals of individuals within an organisation are in line with the goals of the whole organisation

dysfunctional behaviour

behaviour or decision-making by individuals within an organisation which is in their own interests, but not in line with the goals of the whole organisation

budgetary slack

an additional allowance within a budget which has been obtained by over-estimating costs or under-estimating income, in order to make favourable variances easier to achieve

STUDENT ACTIVITIES

11.1 In what circumstances are the following likely to be effective ways of motivating employees?

(a) a budgetary control system

(b) performance related pay.

11.2 What are the advantages which may arise from participative budgeting?

11.3 What is meant by goal congruence?

11.4 Consider the following situation:

Peter Ltd makes and sells a single product, Product P. Peter Ltd uses absorption costing.

The budgeted variable cost of Product P is £5.00 per unit.

The budgeted full cost of Product P is £6.00 per unit, based on absorbing £1,000 per month of fixed production overheads into production of 1,000 units of P. (Non-production overheads budgeted at £1,750 per month are not absorbed).

The original budget for Product P for November 2001 was for 1,000 units to be produced and sold, opening and closing stocks of finished goods and work-in-progress being zero.

The actual results for November were that 800 units of P were sold and 1,000 were produced. The absorption costing budget and actual results for November 2001 are shown below:

	Budget £	Budget £	Actual £	Actual £
Sales 1,000 x £10		10,000		
Sales 800 x £11				8,800
Opening stock	-		-	
Cost of Production	6,000		6,000	
Less: closing stock	-		1,200	
Cost of sales		6,000		4,800
Gross Profit		4,000		4,000
Non-production overheads		1,750		1,650
Net profit		2,250		2,350

Required

Referring to the budgeted and actual results for November 2001 shown above, give two reasons why the additional net profit of £100 does not necessarily give a fair indication of management performance in Peter Ltd in November 2001. Explain briefly how the performance report could be improved.

11.5 Consider the following situation

The managing director of Peter Ltd, which makes and sells a single product P, decided that, for the year 2002, a participative approach to budgeting would be introduced. The draft budget for the year was set at continuing the level of production and sales at 1,000 units of product P per month, but after consultation with the sales manager in the participative process, it was decided to budget for sales and production of 850 units per month. The production manager was involved in setting the cost budgets.

The actual results for January 2002 showed that sales of 900 units had been achieved. The sales manager was very pleased that the revised target of 850 units had motivated the sales staff to exceed it and achieve this level of sales.

The actual results for January 2002 also showed some favourable cost variances, when compared with a flexible budget for 900 units.

Required

(a) Give two reasons why the actual sales volume of 900 units in January may not have been a result of better motivation following the participative budgeting process

(b) Give two reasons why favourable cost variances may have arisen other than as an advantage of participative budgeting.

11.6 Consider the following situation, which we studied in the first Case Study in Chapter 10. The relevant information is repeated here:

PP plc is a manufacturer of photocopying machines, and one of its divisions (Casings Division) makes the outer casings for the machines. The casings are not sold to external customers, only transferred at cost to another division of PP plc, where they are fitted to the machines. The demand for casings therefore depends on the total production of photocopiers in PP plc.

Additional information

The senior management of PP plc has decided to introduce a system of performance related pay, where the measurement of performance is to be based on:

• Keeping unit costs below budget

• Achieving above target levels of production.

Required

Write a memo to the Managing Director of PP plc, explaining:

• In what circumstances performance related pay may lead to improved performance

• Your reservations about applying the scheme to the management of Casings Division, from two aspects:

- the managers of Casings Division being at a disadvantage

- the managers of Casings Division obtaining an unearned benefit

answers to student activities

CHAPTER 1: MANAGEMENT INFORMATION

1.1 (a) The Management Accountant should have these on file.

(b) Trade Press, or Trade Association Database.

(c) Published on behalf of the Government, and reproduced in various printed and electronic forms.

(d) This internal data will probably be held by the Sales Manager, although the Management Accountant will also have a copy.

(e) These will be reported in the financial press, the trade press, and on the Internet.

(f) This is collected on behalf of the Government, and available through Censuses.

1.2 Based on the information given, activity based costing would appear to be most appropriate for the Radical Company. It is the only system that would cope with accurately costing the range of products outlined. For example the developments and design costs for items that are constantly updated are likely to be greater than those with unchanged specifications. Similarly the size of batches and lengths of productions runs would have a cost impact that only ABC would recognise.

1.3 (a) (i)

Profit Statements Using Absorption Costing

	Week 1 £	Week 1 £	Week 2 £	Week 2 £
Sales		24,000		40,000
Less cost of sales:				
Opening Stock	–		5,000	
Cost of Production:				
Direct Materials	5,000		5,000	
Direct Labour	9,000		9,000	
Fixed Overheads	6,000		6,000	
Less				
Closing Stock	(5,000)		–	
		15,000		25,000
Profit		9,000		15,000

(ii)

Profit Statements Using Marginal Costing

	Week 1 £	Week 1 £	Week 2 £	Week 2 £
Sales		24,000		40,000
Less cost of sales:				
Opening Stock	–		3,500	
Variable Cost of				
Production:	14,000		14,000	
Less Closing Stock	(3,500)		–	
		10,500		17,500
Contribution		13,500		22,500
Less Fixed Costs		6,000		6,000
Profit		7,500		16,500

(b)   The stock valuation using absorption costing includes £6,000 ÷ 4,000 units = £1.50 per unit of fixed overheads, which is not included when using marginal costing. This means that the stock of 1,000 units at the end of week one is valued at £1,500 more using absorption costing, and the profit recorded in week one is also £1,500 more. Marginal costing records a profit higher by £1,500 in week two, as the stocks fall by 1,000 units. Both systems show identical profits for the two weeks added together because the stock level at the start of week one is the same as at the end of week two.

1.4 (a)   As can be seen from the workings, this example has a regular trend, increasing by £10 each day, and seasonal variations that are consistent, with each set of 5 totalling zero.

(b)   The forecast for week 4 is calculated as follows:

	Forecast Trend £		Seasonal Variations	Forecast £
Tues	2,130 + (3 x 10)	= 2,160	− 180	1,980
Wed	2,130 + (4 x 10)	= 2,170	− 100	2,070
Thurs	2,130 + (5 x 10)	= 2,180	+ 50	2,230
Fri	2,130 + (6 x 10)	= 2,190	+ 120	2,310
Sat	2,130 + (7 x 10)	= 2,200	+ 110	2,310

Workings

Week	Day	Sales £	5-Point Moving Average (Trend)	Seasonal Variations
Week 1	Tues	1830		
	Wed	1920		
	Thurs	2080	2030	+ 50
	Fri	2160	2040	+120
	Sat	2160	2050	+110
Week 2	Tues	1880	2060	−180
	Wed	1970	2070	−100
	Thurs	2130	2080	+ 50
	Fri	2210	2090	+120
	Sat	2210	2100	+110
Week 3	Tues	1930	2110	−180
	Wed	2020	2120	−100
	Thurs	2180	2130	+ 50
	Fri	2260		
	Sat	2260		

1.5 (a)   Re 2003:

Qtr 1	Sales Trend	=	(42 x £1,200) + £83,000	= £133,400
Qtr 2	Sales Trend	=	(43 x £1,200) + £83,000	= £134,600
Qtr 3	Sales Trend	=	(44 x £1,200) + £83,000	= £135,800
Qtr 4	Sales Trend	=	(45 x £1,200) + £83,000	= £137,000

Incorporating the seasonal variations gives forecasts:

	Trend £	Seasonal Variations %	Forecast £
Qtr 1	133,400	– 10%	120,060
Qtr 2	134,600	+ 80%	242,280
Qtr 3	135,800	+ 15%	156,170
Qtr 4	137,000	– 85%	20,550

(b)   Since amounts in money are based on quantity x price, there are two independent factors influencing the forecast. While quantities may be thought to follow past trends in some circumstances, the effect of price inflation will be a major factor in changing prices. Basing a forecast directly upon monetary amounts will tend to build in additional inaccuracy unless inflation continues in the future at the same rate that it has in the past. It may be better to forecast the two elements of quantity and price separately before combining them in a final forecast.

1.6   (a)   As can be seen from the workings, this example has a regular trend, decreasing by 10 each quarter, and seasonal variations that are consistent, with each set of 4 totalling zero.

(b)   The forecast for year 5 is calculated as follows:

	Forecast Trend		Seasonal Variations	Forecast
Qtr 1	270 – (3 x 10)	= 240	+ 100	340
Qtr 2	270 – (4 x 10)	= 230	+ 40	270
Qtr 3	270 – (5 x 10)	= 220	– 50	170
Qtr 4	270 – (6 x 10)	= 210	– 90	120

Workings

		Sales Units	Moving 4-point Average	Averaged Pairs (Trend)	Seasonal Variations
Year 1	Qtr 1	500			
	Qtr 2	430			
			385		
	Qtr 3	330		380	– 50
			375		
	Qtr 4	280		370	– 90
			365		
Year 2	Qtr 1	460		360	+ 100
			355		
	Qtr 2	390		350	+ 40
			345		
	Qtr 3	290		340	– 50
			335		
	Qtr 4	240		330	– 90
			325		
Year 3	Qtr 1	420		320	+ 100
			315		
	Qtr 2	350		310	+ 40
			305		
	Qtr 3	250		300	– 50
			295		
	Qtr 4	200		290	– 90
			285		
Year 4	Qtr 1	380		280	+ 100
			275		
	Qtr 2	310		270	+ 40
			265		
	Qtr 3	210			
	Qtr 4	160			

CHAPTER 2: STANDARD COSTING – DIRECT COSTS

2.1 To calculate the total actual costs we can reproduce what is effectively a cost reconciliation.

Standard cost for actual production level: £95.40 x 1,060 =   £101,124

Add: Direct Material Price Variance	£1,585	A
Less: Direct Material Usage Variance	(£ 993)	F
Direct Labour Rate Variance	(£2,460)	F
Direct Labour Efficiency Variance	(£1,051)	F
Actual Cost of Actual Production	£98,205	

2.2 Using the budget data to calculate the standard data for one unit:

Direct Materials   40,000 kg ÷ 20,000   = 2 kg,
                    @ £300,000 ÷ 40,000   = £7.50 per kg.
                                              = £15.00 per unit

Direct Labour   10,000 hrs ÷ 20,000   = 0.5 hrs
                    @ £60,000 ÷ 10,000   = £6.00 per hr
                                              = £ 3.00 per unit

Direct Material Price Variance: (37,000 kg x £7.50) – £278,000 = £ 500 A

Direct Material Usage Variance: £7.50 x ([2 kg x 19,000 units] – 37,000 kg) = £ 7,500 F

Direct Labour Rate Variance: (9,800 hrs x £6.00) – £58,600 = £ 200 F

Direct Labour Efficiency Variance: £6.00 x ([0.5 hr x 19,000 units] – 9,800 hrs) = £ 1,800 A

Reconciliation:
Standard Cost for Actual Production Level

19,000 x (£15.00 + £3.00)	£ 342,000	
Add: Direct Material Price Variance	£ 500	A
Less: Direct Material Usage Variance	(£7,500)	F
Direct Labour Rate Variance	(£200)	F
Add: Direct Labour Efficiency Variance	£1,800	A
Actual Cost of Actual Production	£336,600	

2.3 The following comments are valid: (b), (c), (e), (f), (g), (h), (i), (j).
The remaining comments are false.

2.4 Using the budget data to calculate the standard data for one unit:

Variable Materials 3,000 kg ÷ 30,000   = 0.1 kg,
                    @ £75,000 ÷ 3,000   = £25 per kg.
                                            = £2.50 per unit

Variable Labour   15,000 hrs ÷ 30,000   = 0.5 hrs
                      @ £75,000 ÷ 15,000   = £5.00 per hr
                                                = £ 2.50 per unit

Variable Material Price Variance: (3,100 kg x £25.00) – £81,000 = £ 3,500 A
Variable Material Usage Variance: £25 x ([0.1 kg x 32,000 units] – 3,100 kg) = £ 2,500 F
Variable Labour Rate Variance: (15,900 hrs x £5.00) – £77,900 = £ 1,600 F
Variable Labour Efficiency Variance: £5.00 x ([0.5 hr x 32,000 units] – 15,900 hrs) = £ 500 F

Reconciliation:

Standard Marginal Cost for Actual Production Level

32,000 x (£2.50 + £2.50)	£ 160,000	
Add: Variable Material Price Variance	£ 3,500	A
Less: Variable Material Usage Variance	(£2,500)	F
Variable Labour Rate Variance	(£1,600)	F
Variable Labour Efficiency Variance	(£500)	F
Actual Marginal Cost of Actual Production	£158,900	

2.5   Direct Material Price Variance: (71,500 kg x £9.45) – £678,700 = £ 3,025 A
Direct Material Usage Variance: £9.45 x ((96 kg x 700 units) – 71,500 kg) = £ 40,635 A
Note: 5 hours 6 minutes = 5.1 hours.
Direct Labour Rate Variance: (3,850 hrs x £6.30) – £24,220 = £ 35 F
Direct Labour Efficiency Variance: £6.30 x ([5.1 hr x 700 units] – 3,850 hrs) = £ 1,764 A

Reconciliation:
Standard Cost for Actual Production Level

700 x ((96 x £9.45) + (5.1 x £6.30))	£ 657,531	
Add: Direct Material Price Variance	£3,025	A
Direct Material Usage Variance	£40,635	A
Less: Direct Labour Rate Variance	(£35)	F
Add: Direct Labour Efficiency Variance	£1,764	A
Actual Cost of Actual Production (£678,700 + £24,220)	£702,920	

CHAPTER 3: STANDARD COSTING – FIXED OVERHEADS

3.1. (a)   £10,000 ÷ 50,000   = £0.20 per mile
        (b)   Exp   £10,000 – £12,000   = £2,000 adverse
              Vol   £0.20 x (45,000 – 50,000)   = £1,000 adverse
              Total absorbed amount – actual fixed overheads
              (£0.20 x 45,000) – £12,000   = £3,000 adverse (or £2,000 + £1,000)!
        (c)   Under-absorption.

3.2 (a) $50,000 \div 2,000$ = 25 miles per hour.

      (b)   £10,000 $\div$ 2,000   = £5 per hour.

      (c) $45,000 \div 25$ mph   = 1800 hours

      (d)   Exp   £10,000 – £12,000   = £2,000 adverse

            Vol   £5 x (1800 – 2000)   = £1,000 adverse

            Eff   £5 x (1800 – 1850)   = £ 250 adverse

            Cap   £5 x (1850 – 2000)   = £ 750 adverse

            Total absorbed amount – actual fixed overheads

            (£5 x 1800) – £12,000   = £3,000 adverse   (or £2,000 + £1,000)

      (e)   Sickness may relate to capacity variance of 150 hours.

            Roadworks may relate to efficiency variance (lower speed)

            Vehicle insurance costs may relate to expenditure variance.

3.3 (a)   £94,600 $\div$ 2,200   =   £43 per hour

      (b)   Exp = £94,600 – £99,000   =   £4,400 A

            Vol = £43 x (2,500 – 2,200)   =   £12,900 F

            Eff = £43 x (2,500 – 2,600)   =   £4,300 A

            Cap = £43 x (2,600 – 2,200)   =   £17,200 F

            Total = (2,500 x £43) – £99,000 =   £8,500 F

      (c)   True: (iii), (iv), (viii), (x).

3.4 (a)   £448,000 $\div$ 14,000   = £32 per hour

      (b) $14,000 \div 2,000$ = 7 hours each

      (c)   7 x 1800   = 12,600 hours

      (d)   Exp = £448,000 – £455,000   = £7,000 A

             Vol = £32 x (12,600 – 14,000)   = £44,800 A

             Eff = £32 x (12,600 – 12,000)   = £19,200 F

             Cap = £32 x (12,000 – 14,000)   = £64,000 A

      (e)   Reconciliation:

Overhead Absorbed	£403,200
Expenditure Variance	£ 7,000 A
Volume Variance (£64,000 – £19,200)	£ 44,800 A
Actual Overhead	£455,000

3.5   Absorption rate per standard screening:

         £12,000 $\div$ (16 screenings x 4 weeks)   =   £187.50

     Actual number of customers in terms of standard screenings:

         3.240 $\div$ 40   =   81 standard screenings

     Putting this data into a slightly modified version of the diagram gives (see next page):

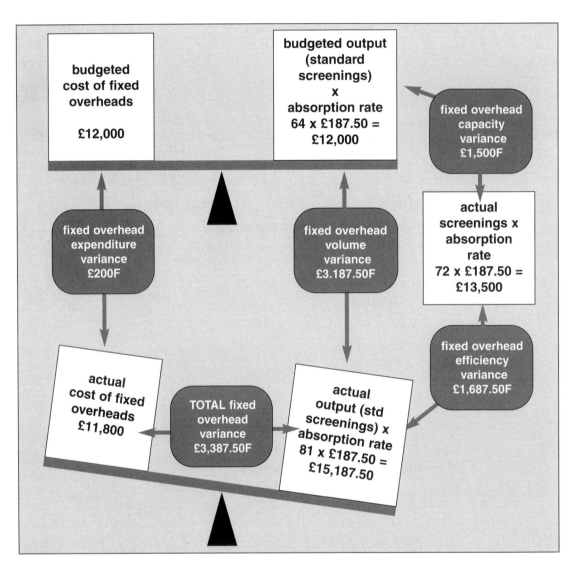

Reconciliation:

Fixed Overhead absorbed		£15,187.50
Less: Expenditure Variance		£200.00 F
Efficiency Variance	£1,687.50 F	
Capacity Variance	£1,500.00 F	
+ Volume Variance		£3,187.50 F
		£3,387.50
Actual Fixed Overheads		£11,800.00

The expenditure variance arises because the expenditure is less than planned. The volume variance arises due to the overheads absorbed by the greater number of customers than was budgeted for (3,240 instead of 40 x 16 x 4 = 2,560).The capacity variance shows the effect of holding an extra 8 screenings than originally planned. The efficiency variance shows the additional overhead absorbed due to the better filling of the building (an average of 3,240 ÷ 72 = 45 attendances per screening instead of the expected 40).

CHAPTER 4: STANDARD COSTING – FURTHER ANALYSIS

4.1 The following statements are true: (b), (c), (d), (f). All the other statements are false.

4.2 **Analysis of March Price Variance:**
Seasonally adjusted standard price per kilo = £16 + 20% = £19.20
Part of variance expected due to seasonality:
1,000 kg x (Original Std – Revised Std)
1,000 kg x (£16.00 – £19.20)   = £3,200 Adverse
Part of variance due to other influences:
(1,000 kg x Revised Std) – Actual Cost
£19,200 – £18,000   = £1,200 Favourable
(£3,200 A + £1,200 F = Original Variance £2,000 A)

Analysis of April Price Variance:
Seasonally adjusted standard price per kilo = £16 – 10% = £14.40
Part of variance expected due to seasonality:
1,200 kg x (Original Std – Revised Std)
1,200 kg x (£16.00 – £14.40)   = £1,920 Favourable
Part of variance due to other influences:
(1,200 kg x Revised Std) – Actual Cost
£17,280 – £18,500   = £1,220 Adverse
(£1,920 F + £1,220 A = Original Variance £700 F)

4.3 (a) Labour Rate Variance:
(3,200 hours x Std Rate) – Actual Cost
(3,200 hours x £7.25) – £23,744   = £ 544 Adverse

(i) Analysed into:
Part due to actual pay award:
3,200 hours x (Std Rate – Revised Std Rate)
3,200 hours x (£7.25 – (£7.00 + 4.5%))
3,200 hours x (£7.25 – £7.315)   = £ 208 Adverse

Part due to other influences:
(3,200 hours x Revised Std Rate) – Actual Cost
(3,200 hours x £7.315) – £ 23,744   = £ 336 Adverse

(ii) Analysed into:
Part due to movement in index:
3,200 hours x (Std Rate – Revised Std Rate)
3,200 hours x (£7.25 – (£7.00 x 150÷140))
3,200 hours x (£7.25 – £7.50)   = £ 800 Adverse

Part due to other influences:
(3,200 hours x Revised Std Rate) – Actual Cost
(3,200 hours x £7.50) – £ 23,744   = £ 256 Favourable

(b)   The first analysis is more useful because it uses the actual pay award implemented for the labour force to calculate a revised standard rate. This effectively amends the standard into what it would have been had the company accurately predicted the pay rise. The £208 adverse variance illustrates for week 12 the effect of the pay rise being greater than was originally expected, whereas the £336 adverse variance is due to other factors (for example bonus payments or overtime premium).

The second analysis is based on the increase of the wage rates in the region as a whole, and does not reflect the actual pay rise awarded in this organisation.

4.4   (a)   Standard weight of materials per unit of production
        = 3,000 kg ÷ 1,500 units   = 2 kg per unit.

Standard weight of materials for actual production
        = 2 kg x 1,700 units   = 3,400 kg.

(b)   Standard cost of one kg material = £15,000 ÷ 3,000 kg = £5

Standard cost of material for actual production = £5 x 3,400 kg = £17,000

(c)   Direct material price variance: (3,600 x £5) – £21,600   = £3,600 Adverse

Direct material usage variance: £5 x (3,400 kg – 3,600 kg)   = £1,000 Adverse

(d)   Standard cost of direct materials for actual production   £17,000
       Direct material price variance   £3,600 A
       Direct material usage variance   £1,000 A
       Actual cost of direct materials   £ 21,600

(e)   Analysis of direct material price variance:
       Part caused by exchange rate movement:
              3,600 kg x (Std price – Revised Std Price)
              3,600 kg x (£5.00 – (£5.00 x 2.5 ÷ 2.00))
              3,600 kg x (£5.00 – £6.25)   = £ 4,500 Adverse

       Part caused by other factors:
              (3,600 kg x Revised Std) – Actual Cost
              (3,600 kg x £6.25) – £21,600   = £ 900 Favourable

CHAPTER 5: MEASURING QUALITY

5.1   'Quality' can be considered as the fitness of a product or service for the purpose for which it is to be used. In the case described, the opinions of the members indicate that the majority of members think that the paper and the printing on the cover are suitable for the journal and changes would not increase its fitness for the purpose for which it is used. More expensive printing and paper would not, in this case, add to the quality of the product.

'Enhancement of value' means increasing the value of a product or service, by adding desirable features for example. In the case described, most members do not want a crossword in the journal, because it would not enhance the value of the journal in terms of its purpose. However, a majority of members would like more pages, provided the cost of postage is not increased. Value for money would be obtained from the postal service and these members think that the journal's value would be enhanced by having more pages.

5.2   Prevention Cost: (b)
Appraisal Cost: (e)
Internal Failure Costs: (a) (d) (f)
External Failure Costs: (c) (g)

5.3   2,000,000 organisers are sold and 1 in 2,000 develop the fault. Therefore 1,000 are faulty, but only 750 of these are returned.

The external failure cost of repairs is 750 x £10 = £7,500.

The internal failure cost of advertising to replace lost customers is £50,000.

Other costs, which cannot be measured on the information available, are the internal failure costs which have been incurred in analysing the fault to find out what repair is necessary.

To improve the situation, the company must eliminate the fault. As repair is possible, it seems likely that the design could be altered to replace the part which develops the fault. Reviewing the specification would be an internal failure cost. Otherwise, stringent quality control or testing of the organisers must be carried out, which would increase prevention and appraisal costs.

5.4   (a)   'Explicit costs of quality' are those which are recorded in the accounting information and can be identified. You may have given as examples in this case:

   •   the cost of replacement decoders at £52 each, ie £52 x 3,860 = £200,720.
   •   the cost of the customer helpline £1,400,000
   •   the proportion of the cost of delivery which is for replacement decoders, which may be calculated on the basis that total deliveries were 8,500 + 3,860 = 12,360.

   £250,000 x 3,860 ÷ 12,360 = £78,074.

   (b)   'Implicit costs of quality' are those which are not recorded or separately identifiable. Examples in this case include:

   •   the part of the subscriptions lost in this period due to customers' dissatisfaction with the speed of the delivery service (some customers may have cancelled for other reasons, but this is not known)
   •   the loss of future subscriptions due to poor quality service and resulting bad publicity, if any
   •   the part of the delivery cost which is due to disruption of schedules in order to ensure replacements reach customers quickly.

5.5   'Cost reduction' refers to a positive programme of reducing costs throughout an organisation, without reducing the value of a product or service. In the case described, recruitment is an important function within the firm, although not its main business. If costs can be reduced for this function, without losing value, this would benefit the firm. It would be necessary to compare the cost of the service offered by Splash Ltd with the current costs. As senior staff time, storage costs and transport costs would be saved, using Splash Ltd may reduce costs. The value of the display stand at conventions would be maintained and possibly even enhanced when looked after by specialists in this field.

'Value analysis' means looking at every aspect of an existing product or service to see whether the same or a better result can be achieved in some other way. In the case of PQR and Partners, the firm offers an accountancy service to customers, but every aspect of the business could be looked at to see whether it contributes value. The value of the display stand and a presence at careers conventions seems to be assumed, but it could be investigated to see whether this assumption is justified. Is there an alternative way of recruiting the best trainees? If not, then Splash Ltd can be considered as a alternative way of carrying out this particular function.

CHAPTER 6: MEASURING PERFORMANCE

6.1 **Consistency** means that performance measures being compared must be prepared using the same policies and methods, so that the comparison is of like with like.

Benchmarking means that performance is measured against standards, targets or industry averages, relating to what is important to the organisation. Benchmarks may be set either internally or externally.

Qualitative data is data which cannot be measured numerically, for example opinions and judgements of performance.

6.2 Answer (c) is correct, because the gross profit = £500,000 x 24% = £120,000

Therefore £500,000 – Cost of sales = £120,000
And cost of sales = £500,000 – £120,000 = £380,000.
Gross profit – Expenses = Operating profit
Therefore £120,000 – expenses = £50,000
And hence expenses = £120,000 – £50,000 = £70,000

6.3

	31 May 2001	31 May 2000
Gross Profit % of Sales	28%	30%
Net Profit % of Sales	16%	18%
Administration expense as % of Sales	4.8%	5.3%
Selling expense as % of Sales	7.2%	6.7%

Comments: Looking at the original figures, it can be seen that Sales Revenue, Purchases and Expenses have all increased in the second year. Administration, which would probably be expected to be a fixed cost, has remained relatively stable. Stock levels have built up in both years. Profits have also increased.

Looking at the ratios, the percentage Gross Profit has decreased slightly, which could be due to increased purchase costs or having to reduce selling prices, or both. The expenses together still represent 12% of Sales, and as would be expected for a fixed cost, the administration percentage has gone down slightly. The selling expense, however, has increased as a proportion of sales, possibly due to increased advertising to generate more sales. The reduction in Net Profit percentage results from the decreased Gross Profit margin.

Toni Jones should consider whether there is a problem with the build-up of stock – are there goods which do not sell? Also the reasons for the decrease in Gross Profit margin and increase in selling expenses should be investigated.

6.4 (a)

Gross Profit margin	= (1,910 ÷ 2,500) x 100%	= 76.4%
Operating profit margin	= (625 ÷ 2,500) x 100%	= 25.0%
Return on Capital Employed	= (625 ÷ 2,840) x 100%	= 22.0%
Asset turnover	= 2,500 ÷ 2,840	= 0.88 times
The average age of debtors	= (160 ÷ 2,500) x 365	= 23 days
Average finished goods stock	= 0.5 x (30 + 90)	= 60

The average age of finished goods stock (using average stock)

$$= (60 ÷ 590) x 365 \qquad = 37 \text{ days.}$$

(b)   Both ROCE and Asset turnover depend on the value of the net assets. During the year ended 30 June 2001, Subsidiary Jack Ltd has considerable additions to the fixed assets, but it is not known at what time of the year these were acquired. It is possible that these new assets have not yet generated additional sales (for asset turnover) or profits (for ROCE). These two measures would be lower as a result.

(c)   If Subsidiary Jack Ltd had achieved the target Asset turnover of 1.5 times, its turnover would have been 1.5 x £2,840,000 = £4,260,000.

(d)   Assuming Subsidiary Jack Ltd had maintained its operating profit margin of 25% on turnover of £4,260,000, its operating profit would be

25% x £4,260,000 = £1,065,000.

With this operating profit, its ROCE would be

(1,065 ÷ 2,840) x 100% = 37.5%.

6.5   (a)   Gross Profit = 35% of £200,000 = £70,000

Turnover – Cost of Sales = Gross Profit

£200,000 – Cost of Sales = £70,000

Therefore Cost of Sales = £130,000

(b) $\dfrac{\text{Current Assets – Stock}}{\text{Current Liabilities}} = \dfrac{\text{Current Assets – Stock}}{£7,000} = 0.9$

Therefore: Current Assets – Stock = 0.9 x £7,000 = £6,300

Current Assets = £6,300 + Stock = £6,300 + £4,200 = £10,500

Current Ratio = Current Assets ÷ Current Liabilities = £10,500 ÷ £7,000

Therefore Current Ratio = 1.5 : 1.

CHAPTER 7: MEASURING PERFORMANCE – FURTHER ASPECTS

7.1   You may have given examples including any of the following:
(a)   Amount of gross profit, net profit, turnover, prices, variances, value added
(b)   Ratios, number of machine hours used, number of units produced, number of rejected units, number of orders processed, number of customer complaints, etc
(c)   Results of customer opinion surveys, peer reviews or appraisals

7.2   The method is to divide each figure by the index for its own year and multiply by the index for the required year, for example year 1 income, put into year 3 terms, becomes:

£260,000 ÷ 115 x 130 = £293,913.

	Year1	Year 2	Year 3
Income (£ in year 3 terms)	293,913	322,358	400,000
Expenditure (£ in year 3 terms)	226,087	253,659	330,000
Surplus (£ in year 3 terms)	67,826	68,699	70,000

It can be seen that the income and the surplus are both increasing in real terms, but not as significantly as the original figures suggest. (Percentages are useful for comparison: for example the surplus figures increased by 16.7% from year 1 to year 3, but in real terms the increase is only 3.2%).

7.3   Exe Ltd, for the year 2000,

(a)   Value Added = £972,000 – (£216,000 + £324,000)

= £972,000 – £540,000 = £432,000

(b)   Value Added per employee = £432,000 ÷ 54 = £8,000

Output = 67,500 product units.

Therefore the Unit Cost is calculated as follows:

(c)   Materials used: £216,000 ÷ 67,500 = £3.20 per unit

(d)   Total cost of inputs: £540,000 ÷ 67,500 = £8.00 per unit

7.4   Wessit Housing Association

(a)   The ratios for each of the two companies are:

	Staylite Ltd	Temeglass Ltd
gross profit margin	45.3%	47.6%
operating profit percentage	5.3%	6.6%
return on capital employed	65.4%	65.9%
current ratio	1.09 : 1	1.97 : 1
quick ratio	0.64 : 1	1.20 : 1
asset turnover	12.44 times	9.99 times
sales per employee	£478,750	£527,778
operating profit per employee	£25,188	£34,833

(b)   Indicators of the profitability of the two companies include the profit percentages and ROCE. Temeglass Ltd appears to be more profitable using any of these indicators. The financial position of the two suppliers can be seen partly from the original figures, in that Temeglass Ltd has no long-term liabilities, whereas Staylite Ltd has significant long-term loans (debentures). Also Temeglass Ltd has a better liquidity position, as can be seen from the current and quick ratios.

(c)   The main performance indicators which may be used to indicate efficiency are ROCE and operating profit percentage. (Profit per employee may also be significant).

(d)   The performance indicator which may be used to indicate the productivity of the companies is sales per employee, although this is not ideal because comparative selling prices and volumes of output are not known. Output per employee would be a better indicator. Profit per employee could also be used here.

(e)   The limitations of the above analysis are:

When using the published accounts of companies, it is not possible to guarantee that we are comparing like with like, as different policies (including those regarding depreciation, stock valuation and goodwill, for example) will affect the results. Also there is the possibility that the Balance Sheet does not show a typical position. In this case, only one year's results are available for each company, so it is not possible to see whether there are any significant trends.

(f)   A further indicator which Wessit Housing Association should seek to obtain would be some measure of quality or value for money. Suggestions include selling prices, product specifications, or some indication of customer satisfaction. The companies may be able to show their previous work and it would be particularly useful to the housing association to obtain opinions or references from previous customers. Numbers of customer complaints would be another possible measure, if available.

7.5   Efficiency ratio = (Standard hours of actual output ÷ Actual hours) x 100%
Standard hours of actual output = 2,400 units x 6 hours = 14,400 hours
Actual hours = 15,000 hours
Therefore Efficiency ratio = (14,400 ÷ 15,000) x 100% = 96%
Capacity Ratio = (Actual hours ÷ Budgeted hours) x 100%
             = (15,000 ÷ 14,700) x 100% = 102%
Activity Ratio = (Standard hours of actual output ÷ Budgeted hours) x 100%
             = (14,400 ÷ 14,700) x 100% = 98%

7.6   The aspects of value for money which are used are:

- *Economy:* controlling expenditure on costs. Economy can be measured in the same way as costs in businesses, by comparing with budgets and calculating variances for example.

- *Efficiency:* relating 'outputs' to inputs, meaning that obtaining more from the money spent shows greater efficiency. A possible indicator for efficiency is the cost per unit, where units of output can be defined.

- *Effectiveness:* relating 'outputs' to the aims of the organisation, so that achieving more of what it sets out to do shows greater effectiveness. Effectiveness may be measured by comparison with targets or with other similar organisations.

Some aspects of non-profit-making activities can only be assessed by qualitative measures: opinions and judgements of experts, users or those who provide the funding.

7.7   Up-to-You Gym: (your suggested indicators may differ from the following and only one is required for each perspective) Nb: 'W' references below refer to the working notes at the bottom of the page.

(a)   The financial perspective: possible appropriate measures from the available information are profit margin (W1) and sales per employee (W2)

(b)   The customer perspective: customer satisfaction and loyalty may be seen from the visits per member (W3) or the percentage of previous years' members who return (W4)

(c)   The internal perspective could be considered by looking at cost per member visit (W5) or the staff : members ratio (W6)

(d)   The innovation and learning perspective could be assessed by measuring the percentage increase in new members (W7) or alternatively the new members as a percentage of the total (W8). Also an indicator of developing new services is opening hours per day (W9).

Workings: the method is shown for 20-2, check that you can agree the answer for 20-1.

		30 Sept 20-2		30 Sept 20-1
W1	profit margin	(230 ÷ 750) x 100%	= 30.7%	28.3%
W2	sales per employee	£750,000 ÷ 22	= £34,091	£42,857
W3	visits per member	60,300 ÷ 1,200	= 50	43
W4	% returning (of prev.)	(470 ÷ 700) x 100%	= 67%	30% (of 580 in 20-0)
W5	cost per visit	£520,000 ÷ 60,300	= £8.62	£14.22
W6	staff:members	1:(1,200 ÷ 22)	= 1:55	1:50
W7	% inc.in new mem.	730 ÷ 525	= 1.39, so 39%	not known
W8	new members %	(730 ÷ 1,200) x 100%	= 61%	75%
W9	open hrs per day	4,368 ÷ 364	= 12 hrs	10.3 hrs

CHAPTER 8: USING BUDGETS

8.1 (i) (c) Since maturity should be a relatively stable period it may provide the data for a sound forecast. However the fact that it will be followed at some point by a period of decline should not be ignored.

(ii) (e) All the factors mentioned will influence the reliability of a forecast based on sampling. The theory of sampling was covered in more detail in chapter 1.

(iii) (b) and (c) Historical trends in price changes can only be valid in the future if the trend is considered likely to continue. The reliability of the data will be improved by choosing as specific an index as possible.

8.2 (a) The speed at which the craftsmen work, and their working hours will determine their output. Since they can sell all that they produce their output will be the principal budget factor.

(b) The transport requirements of the turkey supplier will form the principal budget factor. The transport company and the turkey supplier will have a common activity level over the coming year.

(c) The maintenance requirements of the Manchester trams will form the principal budget factor. This will in turn depend upon maintenance schedules for the current fleet, plus that for any additional trams to be acquired.

(d) The demand from the staff at the business park for baked potatoes seems likely to easily outstrip supply, based on the figures given. The capacity of the outlet would therefore form the principal budget factor.

8.3 (a) Average trend movement is difference between last and first trend figures, divided by number of movements.

$= (6{,}290 - 5{,}800) \div 7 = + 70$

(b) If trend is increasing at an average 70 policies per quarter, then by

Year 3 quarter 3 it will be $6{,}290 + (3 \times 70)$ $= 6{,}500$, and by
Year 3 quarter 4 it will be $6{,}290 + (4 \times 70)$ $= 6{,}570$.

Adjusting these figures by the seasonal variations (which were identical for both years) gives:

Year 3 quarter 3 forecast of $(6{,}500 + 880)$ $= 7{,}380$
Year 3 quarter 4 forecast of $(6{,}570 - 100)$ $= 6{,}470$.

8.4 The production budget in units for month 5 equals:

Budgeted Sales Units	1,800	units
– Opening Stock of Finished Goods	(500)	units
+ Closing Stock of Finished Goods.	400	units
Production budget	1,700	units

The raw materials usage budget is based on the raw material required to satisfy the production budget:

Raw Materials Usage $= (1{,}700 \text{ units} \times 4 \text{ kilos per unit})$ $= 6{,}800$ kilos.

The raw material purchases budget for month 5 will equal:

Raw materials usage budget	6,800 kilos
– opening stock of raw materials,	(1,200) kilos
+ closing stock of raw materials.	1,500 kilos
Raw materials purchases budget	7,100 kilos

8.5 (a)

	Jan	Feb	Mar	Apr	May	Jun	Total
Units of Zapp							
Sales	5000	4000	6500	5000	6500	5000	32000
Less opening stock of Finished Goods	(3000)	(2000)	(3250)	(2500)	(3250)	(2500)	
Add closing stock of Finished Goods	2000	3250	2500	3250	2500	2500	
Production Budget	4000	5250	5750	5750	5750	5000	31500

	Jan	Feb	Mar	Apr	May	Jun	Total
Litres of Woo							
Materials Usage – Woo (Production x 2 litres)	8000	10500	11500	11500	11500	10000	63000
Less opening stock of Woo	(8000)	(10500)	(11500)	(11500)	(11500)	(10000)	
Add closing stock of Woo	10500	11500	11500	11500	10000	10000	
Materials Purchase – Woo	10500	11500	11500	11500	10000	10000	65000

	Jan	Feb	Mar	Apr	May	Jun	Total
Litres of Koo							
Materials Usage – Koo (Production x 3 litres)	12000	15750	17250	17250	17250	15000	94500
Less opening stock of Koo	(16000)	(15750)	(17250)	(17250)	(17250)	(15000)	
Add closing stock of Koo	15750	17250	17250	17250	15000	15000	
Materials Purchase – Koo	11750	17250	17250	17250	15000	15000	93500

	Jan	Feb	Mar	Apr	May	Jun	Total
Direct Labour (Hours) (Production x 0.5 hour)	2000	2625	2875	2875	2875	2500	15750

(b) **Six Months to 30 June**

	£	£
Sales Budget (32,000 units at £70 per unit)		2,240,000
Cost of Sales Budget:		
Opening Stock Finished Goods:		
(3,000 units at direct cost £42* per unit)	126,000	
Cost of Production:		
Direct Costs (31,500 units at £42 per unit)	1,323,000	
Fixed Production Overheads		
(per budget for six months)	600,000	
Less		
Closing Stock of Finished Goods		
(2,500 units at £42 per unit)	(105,000)	
Cost of Sales		1,944,000
Budgeted Gross Profit		296,000

* The direct cost per unit is made up of:	
2 litres of Woo at £3 per litre	£6
3 litres of Koo at £11 per litre	£33
0.5 hour direct labour at £6 per hour	£3
Direct Cost per unit	£42

The budgeted gross profit reconciles with:	
32,000 units at (£70 – £42) per unit	£ 896,000
Less Fixed Production Overheads	£ 600,000
Budgeted Gross Profit	£ 296,000

CHAPTER 9: PRACTICAL ASPECTS OF BUDGET PREPARATION

9.1
(a)	Production Budget
(b)	Raw Materials Purchases Budget
(c)	Production Budget
(d)	Raw Materials Utilisation Budget
(e)	Direct Labour Utilisation Budget
(f)	Production Budget (via Sales Budget)
(g)	Raw Materials Purchases Budget

9.2 (c) 1,875 kilos

Working: Prepared carrots required = 30 x 50 kg = 1,500 kg.
Therefore 1,500 kg represents 80% of unprepared carrots.
Unprepared carrots = 1,500 x 100 ÷ 80 = 1,875 kilos.

9.3 The amount of completed units that passes the quality control check in May will need to be:

Budgeted Sales (Units)	15,000	
– Opening Stock of Finished Goods	(7,500)	(50% May Sales)
+ Closing Stock of Finished Goods	10,000	(50% June Sales)
= production of 'good' units	17,500	units

This amount will equal 87.5% of the total production to allow for the rejection of 12.5%. The total production budget for May, must therefore be:

17,500 units x 100 ÷ 87.5 = 20,000 units.

9.4 (a) The amount of completed bumpers that passes the quality control check in week 9 will need to be:

Budgeted Sales	37,500	
– Opening Stock of Finished Goods	(10,000)	
+ Closing Stock of Finished Goods	2,425	
= production of 'good' units	29,925	bumpers

This amount will equal 95% of the total production to allow for the rejection of 5%. The total production for week 9, must therefore be:

29,925 bumpers x 100 ÷ 95 = 31,500 bumpers.

(b) The number of rejects will therefore be 31,500 x 5% = 1,575 bumpers.

(check: 29,925 + 1,575 = 31,500)

(c) 31,500 completed bumpers will contain 31,500 x 4 kg = 126,000 kilos of plastic. This will be after wastage of 10% during production . . .

So materials usage will be 126,000 x 100 ÷ 90 = 140,000 kilos plastic pellets.

(d) The plastic pellets purchases will allow for the changing stocks of raw materials.

Materials Usage (kilos pellets)	140,000	
– Opening Stock of raw materials	(20,000)	
+ Closing Stock of raw materials	30,000	
= Plastic pellets to be purchased	150,000	kilos.

9.5 (a)

Budgeted Sales (Pies)	150,000	
– Opening Stock of Finished Goods	(10,000)	
+ Closing Stock of Finished Goods	2,500	
= production of apple pies	142,500	pies

(b) The 142,500 pies produced will contain

142,500 x 0.4 kilos = 57,000 kilos cooked apples.

Due to weight loss during cooking this must have started as

57,000 x 100 ÷ 75 = 76,000 kilos of prepared raw apples.

The peeling and coring etc. process will have caused additional wastage.

The quantity of raw apples used in production will therefore have been:

76,000 x 100 ÷ 80 = 95,000 kilos, at a cost of £0.60 per kilo = £57,000.

(c)   The raw apple purchases will allow for the changing stocks of apples.

Materials Usage (kilos raw whole apples)   95,000

– Opening Stock of raw materials   (10,000)

+ Closing Stock of raw materials   15,000

= Raw whole apples to be purchased   100,000   kilos.

This will cost 100,000 x £0.60 = £60,000.

9.6

	Advantages	Disadvantages
Overtime:	Known staff abilities	Overtime premium rate
	Good utilisation of own equipment	Staff may not wish to work overtime.
	Consistent supervision by regular supervisors	Tiredness causing quality problems.
Sub Contacting	Quality may be contactors' responsibility	Cost (a profit is made by sub contractor)
	Credit may be available No overheads.	Process out of organisation's control

9.7   (a)   (i)   Additional cost of using overtime:
Overtime premium   £4 per hour ÷ 20 units = £0.20 per unit.

(ii)   Additional cost of bringing production forward one week:
Financing £150 ÷ 1,000 units = £0.15 per unit.

Therefore it is cheaper to bring production forward one week than to use overtime. However it would be cheaper to use overtime than to bring production forward by more than one week.

(b)   Using the above ranking, and working back from the last week:

Week 14   Demand is 10,000 units above overtime threshold. If made, additional 10,000 units in week 13 additional cost would be financing plus overtime, due to high demand in week 13 already. Therefore use overtime and produce all 75,000 units in week 14, as this is cheaper than making two or more weeks early.

Week 13   Demand is 5,000 units above overtime threshold. 3,000 of the additional units required can be made in week 12 without incurring overtime premium. Remaining additional 2,000 units should be made using overtime in week 13.

Week 12   Produce 62,000 units for immediate sale, plus 3,000 units for week 13 (as above).

Week 11   Produce 65,000 units with no additional cost.

Week 10   Produce 60,000 units with no additional cost.

In summary:

	Production	Additional Cost
Week 10	60,000	–
Week 11	65,000	–
Week 12	65,000	Financing: 3,000 x £0.15 = £450
Week 13	67,000	Overtime: 2,000 x £0.20 = £400
Week 14	75,000	Overtime:10,000 x £0.20 = £2,000
	Total additional cost	£2,850

CHAPTER 10: APPLICATIONS OF BUDGETING METHODS

10.1 (b)

10.2 (a)   Step cost
  (b)   Variable cost
  (c)   Semi-variable cost
  (d)   Fixed cost

10.3 (a)   Variable cost per unit = £(59000 − 43000) ÷ (110000 − 70000) = £0.40
    Fixed cost = £43000 − (£0.40 x 70000) = £15,000
  (b)   Total cost for 80,000 units = £15,000 + (£0.40 x 80,000) = £47,000

10.4 Workings needed:
  (i) Running costs are variable costs: working in thousands of £ and miles:
    37.5 ÷ 250 = 52.5 ÷ 350 = 0.15, that is cost per mile = £0.15.
    £0.15 x 300,000 = £45,500, shown as 45.0 in the table in £000s.

  (ii) Maintenance is a semi-variable cost and the high-low method is used:
    Difference in cost is £10,000 for 100,000 extra miles.
    Variable cost per mile = £0.10
    From the first column, fixed cost = £29,000 − (£0.10 x 250,000) = £4,000.
    Therefore for 300,000 miles, maintenance = £4,000 + (£0.10 x 300,000) = £34,000

  (iii) All other costs are fixed and remain unchanged.

The completed tables are as follows, using the flexed budget for 300,000 miles for comparison with the actual costs for that mileage in the second table.

Transport Fleet Flexible Budgets for the year to 31 March 2001			
Budgeted annual mileage	250,000 £000s	300,000 £000s	350,000 £000s
Running costs	37.5	45.0	52.5
Maintenance of vehicles	29.0	34.0	39.0
Vehicle licences	24.0	24.0	24.0
Insurance	10.0	10.0	10.0
Garaging	12.5	12.5	12.5
Depreciation	40.0	40.0	40.0
Total costs	153.0	165.5	178.0
Cost per mile (to nearest 1p)	£0.61	£0.55	£0.51

Transport Fleet Operating Results for the year to 31 March 2001

	Budget	Actual	Variance
Annual mileage	300,000	300,000	-
	£000s	£000s	£000s
Running costs	45.0	51.5	6.5 A
Maintenance of vehicles	34.0	33.0	1.0 F
Vehicle licences	24.0	24.0	– –
Insurance	10.0	11.0	1.0 A
Garaging	12.5	12.3	0.2 F
Depreciation	40.0	40.0	– –
Total costs	165.5	171.8	6.3 A
Cost per mile (to nearest 1p)	£0.55	£0.57	£0.02 A

10.5   **Task 1: preparatory workings:**

400 prints per month amounts to 400 x 12 = 4,800 prints to be produced and sold in the year.

Copying costs and mounting and framing costs are variable, given as constant amounts per print.

Using the high-low method for power costs gives:

Variable cost per print = £(225 – 175) ÷ 200 = £0.25 per print and hence the fixed part of the cost is £175 – (£0.25 x 300) = £100 *per month*, or £1,200 per year.

Budgeted administration and advertising for the year are £12,000 and £30,000 respectively (fixed).

The **budgeted variable production cost per print** is:

Copying	£5.00
Mounting and framing	£22.00
Power	£0.25
Total variable cost	£27.25

In absorption costing, there would be an additional power cost of £100 ÷ 400 = £0.25 for the budgeted average fixed power cost per print, giving

The **average budgeted production cost per print** can be written

EITHER as:

Copying	£5.00
Mounting and framing	£22.00
Power (variable part)	£0.25
Total variable cost	£27.25
Fixed power cost absorbed	£0.25
Total production cost	£27.50

OR as:

Copying	£5.00
Mounting and framing	£22.00
Power	£0.50
Total production cost	£27.50

Budgets in absorption and marginal costing formats would therefore be:

Historic Print budget for the first year: Absorption Costing **4,800 prints per year**		
	£	£
Sales		240,000
Less: Cost of sales:		
Opening Stock	–	
Cost of production of 4,800 prints		
Copying	24,000	
Mount and frame	105,600	
Power	2,400	
Less: closing stock	–	
Total cost of sales		132,000
Gross profit		108,000
Administration	12,000	
Advertising	30,000	
Total fixed costs		42,000
Net profit		66,000

Historic Print budget for the first year: Marginal Costing **4,800 prints per year**		
	£	£
Sales		240,000
Less: Cost of sales:		
Opening stock	–	
Copying	24,000	
Mount and frame	105,600	
Power	1,200	
Less: Closing stock	–	
Total cost of sales		130,800
Contribution		109,200
Fixed costs		
Power	1,200	
Administration	12,000	
Advertising	30,000	
Total fixed costs		43,200
Net profit		66,000

Task 2: performance statements:

Budgets must be prepared for the situation where 4,000 prints are produced and 3,500 sold. The closing stock of 500 prints is to be valued at budgeted cost, which will be £27.50 per print in the case of absorption costing and £27.25 per print in the case of marginal costing (using the workings in the solution to Task 1). Therefore closing stock will be:

£27.50 x 500 = £13,750 in absorption costing and £27.25 x 500 = £13,625 in marginal costing.

The two required performance statements will therefore be as follows:

Historic Prints: performance statement for the first year using absorption costing					
	Flexed budget		*Actual*		*Variance*
Sales (3,500 prints)		175,000		157,500	17,500 A
Less: cost of sales					
Opening Stock	–		–		–
Cost of production of 4,000 prints					
Copying	20,000		20,000		–
Mount and Frame	88,000		84,000		4,000 F
Power **(W1)**	2,000		1,700		300 F
Less: closing stock Of 500 prints	(13,750)	96,250	(13,750)	91,950	
Gross Profit		78,750		65,550	13,200 A
Administration	12,000		15,600		3,600 A
Advertising	30,000		24,000		6,000 F
Total fixed costs		42,000		39,600	2,400 F
		36,750			
Under-absorption of Fixed cost **(W2)**		(200)			200 F
Net profit		36,550		25,950	10,600 A

W1 The flexible budget figure has been calculated as follows:

£0.50 to be absorbed into each unit produced, giving 4,000 x £0.50 = £2,000.

(An alternative method would be as £1,200 + (£0.25 x 4,000) = £2,200, which would avoid the problem of under-absorption, but would not be consistent with the total production cost of £27.50 calculated in Task 1 for absorption costing. The net profit would still be £36,550 in the flexed budget, agreeing with the adjusted net profit above).

W2 The under-absorption is the *fixed part of the absorbed power* cost on the under-production of prints:

Planned production was 4,800 prints, so 4,000 prints is under-production of 800. The fixed power cost absorbed is £0.25 per print, hence the under-absorption = 800 x £0.25 = £200.

Under-absorption is not shown in the 'Actual' column because the full actual cost has been included in the cost of production.

Historic Prints: performance statement for the first year using marginal costing					
	Flexed budget		Actual		Variance
Sales (3,500 prints)		175,000		157,500	17,500 A
Less: cost of sales					
Opening Stock	–		–		–
Marginal cost of production of 4,000 prints					
Mount and Frame	88,000		84,000		4,000 F
Power **(W3)**	1,000		500		500 F
Less: closing stock of 500 prints	(13,625)	95,375	(13,625)	90,875	
Contribution		79,625		66,625	13,000 A
Power (fixed part)	1,200		1,200		–
Administration	12,000		15,600		3,600 A
Advertising	30,000		24,000		6,000 F
Total fixed costs		43,200		40,800	2,400 F
Net Profit		36,425		25,825	10,600 A

W3   The budget is 4,000 x £0.25 variable cost.

The actual figure is £1,700 less the fixed cost of £1,200 (given as equal to budget).

CHAPTER 11: MANAGEMENT ISSUES IN RELATION TO BUDGETING

11.1   (a)   A budgetary control system can be an effective way of motivating employees providing they accept the system as fair and reasonable. Most importantly, the standards or targets set in the budgets should be challenging, but achievable. Targets which are too low or impossibly high will not motivate people.

Measurement of performance against budget should be based only on aspects of performance over which the person has some influence. Participation in the budget setting process may improve motivation, although some employees prefer to have targets set for them.

(b)   Performance related pay can be an effective way of motivating employees providing they are aware of what constitutes good performance and see the measurement being used as fair and reasonable. This means that they need to:

- know the organisation's objectives
- have budgets which are in line with those objectives
- accept the budgets as their own targets
- feel that they can improve performance, ie they have both the skills and the authority to do so
- feel that the financial and non-financial rewards for improved performance are worthwhile.

11.2 The advantages that may arise from participative budgeting include:

- There is an input of information from those who have more detailed, specialist knowledge of the work to be done

- Those who participate should have a more positive attitude towards the budgeting system

- Those who participate should more readily accept the budget as their personal target, which improves motivation

- Those who participate may broaden their job experience and acquire new skills

- The participation process should improve communication through the different levels of management, in particular regarding the organisational goals.

11.3 Goal congruence means that the goals of individuals within an organisation are in line with the goals of the organisation as a whole. This is the desirable situation where achievement of individual goals will contribute towards the progress of the whole organisation in the desired direction.

11.4 The absorption costing report shows that the costs of production were in line with the budget and that the non-production overheads were below budget. However, the sales volume was 200 units below budget, and the level of gross profit was only maintained by the increase in the selling price (which could have caused the reduction in demand). The reasons why the higher net profit does not necessarily reflect performance are:

- The production was not all sold as planned, and the closing stock value includes £200 of fixed production overhead which is carried forward into December. Continually building up unsold stock can show higher recorded profit in absorption costing, but is not necessarily a favourable situation.

- The non-production overheads were lower than budget, but this may or may not be a result of management action. It is possible that these are affected by external factors, for example the prices of some bought-in services such as electricity or telephone costs may have been reduced by the providers because of competition in their markets.

The report could be improved by:

- Using marginal costing. This would mean that the fixed production overhead of £1,000 per month would all be charged in November. The emphasis on contribution in marginal costing would show the difference between the original budget and the actual results in terms of total contribution:

- Original budget: £(10 – 5) x 1000 = £5,000 total contribution

- Actual results: £(11 – 5) x 800 = £4,800 total contribution

- This shows clearly the net effect of the higher selling price but lower sales volume. A marginal costing statement is shown opposite.

- Using flexible budgeting. This would mean that the actual results for sales of 800 units would be compared with the budget for the same sales volume.

- Give more information regarding non-production overheads, so that the reason for the reduction can be investigated.

The marginal costing statement would be:

	Budget £	Budget £	Actual £	Actual £
Sales 1,000 x £10		10,000		
Sales 800 x £11				8,800
Opening stock	–		–	
Cost of Production	5,000		5,000	
Less: closing stock	–		1,000	
Cost of sales		5,000		4,000
Contribution		5,000		4,800
Fixed production overheads		1,000		1,000
Non-production overheads		1,750		1,650
Net profit		2,250		2,150

11.5 (a) Two reasons why the actual sales volume of 900 units in January may not have been a result of better motivation following the participative budgeting process are:

- The demand for Product P may have increased for some reason unconnected with the effort of the sales staff, for example customers restocking the product after the Christmas period.

- The consultation with the sales manager may have resulted in the budget being set lower than sales staff really expected, so that they had a better chance of achieving higher sales than budget.

(b) Two reasons why favourable cost variances may have arisen other than as an advantage of participative budgeting could be any of the following:

- There may have been a reduction in costs for reasons external to Peter Ltd, not due to the control of managers within the company.

- There may have been an overestimation of costs in the budget, that is the production manager may have introduced 'budgetary slack' to make favourable variances more likely.

- There could have been cost savings (possibly emphasising the short-term view) which do not represent a favourable situation, such as cutting back on quality or on machine maintenance.

11.6

MEMORANDUM

TO: Managing Director, PP plc

FROM: ...　　　　　DATE: ...

SUBJECT: Performance related pay.

The circumstances in which performance related pay is likely to lead to improved performance are:

- managers are working towards known company objectives
- managers want to work towards those objectives
- budgets are set in line with those objectives
- managers see the budgets as a challenge, but achievable
- managers feel they can influence achievement of objectives
- managers are able to improve performance
- managers are motivated to achieve improved performance by financial and non-financial rewards

I have reservations about applying the scheme to the management of Casings Division in two respects:

1　The managers of Casings Division being at a disadvantage:
- the volume of output is not under their control, it is determined by the company requirement for casings
- cost savings would not benefit Casings Division as the casing is sold internally only, at cost
- not all costs in the division are necessarily controllable by them

2　The managers of Casings Division obtaining an unearned benefit
- they may achieve higher production levels and lower unit cost (without any effort) if higher volumes are demanded (lower unit cost will result if fixed costs are shared over more units)
- they may drive costs down to achieve lower unit cost, by cutting back on the quality of materials or of workmanship

---

INDEX